Multicultural Education Policies
in Canada and the United States

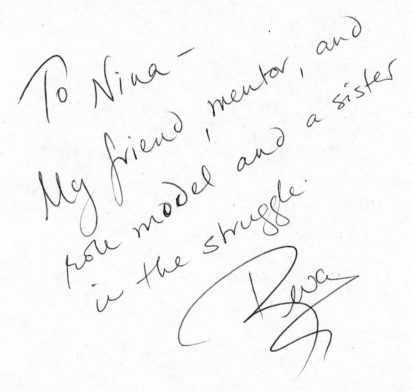

To Nina —
My friend, mentor, and
role model and a sister
in the struggle.

APRIL 2007

Edited by Reva Joshee and Lauri Johnson

Multicultural Education Policies in Canada and the United States

UBCPress · Vancouver · Toronto

We dedicate this volume to a friend and mentor who has been a beacon for many in the field of multicultural education, James A. Banks.

16 15 14 13 12 11 10 09 08 07   5 4 3 2 1

Printed in Canada on ancient-forest-free paper (100 percent post-consumer recycled) that is processed chlorine- and acid-free, with vegetable-based inks.

Library and Archives Canada Cataloguing in Publication

Multicultural education policies in Canada and the United States / Reva Joshee and Lauri Johnson, editors.

Includes bibliographical references and index.
ISBN 978-0-7748-1325-9

1. Multicultural education – Canada. 2. Multicultural education – United States. I. Joshee, Reva, 1960- II. Johnson, Lauri

LC1099.M8375 2007   370.117'0971   C2007-900346-X

Canadä

UBC Press gratefully acknowledges the financial support for our publishing program of the Government of Canada through the Book Publishing Industry Development Program (BPIDP), and of the Canada Council for the Arts, and the British Columbia Arts Council.

This book has been published with the help of a grant from the Canadian Federation for the Humanities and Social Sciences, through the Aid to Scholarly Publications Programme, using funds provided by the Social Sciences and Humanities Research Council of Canada. Additional support for this publication came from the Baldy Center for Law and Social Policy and the Canadian American Studies Committee at the University at Buffalo.

Printed and bound in Canada by Friesens
Set in Stone by Blakeley
Copy editor: Sarah Wight
Proofreader: Gail Copeland
Indexer: Rebecca Lewis

UBC Press
The University of British Columbia
2029 West Mall
Vancouver, BC V6T 1Z2
604.822.5959 / Fax 604.822.6083
www.ubcpress.ca

Contents

Figures and Tables / viii

Foreword / ix
Charles Ungerleider

Acknowledgments / xv

Introduction: Cross-Border Dialogue and Multicultural Policy Webs / 3
Lauri Johnson and Reva Joshee

Part 1: Historical Context

1 Past Crossings: US Influences on the Development of Canadian
Multicultural Education Policy / 17
Reva Joshee and Susan Winton

2 Diversity Policies in American Schools: A Legacy of Progressive School
Leadership and Community Activism / 28
Lauri Johnson

3 We Are Already Multicultural: Why Policy and Leadership Matter / 42
Yoon K. Pak

Part 2: First Nations and Native American Education

4 First Nations Education Policy in Canada: Building Capacity
for Change and Control / 51
Jan Hare

5 Policy Issues in the Education of American Indians and Alaska Natives / 69
John W. Tippeconnic III and Sabrina Redwing Saunders

6 What We Know about Native Participation in Higher Education / 83
Augustine McCaffery

Part 3: Immigrant and Language Education

7 Canadian Policies on Immigrant Language Education / 93·
Tracey M. Derwing and Murray J. Munro

8 Language Education in the Conflicted United States / 107
Carlos J. Ovando and Terrence G. Wiley

9 A Critical Examination of Language Policies and Practices in Canada and the United States / 120
Karen M. Gourd

Part 4: Race-Based Policies

10 Race-Based Policies in Canada: Education and Social Context / 131
Adrienne S. Chan

11 Education, American Style: Race-Based School Policies and Practices in the United States / 146
Christopher M. Span, Rashid V. Robinson, and Trinidad Molina Villegas

12 Canadian and American Race-Based Education Policies / 159
Njoki Nathani Wane

Part 5: Employment Equity and Affirmative Action

13 Canada's Employment Equity Act: Perspectives on Policy and Implementation / 167
Carol Agocs

14 Critical Race Theory and Interest Convergence in the Backlash against Affirmative Action: Washington State and Initiative 200 / 188
Edward Taylor

15 Dialogue across Borders on Employment Equity/Affirmative Action / 204
Michelle Goldberg

Part 6: Extending the Dialogue

16 Institutional Racism in Education Policy and Practice:
A View from England / 217
David Gillborn

17 Multicultural Policies and Practices in North America:
A Dialogue with the View from England / 241
Catherine Cornbleth, Rinaldo Walcott, Carlos J. Ovando, and Terezia Zoric

Contributors / 248
Index / 252

Figures and Tables

Figures

16.1 Tiering in GCSE examinations / 225

16.2 Relative attainment by age and ethnicity / 227

Tables

7.1 Top ten source countries for Canadian immigrants, 2001 / 94

13.1 Representation of employees who are members of designated groups in firms covered by the Employment Equity Act, Canada, 1987 and 2001 / 174

16.1 Ethnic origin and GCSE attainment / 222

Foreword

Charles Ungerleider

Over the last sixty-five years, Canada has charted a course unique among nations in pursuit of a sometimes elusive and controversial vision of a multicultural society. In this vision, people retain their heritage languages and their cultural identifications while enjoying the full benefits of a citizenship founded on shared rights, freedoms, and obligations: "Canada, with its policy of 'multiculturalism within a bilingual framework' and its recognition of Aboriginal rights to self-government, is one of the few countries which has officially recognized and endorsed both polyethnicity and multinationality" (Kymlicka 1995, 22).[1]

Canada's journey toward the vision of a cohesive, multicultural society has taken a number of detours and experienced a number of delays. Not all Canadians have benefited equally from or embraced with enthusiasm the goals of multiculturalism. Nor have all of the implied promises of multiculturalism been fully realized. Some critics have said that multiculturalism has been a way for political parties to win the support of immigrants by offering them multicultural programs actually designed to promote their assimilation. Other critics have said that multiculturalism was an attempt to reduce anti-French feelings among nonfrancophones angered by Canada's policies of bilingualism and biculturalism. Still others have expressed concern that the emphasis on multiculturalism might increase cultural group identification at the expense of Canadian social cohesion. Now, after more that thirty years of multiculturalism as *official* state policy, it is appropriate to ask what Canada has achieved that distinguishes it from the United States, where multiculturalism is neither an official nor unofficial state policy but where it is possible nonetheless to speak of multicultural policy.

This volume is dedicated to a cross-border dialogue on the development and impact of multicultural policies in Canada and the United States. As a border crosser, I am well positioned to comment on the benefits and pitfalls of cross-border dialogues – especially ones involving the United States and Canada. I was born and educated in the United States and have spent more

x *Charles Ungerleider*

than half of my life in Canada. I often traverse what is frequently called "the longest undefended border in the world." My educational preparation in political science, sociology, and education, and my vocation in applied sociology and educational research, incline me to the analysis of social phenomena and the application of such analyses to public policy.

In my capacities as associate dean for teacher education at the University of British Columbia and deputy minister of education for the Province of British Columbia I had many opportunities to host international visitors interested in various dimensions of Canadian society. Over time I came to realize that I was as much a beneficiary of these sessions as the visitors were. My ability to describe and explain the phenomena of interest to my guests improved over time. Recurrent themes included concern for Canadian identity, social cohesion, the role of the state in the lives of citizens, collective versus individual orientations, and policies that addressed issues of equity and social justice. The clarity of my expositions and their intelligibility to my visitors increased as I learned to connect them with contexts familiar to my visitors and identify important similarities and differences. Many of those conversations were catalytic in promoting my understanding. The questions prompted me to consider taken-for-granted experiences in new light or to penetrate surface understanding in search of deeper meaning. These sessions heightened my own understanding of familiar Canadian policies and practices as well as my appreciation of their strengths and shortcomings.

Identity was an inevitable point of entry to conversation with many visitors. Some visitors from the United States were interested in exploring the application of the "melting pot" to the Canadian context. In the United States, democracy was considered the crucible in which differences among immigrants would be melted and forged into a new American alloy. Many US visitors challenged the American melting pot shibboleth and were curious how – and how successfully – Canada had responded to the challenge of integrating newcomers into the social fabric and ensuring that Canadian society accommodated immigrants.

I explained that Canada has developed a different response to the questions of how much and what kind of diversity it can and should accommodate while preserving its identity and cohesion as a nation. Over the last sixty-five years, Canada has tried to become a society in which its citizens can retain the characteristics and values of the groups with which they identify. The belief – and *belief* is the operative word – is that Canadians should be able to retain the characteristics and values of their ancestors, so long as that retention does not create inequality.

Many visitors from the United States commented on the American penchant for, and preoccupation with, the individual. Some opined that the emphasis on the individual was attributable to two of the animating forces of the American state – liberty and the pursuit of happiness – and consequent efforts to ensure that the rights of the individual take precedence over those of the group. These border crossers were eager to know how Canada managed the tensions between the individual and the group.

I acknowledged that Canada has tried – not always successfully – to achieve a balance between the rights of the individual and the rights of the group. Canadians enjoy protections of fundamental freedoms – of speech, association, and religion – similar to those enjoyed by Americans. But Canada recognizes group rights. What is addressed less formally in the United States, receives formal attention in the Canadian context. For example, Canada protects minority language education rights of French and English speakers as denominational, separate, and dissentient rights and privileges. Canadians value their multicultural heritage and mention it explicitly in their Constitution. Canadians seek to preserve and enhance links to their ancestral origins by ensuring that their Charter rights are interpreted in a manner consistent with that heritage. Treaty rights of Aboriginal peoples, their rights and freedoms enshrined in the Royal Proclamation of 1763, and the rights they have obtained or may obtain by means of land claims settlements are also guaranteed. Canadians have also committed themselves to addressing disparities by promoting equal opportunities for all Canadians no matter where they live. The Canadian government encourages economic development so that inequality of opportunity is reduced or eliminated. Essential public services, such as health care and education, are provided to all Canadians.

American visitors have observed that although recent immigration to the United States continues to belie the melting pot thesis, the United States still enjoys strong allegiance to the state – even among groups for whom the American dream has remained elusive. The apparent success of the United States in securing the attachment of newcomers is attributed to the communication of American norms and values, intensified in recent years by external threats. These values permeate the mass media, school, religion, and even the workplace to reinforce a "we-feeling" among Americans despite their social location or circumstance.

According to some of my border-crossing informants, the self-confidence of the United States is due to more than simply its military and economic might, though these factors certainly contribute to a strong national self-image. Its revolutionary origins contribute to an image of the United States as uncompromising. Its survival of a civil war – which they point out is commonly defined in moral rather than economic terms – seems designed to reinforce the image of an enduring and strong central government. Even its enduring racial conflict, they say, helps to contribute to the self-image of a nation struggling to ensure that freedom and equality triumph over bigotry and discrimination.

After spending some time in Canada, many of these same visitors observe that Canada's sense of self seems weak in comparison with the United States.

Some ask directly what is on the minds of all who visit Canada: how does Canada manage to remain a socially cohesive society with an apparently weak sense of self in the face of such forces as regional alienation, Quebec nationalism, ethnocultural diversity, economic globalization, proximity to the most powerful nation on earth, and increasing individualism?

They observe that demographic and social patterns seem to militate against social cohesion of the Canadian state. They note that Canada is sparsely populated for its size, with its 32 million people living primarily in cities along a narrow corridor in close proximity to the US border. Canadian travel patterns seem to follow a geography that has them moving from north to south rather than east or west. So many Canadians live in Los Angeles someone quipped that it is Canada's second-largest city.

Many have observed that, unlike the United States, Canada is unable to sustain its population through childbirth alone. To maintain its population and a standard of living that depends on maintaining a workforce sufficiently large to support social services, Canada's survival depends on immigration. Immigrants have typically comprised about 15 percent of Canada's population. Recent immigration to Canada is about 18 percent of the population, while current US immigration is closer to 11 percent. Because a constant influx of newcomers is necessary for Canada's survival, ensuring the integration of immigrants into Canadian society is a continuing task.

While the United States has a strong, enduring, and reasonably well-integrated two-party political system at both the national and state levels, Canada's political landscape is more fragmented. Four official parties are represented in the House of Commons, each with a more or less regional base. The Conservative strength is in the West and East, the Liberal strength is in Ontario and Quebec, the Bloc Québécois is exclusive to Quebec, and the New Democratic Party is supported here and there outside of central Canada. These regional differences and party differentiation account for the fact that the Liberals formed a majority government in 2000 even though they earned only 40 percent of the popular vote. In more recent years these regional differences have led to two successive minority governments.

Canada's symbols are not evocative. Where the United States has the bald eagle, a commanding presence, Canadians have the beaver – a furry creature with a dental structure that is easily caricatured. Canada's flag is less than forty years old, and "O Canada" is sung in both official languages, each version conveying subtle and not-so-subtle differences in meaning.

Observers comment that the image of Canada communicated by its media is dominated by political fragmentation and differences. Whereas American media provide a clear and constant image of the United States, the image of Canada reflects its fragility. Observers are puzzled that even the national media – the Canadian Broadcasting Corporation and the National Film Board of Canada – communicate different messages about Canada in English and French. That Canadians have greater access to cable television networks than any other country in the world – many originating outside of Canada's borders – makes the communication of common norms and values tenuous. Canada has systematically fettered its national broadcasting service to the point that its audiences are small, demographically isolated, and linguistically fragmented. Despite assertions to the contrary, Canada has no national newspaper and no national news magazine to convey to Canadians a sense of themselves as a cohesive nation.

Canada's indigenous film industry is insignificant in comparison to that of the United States. Canadian films do not draw the audiences that films from the United States do. Canadian radio and television must meet quotas for the inclusion of "Canadian content," but no Canadian content quotas ensure that Canadian films receive screen time or distribution. Canada dares not even dream of invoking preferential measures for its film industry for, if it did, representatives of American producers would fly north to threaten Canadian policy makers and theatre owners with retribution.

Like the United States, Canada is a confederation. Like the US states, Canadian provinces have fought to retain and exercise powers not accorded to the Government of Canada and have successfully maintained their distinctive identities. While American politicians seem anxious to proclaim their allegiance to the United States, few Canadian politicians seem capable of seeing beyond the horizon of their local and regional interests. As a consequence, Canada's central institutions do not exert the influence that is exercised by the US federal government.

Canadians do not refer to the Government of Canada as their "national" government, since "nation" – in the Canadian context – refers to founding nations: English, French and more recently Aboriginal, implying differences based on ancestry. Consider that the provincial legislature of Quebec is called the National Assembly – proclaiming what many of its residents regard as both reality and aspiration.

As this volume makes clear, ironies are at work with respect to multicultural policies in both countries. For example, despite its self-definition as the crucible for ethnocultural differences, the United States is populated by people who cling tenaciously to their heritage cultures and languages. Neither sustained messages encouraging assimilation nor episodic attacks such as English-only laws seem capable of completely eradicating difference. In Canada, with its officially declared vision of a society in which it is permissible – even desirable – to retain one's cultural self-identification and home language, heritage-language retention beyond the second generation is infrequent and beyond the third a rarity, and exogenous marriage is commonplace.

This suggests that while our heritage culture and languages are important reference points for self-definition, they are susceptible to influence by the context in which we find ourselves. It also suggests that the state – though influential – is not determinative in matters such as self-identification. The state can affect the environment in which ethnocultural identities develop and contend. But as the events of the last ten or fifteen years have shown, the state can neither eradicate ethnocultural identifications that provide salient points of self-reference or attachment for those who wish to retain them, nor cause them to flourish when they no longer serve us.

In addition to important insights into multiculturalism in the United States and Canada, this volume contains lessons for those interested in border-crossing policy analysis. The policies pursued under the ambit of multiculturalism are indicative of the value preferences at work when the policies were adopted and pursued. Policy change also reflects contemporary exigencies and values. Thus, it is important to inquire about the implications of the policies implemented at a particular time and the values that underpin them, as well as the universe of alternatives available to decision makers and the constraints – cultural, social, political, economic, and historical – under which they worked.

Border-crossing policy analysts should be sensitive to context. The successful analyst is part historian, part sociologist, part economist, and so on, avoiding the temptation to judge past decisions by today's standards. For if today's standards had existed at the time, it is likely that different decisions would have been made and different policies adopted. As this volume makes very clear, real-world policy making is temporally and contextually specific. It is the contextual sensitivity and temporal immediacy that cause the adrenalin rush for border-crossing policy analysts. Enjoy it!

Notes
1   Canada is a state that incorporates distinct and potentially self-governing groups – First Nations, Métis, Inuit, English, and French – as well as immigrants from many national communities. See Kymlicka 1995, 10-33.

References
Kymlicka, W. 1995. *Multicultural citizenship: A liberal theory of minority rights*. Oxford: Clarendon Press.

Acknowledgments

Earlier versions of many of the chapters in this book were presented at two Canada/US cross-border conferences. The first, "Canadian/US Conference on Multicultural Policy," was held on 8 June 2002 and sponsored by the Canadian Studies Center at the University of Washington. The second conference, "Dialogue on Multicultural and Diversity Policies in Canada and the United States: Symbol or Substance?," was sponsored by the Baldy Center for Law and Social Policy at the University at Buffalo on 22-23 May 2003, with additional support from the Canadian American Studies Committee and the Graduate School of Education at the University at Buffalo.

Work like this inevitably involves a number of people, many of whom toil in the background with little recognition. In particular we'd like to thank Emily Andrew, Camilla Blakeley, Nadine Fabbi, Jane Goodlet, Becky Lewis, Laura Mangan, Kara Olidge, and Michael Stanford for their invaluable help at various points in this process. We thank the participants in the two conferences and the students in our three cross-border classes for their contributions to the dialogue. Many thanks as well to all of the contributors for their excellent work and cooperation. Most especially we'd like to thank our respective families for the support, understanding, and love that took us through the most difficult moments.

Introduction: Cross-Border Dialogue and Multicultural Policy Webs

Lauri Johnson and Reva Joshee

Since at least the 1990s there has been considerable interest in comparative studies of multicultural policies. In part this interest has been fuelled by a growing awareness of the multiethnic nature of most contemporary nation-states and the need to account for this aspect of pluralism in public policy. The Management of Social Transformations program of UNESCO, for example, was initiated in the 1990s to bring the attention of researchers and policy developers to issues of public policy in multiethnic societies (see, for example, Inglis 1996; Premdas 1998). The International Metropolis project, also launched in the 1990s, is dedicated to increasing knowledge on issues related to immigration and to providing a forum for discussions among researchers, policy developers, and nongovernmental organizations. It now involves participants from over twenty countries and several international organizations. As a result of these and other initiatives the past decade saw several international and comparative publications on multicultural policies (such as Inglis 1996; Wieviorka 1998; Young 1998) and immigration policies (such as Cohen and Layton-Henry 1997; Favell 2001; Joppke and Morawska 2003). While many of these works made some reference to education, it was not a central concern in much of this research.

Comparative multicultural education has attracted some interest since the 1970s – the beginning of the current era of multiculturalism in Canada and the United States (for example, Tonkin 1977). But sustained interest in comparative multicultural education has been a recent development (Sutton 2005). As Sutton notes, most of the current comparative work done in the name of multicultural education focuses on "issues of identity, diversity, and citizenship" (97). Typical comparative volumes present chapters on individual countries. Carl Grant and Joy Lei (2001), for example, edited an international volume that includes chapters on multicultural education in North America, South America, Europe, Asia, and Africa. More recently James Banks (2004) has prepared a volume on citizenship education in diverse societies that also includes chapters from each of these five continents. In addition, there have been several works on comparative bilingual and multilingual education (for example, Baker and Jones 1998; Cenoz and Genesee 1998; Cummins and Corson 1997; Schiffman 1996). While the works on bilingualism and multilingualism recognize the multiethnic nature of societies, any discussion of policy is typically limited to language policy. Among the studies on language, only one has focused specifically on Canada and the United States (Ricento and Burnaby 1998). To date there has been no attempt to look in depth at the full array of multicultural education policies in Canada and the United States.

Despite a deep-rooted multicultural policy history (see Chapters 2 and 3), we live in a time when diversity initiatives do not receive much support in either of our countries. Some scholars attribute this to the recent neoliberal turn in political and popular thought (see, for example, Apple 2004; Ball 1998). Others contend that undermining diversity is consistent with the underlying premises of the democratic liberal state, which require drawing boundaries between those who are members and those who are not (for example, Cole 2000; Goldberg 2002). While we recognize these claims, we believe the competing impetus for equality, also foundational to the liberal democratic state, provides an avenue for work for diversity. As scholars interested in the study of multicultural and diversity policies, we are also activists committed to exploring ways to think about these policies that provide for possibility as well as critique. Our mutual quest has led us to engage in an extended dialogue over the last seven years about policy issues in our two countries, Canada and the United States, and to recognize the power of dialogue as a method for understanding policy. In the remainder of this introduction we recount briefly the major components of our own policy dialogue, speak to the insights we have gained though the process, and argue that systematic cross-border dialogue, as evidenced by the chapters in this book, is a productive approach to comparative policy study.

As policy researchers, we identify as pragmatic postpositivists. We are attracted to postpositivist approaches that emphasize critique and deconstruction and draw attention to issues of power and discourse. As activists, however, we feel compelled to use our insights to engage with policy developers in ways that will move the policy process forward. We are sympathetic with Piers Blaikie (2001, 2), who notes, "There comes a point in the deconstruction of policy truth claims and the rational model for policy making, when the reader asks, having witnessed another deft act of deconstruction, yet another description of contested terrains, 'So what?' and 'What now?'" Indeed, these are questions we have asked each other and our colleagues. In part our response to these questions has been a historical examination of diversity policies that allows us to examine issues of power, uncover the competing discourses that structured earlier struggles, and produce what Emery Roe (1994) might call new policy narrative contenders. By engagement in cross-border policy dialogue we have attempted to use these alternate narratives to rethink current approaches to issues in multicultural education.

What Do We Mean by Policy Dialogue?

The term *policy dialogue* is used in a variety of ways in the literature. Several scholars talk about deliberation or discussion as a central component of their approaches to policy analysis (for example, DeLeon 1997; Dryzek 1990; Fischer and Forrester 1993; Mansbridge 1997; Reich 1990). As Yusuf Bangura (1997) notes, the literature outlines at least five different models of policy dialogue. Common to all models is the understanding that dialogue involves discussion about a specific policy issue that brings together individuals and groups deemed to be stakeholders. Bangura explains, "Policy dialogue is defined as an organized deliberation between two or more actors on the allocation of values that is likely to result in new policies or modifications of existing ones. Implicit in the concept of policy dialogue is a clarification of the issues and an understanding of the interests and concerns of contending parties" (5). While some of these elements apply to our notion of policy dialogue, in our current endeavour we are more concerned with dialogue as a process that allows us to engage across national contexts about common policy issues that may have had different trajectories in our two countries.

For us, policy dialogue is a process through which the parties involved convey their own sense of, position on, and story about an issue. Unlike a simple conversation or discussion, dialogue implies coming to new understandings about issues of common concern by listening, asking clarifying questions, recognizing and talking about points of disagreement, engaging in critique and reflection on our own national contexts, and moving the project forward by asking the question: what new insight does this bring to our policy project?

Our particular approach to cross-border policy dialogue demands first that we understand that the policy area under study is broader than simply one policy statement or group of policy statements. We believe that the entire context and scope of the policy area must be taken into account and that dialogue helps us to uncover the links between specific policies in each country, identifying the "policy webs" (Joshee and Johnson 2005) within each country and internationally.

Multicultural Policy Webs

Most studies of multicultural education in Canada and the United States focus on explicating different theoretical approaches (for example, Dei 1996; Sleeter 1996), critiquing work in the field (for example, Lesko and Bloom 2000; Rezai-Rashti 1995), understanding how multiculturalism looks in practice (for example, Hudak 2000; Solomon and Allen 2001), or some combination of the above. While all of these approaches have implications for policies, policy is generally not their focal point. The few policy studies in multicultural education that do exist have generally taken a narrow view by starting from a discrete policy statement and making links between that statement and what is happening in classrooms and schools (for example, McCaskell 1995). Because the statements and practices rarely match, policy analysts conclude that there is resistance or a lack of commitment to implementing the policy, or that teachers lack multicultural resources and a sufficient knowledge base about diversity (for example, Echols and Fisher 1992; Harper 1997; Tator and Henry 1991). This approach to linking policy and practice does not account for the fact that multicultural policies are generally embedded in states and organizations with histories of racism and exclusion.

We believe that rather than being analyzed individually, diversity policies should be considered within the complex of policies that address the range of issues associated with multiculturalism. In both Canada and the United States, multicultural education is part of a larger complex of policies and programs meant to address social and cultural inequality. As Julia O'Connor (1998, 193) has noted with respect to education and class-based inequality, "Equality of educational opportunity does provide working-class children the right of access to a mobility route that is absent without such equality. The extent to which this right can be exercised is related to the degree of income inequality and the scope and effectiveness of programs directed to addressing this inequality." We believe that this parallels the reality of policies in multicultural education. Their relative success is dependent on the scope and effectiveness of other policies and programs addressing related concerns.

Considering policy in the context of a web of interrelated, ongoing policies (Oquist 2000) provides a powerful metaphor for thinking about and mapping multicultural education policies in both the United States and Canada. In our view, this web has rings that represent different levels at which policy is formally located, and cross-cutting threads that, while connected, are not necessarily straight lines. These threads represent policies at different levels that address similar issues but are not necessarily harmonious. The points at which the threads cross the rings represent discrete policy texts, each of which is the result of historical struggles. Significantly, the web draws our attention to the open spaces between the threads. In these spaces individuals have some freedom to act in ways that support, extend, or undermine stated policy objectives and to introduce new ideas that may influence the policy discourse. The web metaphor acknowledges that the policy process is complex and involves actors from both within and outside of the state.

The History of the Canada-US Dialogue

This ongoing dialogue about diversity policies in Canada and the United States began with a cross-border conference on multicultural education organized by graduate students from the University of British Columbia and the University of Washington that took place in Vancouver, British Columbia, in June 1998. Out of the conference grew a cross-border course that was designed to allow students from the United States and Canada to learn together about multicultural education policy in both countries. The course has been conducted twice with students from the University of British Columbia and the University of Washington and once at the University of Toronto and the University at Buffalo, with students travelling between the two universities for classes. Students engage with readings on the historical bases for policy, federal policies in the United States and Canada, immigrant education, multiculturalism and antiracism in the schools, and multiculturalism in higher education. Working in cross-border groups to facilitate online dialogues, they end the class by creating presentations related to the five areas.

We also built on our growing understanding of the dialogue process through engagement in joint scholarship. In the fall of 1999 we co-wrote a paper comparing multicultural education policy and practice in New York City and Vancouver, British Columbia. It took us about four months to realize we had very different frames of reference, in terms of both our national contexts and our approaches to policy. In the end we wrote a draft that we presented as a work-in-progress at a conference but never finished, because we realized that presenting side-by-side examples of diversity policies was not enough. We needed to find a truly comparative approach to policy analysis, a way to think about how our understanding of what happened in one context might inform our understanding of what happened in the other.

The resolution to our dilemma came as a result of a fortuitous conversation about some historical work we had been doing separately, one examining the intercultural education movement in the United States in the 1930s and 1940s and the other the development of federal policy on multiculturalism and education in Canada. Comparing notes, we discovered that in the United States a radio program had been developed titled *Americans All, Immigrants All*, while in Canada a program called *Canadians All* was developed and broadcast in the 1940s. Working together with our colleague Yoon Pak from the University of Illinois, we eventually uncovered a number of links between the work of activists and educators in the United States and Canada at this time. Our ongoing conversations about this research led us to think more deeply about the differences and similarities between the two contexts. We developed a more comprehensive understanding of the historical development of diversity policies and started to articulate the multicultural policy web in each country. We were also reminded that though Canadians freely took from what was happening in the United States, Americans rarely paid much attention to what was happening in Canada, even when they were invited to participate. We were determined not to repeat this pattern.

By the spring of 2002 we had developed a plan for a publication that would bring together colleagues from the United States and Canada who could talk face-to-face on race-based policies, immigration and language policies, policies for First Nations and Native Americans, and employment equity and affirmative action policies. We chose these areas because multicultural education in both countries has a history of focusing on issues of culture, race, and ethnicity. In Canada, the official multicultural policies have been defined largely in these terms. In the United States, the origins of multicultural education are in the intercultural education movements of the 1930s (see Chapter 2), whose approaches and practices were revived and revised following the civil rights movement of the 1960s. Both movements were linked to struggles related to race, ethnicity, and language. While US multicultural education has expanded over the years to include gender, ability, sexual identity, and class, many still define it largely in terms of its original mandate (see, for example, Sutton 2005).

We began with a mini-conference sponsored by the Canadian Studies Center of the University of Washington in June 2002. A larger conference in May 2003, sponsored by the Baldy Center for Law and Social Policy at the University at Buffalo, brought together many of the people who contributed to this volume, as well as other scholars, educators, and activists. At this point we realized that we needed to think more deliberately about international rather than just cross-border dialogue. We also realized that whenever two people were involved in discussion we needed at least a third person to move us from discussion to dialogue. The third person helped us to read our papers together in a way that created new insights. This is the pattern you will encounter throughout this book.

Organization of the Text
This book aims to simulate a policy dialogue process to help us better understand the policy webs in Canada and the United States. To this end we have divided the book into parts by policy area; five include a chapter each on Canada and the United States, with a third dialogue chapter intended to draw insights from the previous two chapters and take our project forward. The first part of the book provides some historical context for what follows, the second examines policies for Native American and First Nations peoples, the third discusses policies for immigrants and language policies, the fourth investigates race-based policies, and the fifth looks at affirmative action and employment equity. Part 6 moves from our position in North America to examine race and policy in the United Kingdom, with a dialogue response by a panel of Canadian and American scholars. The chapter on England stands in dialogue with the previous five parts. Having thought through the issues related to multicultural education in Canada and the United States, we felt the need for a voice from outside to help us think again about the questions

we may have missed. A voice from Britain was the obvious choice because, as we see in Chapter 16, current policy trends in education in the United States and Canada echo earlier moves in the United Kingdom. The organization of the book responds to the question, What can we learn from these policy studies in relation to each other that we may not have learned from each individually? In this way we have attempted to bring our ongoing comparative policy dialogue to this book.

Part 1 explores the historical context of diversity policies. Both the chapter on Canada and the one on the United States find multicultural education more deeply rooted in the history of our respective countries than do conventional policy narratives. The stories begin in the 1930s and 1940s. Reva Joshee and Susan Winton link diversity work in Canada to work in the United States, showing how it was the source of a variety of initiatives that helped define early Canadian multicultural education policy. They postulate reasons why these initiatives took root in Canada in ways they did not in the United States and suggest that the comparatively deep roots of multiculturalism in Canada, no matter how symbolic in nature, persist in the face of the neoliberal assault on social justice and equity. Lauri Johnson's chapter shows that from the beginning multicultural education policy in the United States has been reactive, a strategy to address problems of racial conflict and intolerance by educating children about the equality of all. Johnson demonstrates historical moments that created spaces for innovative leadership and community activism around diversity issues. In her dialogue chapter, Yoon Pak reminds us that the work done in the name of multicultural education can exoticize and marginalize some groups through its own kind of myth making, underscoring the need to look at policies in connection with existing discourses and relations of power.

Part 2 introduces issues in the centuries-old struggles surrounding educational policies for Native American and First Nations peoples. Both chapters show that policies designed by the federal governments of the United States and Canada have largely failed by standard measures. Jan Hare points out that the Canadian government's policy stance of Indian control of Indian education will never be a reality until capacity building is introduced to the equation. She argues that earlier discourses of "civilizing," "assimilating," and "integrating" First Nations have effectively stripped these communities of the capacity to exercise true authority over their own education. John Tippeconnic and Sabrina Redwing Saunders suggest that we need to introduce new questions as well as new approaches into existing policy processes to address the issues facing American Indian and Alaskan Native communities in terms of schooling. Augustine McCaffery's dialogue chapter extends Tippeconnic and Saunders' discussion by considering the participation of American Indian and Alaskan Native students in higher education and connects the issue of capacity building to their participation in graduate education.

Part 3 examines immigrant and language policies. Tracey Derwing and Murray Munro note that the Canadian context differs from the United States because of Canada's official policy of bilingualism. While some programs encourage the acquisition and retention of languages other than English or French, the major focus of language policies for immigrants is on the acquisition of one of the two official languages. Yet there is little attention to ensure that students are given adequate instruction in English. Derwing and Munro warn that without serious and sustained attention to this matter Canada risks creating a perpetual immigrant underclass. Carlos Ovando and Terrence Wiley discuss the conflicted nature of language education policy in the United States. This conflict arises when a strong national identity, linked to a monolingual English populace, meets the ideal of equal educational opportunities for all. The continuing opposition to bilingual education in the United States indicates that this conflict is far from being resolved. In her dialogue chapter Karen Gourd notes that in both countries, language policies have served as both a means of control and a space for dissent and change. Educators need to be cognizant of this tension if they are to implement language programs that respond to the needs of learners and, where necessary, push the limits of existing policies.

Part 4 examines race-based policies. Adrienne Chan argues that Canadian policies have historically sanctioned race-based inequality, with patterns of segregation similar to those in the United States. Despite more recent race-based policies that attempt to create the conditions for racial equality, she posits that the discursive legacy of racialization continues to limit the educational experiences of students of colour. Christopher Span, Rashid Robinson, and Trinidad Molina Villegas demonstrate that race-based policies are deeply rooted in the US educational system and that historically race has played a more significant role in educational success than any other factor. Through the efforts of community and parent activists, policies that systematically segregated or denied education to minoritized racial groups were challenged and ultimately changed. In her dialogue chapter, Njoki Nathani Wane shows that we find greater similarity between the two countries in race-based policies than in any other area of policy related to multicultural education. The most notable differences arise between the racialized groups in each national context. That is, racism affects different racialized groups differently. Until we can have productive conversations about racism and race-based policies in multiracial settings, we will fail to move beyond understanding to action.

Part 5 moves us from discussions of policy in K-12 schools to an examination of an issue more central to the postsecondary realm: affirmative action and employment equity. Carol Agocs notes that, unlike affirmative action, employment equity policies in Canada do not address student recruitment at the postsecondary level. While employment equity policies apply to only a small percentage of the Canadian workforce, they have provided a framework for thinking about equity beyond the more narrowly defined terms of multiculturalism policies. Centring her discussion on the parliamentary review of the federal Employment Equity Act, Agocs shows how larger political discourses inhospitable to diversity can limit possibilities for action. Edward Taylor's critical account of affirmative action policy, using the case of Washington State, shows how tenuous equity policies can be. Through the lens of critical race theory he argues that policies based in a liberal paradigm, like affirmative action, can be successful only to the extent that they benefit the White majority. He argues for a new paradigm based on racial realism. In her dialogue chapter, Michelle Goldberg draws on critical race theory and postpositivist approaches to policy to think more deeply about issues of discourse, particularly in relation to the dismantling of employment equity policies in the province of Ontario. Collectively these three chapters provide specific examples of how multicultural and diversity policies can be challenged and overturned. They also provide tools for activists to deconstruct prevailing discourses so we might mount our own challenges.

The final part of the book extends the cross-border dialogue to England, where the diversity of the student population provides similarities as well as contrasts to the US and Canadian contexts. David Gillborn asks us to consider a current incarnation of citizenship education, a movement that spurred the development of progressive diversity policies and practices in Canada in the 1940s and 1950s and is now being used in England to mask the fact that issues of racism in education are not being addressed. In their panel response, Catherine Cornbleth, Rinaldo Walcott, Carlos Ovando, and Terezia Zoric each reflect on the issues Gillborn raises in light of the United States and Canadian policy contexts. We end with the understanding that while diversity policies may not ensure that multicultural educational programs are enacted in schools, they can create spaces of possibility that exist when we recognize the limits of policy texts, the possibilities of prevailing discourses, and the necessity of everyday political action.

Conclusion

The current dominant ideology guiding educational policy development is rooted in a neoliberal approach that replicates existing inequalities based on race, class, and gender. This approach to policy making stands in stark opposition to efforts to create a more socially just society. As Apple (2004) notes, however, struggles for social justice in education continue. In this book we aim to document the erosion of diversity policies, as well as form cross-national alliances to continue the struggle for socially just policy making. Like Blaikie (2001), we believe we must advocate for the kinds of policies we believe are necessary. He argues, "It would seem ... that there are good rational grounds for talking reason to power, but also to engage policy actors with the demonstrable results of previous courses of action. Of course this engagement will be political and involve alliance making across national boundaries and with a wide cast of actors in civil society" (7). A central challenge is that multicultural and diversity education policies have traditionally been studied in ways that produce few demonstrable results. Consequently, we cannot say with any certainty what difference a single multicultural education policy might make. But we do know from history and the present what can happen when social injustice is allowed to flourish. Using policy dialogue to compare the policy webs in both nations and examine their discursive struggles over time, we hope to show how a complex of policies can make a difference.

References

Apple, M.W. 2004. Creating difference: Neo-liberalism, neo-conservatism, and the politics of educational reform. *Educational Policy* 18(1): 12-44.

Ball, S.J. 1998. Big policies/small world: An introduction to international perspectives in education policy. *Comparative Education* 34(2): 119-27.

Baker, C., and S.P. Jones. 1998. *Encyclopedia of bilingualism and bilingual education.* Clevedon, UK: Multilingual Matters.

Bangura, Y. 1997. *Policy dialogue and gendered development: Institutional and ideological constraints.* Geneva: United Nations Research Institute for Social Development. http://www.unrisd.org.

Banks, J.A., ed. 2004. *Diversity and citizenship education: Global perspectives.* San Francisco: Jossey-Bass.

Blaikie, P. 2001. *Is policy reform pure nostalgia? A Himalayan illustration.* Berkeley Workshop on Environmental Politics Working Paper 01-9. Berkeley: Institute of International Studies, University of California. http://globetrotter.berkeley.edu/EnvirPol.

Cenoz, J., and F. Genesee, eds. 1998. *Beyond bilingualism: Multilingualism and multilingual education.* Clevedon, UK: Multilingual Matters.

Cohen, R., and Z. Layton-Henry, eds. 1997. *The politics of migration.* Cheltenham, UK: Edward Elgar.

Cole, P. 2000. *Philosophies of exclusion: Liberal political theory and immigration.* Edinburgh: Edinburgh University Press.

Cummins, J., and D. Corson, eds. 1997. *Second language education.* Vol. 5 of *Encyclopedia of language and education.* Dordrecht, Netherlands: Kluwer Academic Publishers.

Dei, G.S. 1996. *Anti-racism education: Theory and practice.* Halifax: Fernwood Publishing.

DeLeon, P. 1997. *Democracy and the policy sciences.* Albany: State University of New York Press.

Dryzek, J.S. 1990. *Discursive democracy: Politics, policy, and political science.* New York: Cambridge University Press.

Echols, F., and D. Fisher. 1992. School action plans and implementation of a district race relations policy. *Canadian Ethnic Studies* 24(1): 58-78.

Favell, A. 2001. Multicultural nation-building: "Integration" as public philosophy and research paradigm in Western Europe. *Swiss Political Science Review* 7(2): 116-24.

Fischer, F., and J. Forrester. 1993. *The argumentative turn in policy analysis.* Durham, NC: Duke University Press.

Grant, C.A., and J.L. Lei, eds. 2001. *Global constructions of multicultural education: Theories and realities.* Mahwah, NJ: Lawrence Erlbaum.

Goldberg, D.T. 2002. *The racial state.* Malden, MA: Blackwell Publishers.

Harper, H. 1997. Difference and diversity in Ontario schooling. *Canadian Journal of Education/Revue canadienne de l'éducation* 22(2): 192-206.

Hudak, G.M. 2000. Reaping *The Harvest of Shame*: Racism and teaching in a time of radical economic insecurity. In *Multicultural curriculum: New directions for social theory, practice, and policy*, ed. R. Mahalingam and C. McCarthy, 286-301. New York: Routledge.

Inglis, C. 1996. *Multiculturalism: New policy responses to diversity*. Management of Social Transformations (MOST) – UNESCO, policy paper no. 4. http://www.unesco.org/most.

Joppke, C., and E. Morawska, eds. 2003. *Toward assimilation and citizenship: Immigrants in liberal nation-states*. New York: Palgrave Macmillan.

Joshee, R., and L. Johnson. 2005. Multicultural education in the United States and Canada: The importance of national policies. In *International handbook of educational policy*, ed. N. Bascia, A. Cummings, A. Datnow, K. Leithwood, and D. Livingstone, 53-74. Dordrecht, Netherlands: Kluwer Academic Publishing.

Lesko, N., and L. Bloom. 2000. The haunting of multicultural epistemology. In *Multicultural curriculum: New directions for social theory, practice, and policy*, ed. R. Mahalingam and C. McCarthy, 242-60. New York: Routledge.

Mansbridge, J. 1997. What does a representative do? Descriptive representation in communicative settings of distrust, uncrystallized interests, and historically denigrated status. Paper presented at the Canadian Centre for Philosophy and Public Policy conference on "Citizenship in Diverse Societies: Theory and Practice." 4-5 October, Toronto.

McCaskell, T. 1995. Anti-racist education and practice in the public school system. In *Beyond political correctness: Toward the inclusive university,* ed. S. Richer and L. Weir, 253-72. Toronto: University of Toronto Press.

O'Connor, J.S. 1998. Social citizenship and the welfare state, 1965-1995: Canada in comparative context. In *The vertical mosaic revisited*, ed. R. Heles-Hayes and J. Curtis, 108-231. Toronto: University of Toronto Press.

Oquist, P. 2000. Governance policy formulation and implementation. Paper presented at the seminar on "International Experiences on Good Governance and Fighting Corruption," 17 February, Bangkok. http://www.info.tdri.or.th.

Premdas, R.R. 1998. *Public policy and ethnic conflict*. Management of Social Transformations (MOST) – UNESCO, discussion paper no. 12. http://www.unesco.org/most.

Reich, R.B. 1990. Policy making in a democracy. In *The power of public ideas*, ed. R.B. Reich, 123-56. Cambridge, MA: Harvard University Press.

Rezai-Rashti, G. 1995. Multicultural education, anti-racist education and critical pedagogy: Reflections on everyday practice. In *Anti-racism, feminism and critical approaches to education*, ed. R. Ng, P. Staton, and J. Scane, 3-19. Westport, CT: Greenwood Publishers.

Ricento, T., and B. Burnaby, eds. 1998. *Language and politics in the United States and Canada: Myths and realities*. Mahwah, NJ: Lawrence Erlbaum.

Roe, E. 1994. *Narrative policy analysis: Theory and practice*. Durham, NC: Duke University Press.

Schiffman, H.F. 1996. *Linguistic culture and language policy*. New York: Routledge.

Sleeter, C.E. 1996. *Multicultural education as social activism*. Albany: State University of New York Press.

Solomon, R.P., and A.M.A. Allen. 2001. The struggle for equity, diversity, and social justice in teacher education. In *The erosion of democracy: From critique to possibility*, ed. J.P. Portelli and R.P. Solomon, 217-44. Calgary: Detselig Enterprises.

Sutton, M. 2005. The globalization of multicultural education. *Indiana Journal of Global Legal Studies* 12(1): 97-108.

Tator, C., and Henry, F. 1991. *Multicultural education: Translating policy to practice*. Ottawa: Department of Multiculturalism and Citizenship.

Tonkin, H. 1977. Language and the international context. *ADFL Bulletin* (Association of Departments of Foreign Languages) 9(2): 17-23.

Wieviorka, M. 1998. Is multiculturalism the solution? *Ethnic and Racial Studies* 21(5): 881-910.

Young, C., ed. 1998. *Ethnic diversity and public policy: A comparative enquiry*. Basingstoke, UK: Palgrave.

Part 1:
Historical Context

1
Past Crossings: US Influences on the Development of Canadian Multicultural Education Policy

Reva Joshee and Susan Winton

Throughout the nineteenth and early part of the twentieth century, Canada saw itself as the North American outpost of Britain and a key defender of the empire. As a colony, its citizens were British subjects and its policies either came directly from Britain or were influenced by British precedents. After the First World War, Canada became more concerned with establishing an independent identity. This quest continued through the interwar period and eventually bore fruit after the Second World War. An important part of this evolution was the passage of the Citizenship Act (1947) and the programs associated with it. An integral part of the discourse around the new Canadian citizenship was a concern with cultural diversity (Joshee and Johnson 2005; Joshee 1995, 2004). In the search for policies and practices to support diversity, Canadians continued to look outside their borders for inspiration. A chief source of models was the United States (Hare also notes in Chapter 4 that residential schools in Canada were based largely on American models). To date, this connection has received little attention, we believe, because multiculturalism has long been purported to be the main feature distinguishing Canada from the United States. But there is much to learn from exploring this connection as we try to unearth the roots of Canadian multiculturalism. Our discussion asks two questions: Why did these ideas take root in Canada and not in the United States? And how might knowing this help multiculturalists in the United States and Canada think differently about policy process in this field?

We concentrate on the period from the 1940s to the early 1950s, not because this marks either the beginning or the end of US influence on Canadian thinking, but because the period was fundamental to the development of policy in multicultural education and multiculturalism more broadly (Joshee 1995). US influence was felt in Canadian policies and practices of the day in three principal ways. First, Canadian policy developers looked to US policies and practices as models for their own; second, the work of some American scholars shaped the thinking of key decision makers; and third, policy developers and educators "borrowed" US curriculum materials and educational approaches. Although we will touch on all three in this discussion, we will concentrate on the third.

The Context for Cultural Diversity Policy

The period of the Second World War was a turning point for cultural diversity policy in Canada. Five key features came together to change the way Canadians thought about diversity:

1 Even with restrictive immigration policies, by 1940 almost one-fifth of the Canadian population was of origins other than British or French.
2 The railways, which were very influential in Canada at the time, supported multicultural fairs across the country and were actively redefining Canadian identity as a mosaic of cultures.
3 A number of scholars, who also had influence on the direction of public policy, were beginning to study cultural diversity and define it as an asset.
4 The federal government was interested in ensuring that all Canadians regardless of origin would support the Canadian war effort. Therefore it established ethnocultural community organizations and a network of ethnic presses through which it could communicate with various groups.
5 The desire to define Canadians as different from the intolerant Nazis led to wartime propaganda describing Canada as a country that had always welcomed diversity. (Joshee 2004)

Thus the Canadian government began to lay the foundations for the present multiculturalism policy in 1940.

As the war ended, the government began work on the Citizenship Act. Prior to 1947, when the act was passed, Canadians held British passports and were legally considered British subjects residing in Canada. Even here there was an American connection. In opening the House of Commons debate on the bill, Paul Martin, Sr., secretary of state for Canada, proclaimed, "We are convinced of the desirability of emulating the sort of ceremony which characterizes the admission of persons into United States citizenship" (Martin 1946, 6). Unlike the rhetoric of American citizenship, however, much of the rhetoric surrounding the Canadian Citizenship Act spoke of the importance of cultural diversity. Martin himself, in moving the second reading on the bill, noted: "Fortune has placed this country in the position where its people do not all speak the same language and do not all adore God at the same altar. Our task is to mould all these elements into one community without destroying the richness of any of those cultural sources from which many of our people have sprung" (19). This identification of cultural diversity with citizenship remained in place until the 1960s, and a link between multiculturalism and citizenship exists even today.

Initiatives in Education

Under the banner of citizenship education, government officials working with key nongovernmental organizations began to develop a variety of programs. During the Second World War, the term *citizenship education* had designated a range of activities designed to promote patriotism and a sense of common identity. Included in this category were initiatives aimed at developing a sense of Canadianism among members of the so-called foreign-born population and related projects meant to educate "old stock" Canadians about the threat that prejudicial attitudes posed to national unity.

In their work with both newcomers and the old stock, Canadian educators took inspiration and ideas from their American colleagues. For newcomers, citizenship education was seen as having two distinct components: English or French language training and a civics program including information about history, government, geography, and rights and responsibilities. For members of the "old stock," citizenship education was meant to include information that would reduce prejudice toward newcomer communities.

In 1944, the Canadian Council of Education for Citizenship, later the Canadian Citizenship Council (CCC), suggested in a memo to its members that it take on responsibility for the citizenship education of newcomers. The author of the memo noted that the council "should make a further study of methods that are being adopted in other countries, and in the United States in particular." By 1948, the CCC had hired Florence Gaynor, acknowledged as the leading expert in the field in Canada, to develop a program for teachers of English as a second language. Gaynor based much of her work on a program developed by researchers at Harvard, and the CCC became the Canadian distributor for the Harvard materials. The federal government's Citizenship Branch later created Canadian adaptations of the material (Canada, Senate 1949). The CCC later claimed that Gaynor and her work were "largely responsible for promoting one basic system of language teaching being adopted by all ten provinces, and by voluntary organizations" (CCC 1957).

The CCC also developed and distributed civics materials. These, too, took their inspiration from American sources. In 1944, Robert England was asked to prepare a report on the future of the Nationalities Branch, the arm of the Department of National War Services responsible for working with ethnic communities. The bulk of his recommendations focused on citizenship and citizenship education (Joshee 1995). In researching his report he consulted with the US Department of Justice Immigration and Naturalization Service. On the basis of material on education for naturalization that he obtained from the department's chief of educational services, England suggested that the Nationalities Branch be renamed the Citizenship Branch and that its new duties should include developing a program of citizenship training (England 1944). After being stymied in their efforts to get approval to produce and distribute educational materials similar to American ones, officials of the Citizenship Branch funded the CCC to produce a series of booklets on Canada (Minutes 1944).

Citizenship education for old stock Canadians was meant to promote acceptance of newcomers. The direction of this work was largely influenced by the research of American scholars such as Ashley Montague, Louis Wirth, and Robert Park. Montague was instrumental in preparing the *Statement on Race* published by UNESCO in 1950. Working with a panel of international scholars, Montague argued that race was a concept with no scientific foundation. Wirth and Park were sociologists associated with the Chicago School. Wirth initiated the Committee on Education, Training and Research in Race Relations, whose publications were deemed by officials of the Canadian Citizenship Branch to be outstanding examples of research in the area (Falardeau 1953). Park studied intercultural relations in Quebec and appears to have been at least indirectly responsible for the development of intercultural programs for members of Canadian francophone and anglophone communities (Helpful n.d.).

US programs addressing intergroup relations were at least as important as US research to establishing the direction of multicultural education. One of the key wartime initiatives of the Bureau of Public Information, the propaganda arm of the Canadian government during the war, was the production of a radio series called *Canadians All*. It focused on the contributions of different ethnic groups to the development of civilization as a whole and to Canadian society more specifically. In addition, several of the broadcasts mentioned the contribution of members of that ethnic group to the Canadian war effort. The radio series was followed by a film called *Peoples of Canada* produced by the National Film Board, and a pamphlet called *Canadians All* produced for and distributed by the Wartime Information Board. The pamphlet described Canada as a diverse society and emphasized the importance of accepting all members of the society as part of the Canadian family. In addition, the radio series inspired a short-lived magazine, also called *Canadians All*, published in 1945 and 1946. The magazine contained fiction and nonfiction that addressed aspects of cultural diversity in Canada. For example, one article described how serving in the armed forces was making young men more aware of diversity within Canada (McKeown 1945).

Although the US roots of these initiatives were not specifically acknowledged, in the 1930s educators in the United States had produced a radio series called *Americans All, Immigrants All* and a film called *Americans All* (for a fuller discussion of this radio series, see Chapter 3). These were also aimed at mainstream Americans with a view to reducing prejudice toward different ethnic groups. Other American films addressing cultural diversity found their way into Canada, largely through the work of the Jewish Labor Committees in Canada and the United States. After the war, the US Jewish Labor Committee became increasingly active in addressing racism in the labour movement and in the community more generally (Jewish Labor Committee 1960). In 1946, the well-known labour activist Kalmen Kaplansky was asked to head a similar initiative in Canada (Activities 1946). Despite initial concerns about using US material for educational purposes in Canada, Kaplansky and his associates used numerous US films, cartoons, and publications in their work.

The Jewish Labor Committee was only one of several organizations involved in adapting US material for Canada after the war. The Canadian Committee on Cultural Relations undertook an inventory of intercultural programs and policies in Canada in 1948. Among the programs discussed in this report was a session at the YMCA conference on "Inter-racial and Inter-cultural Advance." The films *The Springfield Plan, Americans All,* and *Don't Be a Sucker* were shown in order to start discussions on racism. These discussions led YMCA officials to develop an extensive program in intercultural relations. This process seemed to be patterned on the work that was being done by the Joint Labour Committee to Combat Racial Intolerance, through which the Jewish Labor Committee was doing its work in Canada (Jewish Labor Committee 1960). The National Film Board put together a "Canadianized" version of the three US films used by the YMCA, and the 1946 report on the publications and program of the Citizenship Branch noted that the NFB had prepared an introduction for the combined version of the three films "in which Mr. Foulds [the Director of the Citizenship Branch] shows the applicability of the film to Canadian conditions" (Canada 1946).

Apart from the films, Canadians were aware of other materials and approaches that were being used in the United States to address intergroup relations. The Springfield Plan was an intercultural education program that, at least in its Canadian interpretation, was understood as "a unified programme of intercultural democratic education which would affect the entire school population and adult community" (Welland Public Library 1946; for a detailed description of the Springfield Plan, see Johnson 2005). On the instigation of the Toronto Civil Liberties Association (1946), the Springfield Plan was intro-duced to at least two school districts in Ontario (Kirkland Lake and Welland). The Springfield Plan was widely known by educators and policy developers in Ontario in the 1940s. Other intercultural programs were introduced by bringing their originators to Canada. For example, the Toronto Committee on Intercultural Education "brought leaders from the United States, including Miss [Hilda] Taba ... to lead workshops, conferences of teachers and parents, and to speak in the schools" (Canadian Committee 1948, 74).

Canadian educators and policy developers did not simply adopt every US program they learned about. At the annual meeting of the Canadian Citizenship Council in 1948, for example, a US-based educational program called the Freedom Train Project was discussed. The fact that there is no explanation of the program in the minutes of the meeting indicates that the members of this group were at least familiar with it. The decision was made, however, not to attempt a Canadian version of the program because of the projected cost of the undertaking.

All of the programs and materials discussed above were connected with intercultural education in the United States and citizenship education in Canada. This work in citizenship education in the 1940s and 1950s was central in establishing the direction of later policies in multiculturalism and multicultural education in Canada (Joshee 1995). Thus there was a profound US influence on the development of multiculturalism and multicultural education in Canada. Why, then, did these ideas and programs result in long-standing policies in Canada but not in the United States?

Canadian Particularities in Support of Multiculturalism
We propose that at least six significant differences between the United States and Canada allowed these ideas to become established in Canada. These differences fall into two groups. The first set has to do with Canadian society as a whole and Canadians' ideas about themselves. The second set is related to the specific policy development process in the area of cultural diversity.

First, as we have implied above, the founding compact of Canada implicitly recognized the value of retaining a connection to one's ancestral culture. The British who lived in Canada were loyalists who did not want to sever their connection with their homeland. Some (for example, Ignatieff 2000) point to the Royal Proclamation of 1763, which confirmed the right of Aboriginal peoples to self-government, as evidence of how tolerance and diversity were structured into early Canadian policy. Others note that the Royal Proclamation was a pragmatic response to the British need for the support of the First Nations in the war against the French (Armitage 1995), and that the subsequent Quebec Act of 1774, which sanctioned the continued existence of the French language, culture, and legal system, was enacted because assimilation of the French Canadian population was an unrealistic goal at the time (Kelley and Trebilcock 1998). Even though few would argue that either of these policies led to truly enlightened treatment of minority groups in Canada, they did build some measure of respect for minority cultures into the framework of the country while also incorporating the principle of limits to the kind of diversity that was allowable.

Second, Canada is a younger country than the United States with a different set of foundational myths. Slavery, for example, which was a feature of early Canada, had a relatively short history and does not form part of the current consciousness of most Canadians. Most Canadians are far more aware that Canada was a destination for people seeking freedom from slavery in the United States. This is part of the foundational myth that declares Canada to be, and to always have been, a more tolerant country than the United States. Although much research refutes the reality of this claim (for example, Reitz and Breton 1994; Walker 1997) the myth has allowed for a basis from which policy developers and activists are able to press their claims for diversity and equity. The fact of being younger has also meant that there was, and to some extent continues to be, a sense that Canada is still developing its identity.

Third, at least since the late 1940s, Canada has seen itself as a progressive country with something to offer the international community. Canadian adult educators in the 1940s and 1950s were acknowledged internationally as having developed some of the most innovative programs addressing democracy and citizenship (Selman 1991). It was a Canadian, John Humphrey, who drafted the UN Declaration on Human Rights. Another Canadian, Lester B. Pearson, developed the notion of the UN peacekeeping force and, until recently, international peacekeeping was the main function of the Canadian Armed Forces. We believe that this sense of connection to the international community has also led to a sense of commitment to international instruments addressing diversity and equity. As Hunsley (2000) has noted, although these instruments are unenforceable in Canada, they do carry moral sway. They have provided useful levers for policy advocates and developers.

The fourth difference connects more directly to the policy process. At least since the 1940s a close connection has existed between government agencies and certain nongovernmental organizations. In his 1947 dissertation on the Canadian Citizenship Council, J. Roby Kidd, a noted adult educator, commented that in Canada government agencies often had parallel nongovernmental partners. The public and private organizations involved in such relationships had similar foci and concerns and complemented each other's work. In the case of the work in cultural diversity and education, information about US initiatives came into Canada through both the public and private sectors and was often supported by both.

The fifth significant difference appears to have been the link made between cultural diversity and citizenship. In wartime rhetoric, citizenship was equated with patriotism, and being tolerant of diversity was seen as a feature of both (Joshee 2004). Postwar Canada was ripe for the new Citizenship Act. The fact that Paul Martin, Sr., introduced the legislation with references to cultural diversity as a strength of the country further sanctioned the association of cultural diversity and citizenship. While activists in the United States made equally strong links between diversity and democracy (Joshee and Johnson 2005), democracy is an ideal rather than a policy sphere. The link to citizenship gave work in intercultural education a strong "hook" in Canada that it lacked in the United States.

Finally, many people who were influential in the early policy development process had some measure of commitment to cultural diversity. Aside from Paul Martin, Sr., these included Frank Foulds and V.J. Kaye, both longtime employees of the Citizenship Branch; John Kidd, the director of the

Canadian Citizenship Council; and Roby Kidd, the director of the Canadian Association for Adult Education. The latter two organizations functioned as the "parallel private organizations" to the Citizenship Branch in the 1940s and 1950s. Other influential senior civil servants, scholars, activists, and educators were also committed to cultural diversity. While the majority of the Canadian public may not have been supportive of diversity, there was enough support within the leadership of various sectors that significant work could be accomplished.

Conclusion

Canada continues to borrow educational approaches and policy models from the United States, although today's climate of neoliberalism means those models have changed. As multicultural policies "retreat" (Joppke 2004), diversity is increasingly addressed in the context of social cohesion. As Helly (2003) has noted, government discourses and programs related to social cohesion are concerned with creating the conditions for economic prosperity. Among other things, this means a focus on the individual, economic participation, and compliance rather than on social protest and working toward equality and social justice. This focus has precipitated a turn toward character education. The US-based Character Education Partnership (2003) describes character education as "the intentional, proactive effort by schools, districts, and states to instill in their students important core, ethical values." Similarly, Dalton McGuinty (2003, 15), the premier of Ontario, defines character education as "the deliberate effort to develop virtues that are good for the individual and good for society."

Character Counts and the Character Education Partnership are two of the largest character education initiatives in the United States. Both advocate that schools develop certain values in students through all aspects of schooling. Character Counts identifies and defines the six values to be taught, whereas the CEP believes school communities must decide the values through consensus. Values are defined in terms of behaviours. Teaching methods advocated include teacher modelling, cooperative learning, moral reflection, conflict resolution training, schoolwide discipline, community service, and celebration. Character Counts (2003) claims to be the United States' "most widely adopted framework" and asserts that "thousands of diverse groups" are currently using it.

The York Region District School Board in the greater Toronto area has developed and implemented a formal character education program and policy called Character Matters. This program has much in common with the CEP initiative and Character Counts. Character Matters actively promotes ten attributes deemed to be "universal attributes that transcend racial, religious, and socio-economic lines" (Glaze, Hogarth, and McLean 2003, 2).

Examination of the values promoted by Character Matters and Character Counts finds differences in how they are defined as well as in the list of values themselves. For example, *fairness* appears on both lists. Character Counts defines fairness in terms of following rules, sharing, taking turns, listening, and not blaming or taking advantage of others. Character Matters, on the other hand, defines fairness much more broadly as being sensitive to others' needs, treating others as we wish to be treated, interacting without stereotyping, prejudice, or discrimination, and standing up for human rights. In addition to raising questions about the assumed universality of values associated with character education, this example leads us to speculate that the principles that allowed multicultural education to take root in Canada will persist even in the face of neoliberal assaults. Even an essentially neoliberal program such as character education provides an opening for activists to continue working for social justice.

A considerable body of literature now exists on policy transfer (see, for example, Stone 2004; Mossberger and Wolman 2003; Dolowitz and Marsh 2000; Hulme 1997). Like the related literature on policy borrowing (for example, Phillips and Ochs 2003) and policy convergence (for example, Taylor and Henry 2003), the work on policy transfer examines cross-national influences on policy. All three of these approaches to the study of policy seek to explain how policy ideas travel across time and space. Policy transfer, in particular, focuses on the role of agency in the policy process but, until recently, nonstate actors have been peripheral to, if not ignored in, most accounts of policy transfer (Stone 2004).

This chapter provides a detailed account of policy transfer between the United States and Canada and demonstrates the necessity of noticing a variety of state and nonstate actors. More than simply noticing what happens, however, as researchers and activists we feel it is our role to find ways to explicitly involve ourselves in transfer processes. Our attention here and elsewhere to current multicultural, citizenship, and character education initiatives speaks to that commitment (Joshee and Johnson 2005; Joshee 2004; Winton 2004). Our colleagues from the United States who have worked on this volume, unlike their predecessors in the 1940s, are learning from and drawing on Canadian examples. Thus the work of the Canadian pioneers in multicultural education policy continues to echo on both sides of the border.

References

Activities in the field of racial tolerance. 23 August 1946. MG 28, V 75, vol. 29, Library and Archives Canada.

Armitage, A. 1995. *Comparing the policy of Aboriginal assimilation: Australia, Canada, and New Zealand*. Vancouver: UBC Press.

Canada. Citizenship Branch. 1946. *Publications and programme, 1946*. 18 January. MG 28, I 179, vol. 25, Library and Archives Canada.

Canada. Senate. 1949. *Proceedings of the Standing Committee on Immigration and Labour*. Minutes of evidence, 29 May. RG 26/66/2-18-1, Library and Archives Canada.

Canadian Committee on Cultural Relations. 1948. *Inventory of intercultural programs and policies in Canada*. MG 28, I 85, vol. 78, Library and Archives Canada.

Canadian Council of Education for Citizenship. 1944. Draft memo re. naturalization and training for citizenship. MG 28, I 85, vol. 45, Library and Archives Canada.

CCC (Canadian Citizenship Council). 1948. Annual meeting minutes, January. MG 28, I 85, vol. 45, Library and Archives Canada.

–. 1957. *Immigrant language and citizenship training program*. MG 28, I 179, vol. 26, Library and Archives Canada.

Character Counts. 2003. Home page. http://www.charactercounts.org.

Character Education Partnership. 2003. About CEP. http://www.character.org.

Dolowitz, D., and D. Marsh. 2000. Learning from abroad: The role of policy transfer in contemporary policy-making. *Governance: An International Journal of Policy and Administration* 13(1): 5-24.

England, R. 1944. *Report on the reorganization of the Nationalities Branch*. June. RG 26/13 A, Library and Archives Canada.

Falardeau, J.C. 1953. Statement on research relating to the integration of newcomers in Canada. Paper presented at the National Seminar on Citizenship, Ottawa.

Glaze, A.E., B. Hogarth, and B. McLean. 2003. Can schools create citizens? *Orbit* 33(2): 1-3.

Helly, D. 2003. Social cohesion and cultural plurality. *Canadian Journal of Sociology* 28(1): 19-42.

Helpful suggestions on racial background study. n.d. MG 28, I 85, vol. 71, Library and Archives Canada.

Hulme, R. 1997. The global development and spread of policies and political institutions. Contemporary Political Studies Annual Conference Papers. Available at Political Studies Association, http://www.psa.ac.uk/cps.

Hunsley, T. 2000. Canada: Experience and lessons for the future. In *Reforming social policy*, ed. D. Morales-Gomez, N. Tschirgi, and J.L. Moher, 83-114. Ottawa: International Development Research Centre.

Ignatieff, M. 2000. *The rights revolution*. Toronto: Anansi Press.

Jewish Labor Committee. 1960. *Triennial report on the anti-discrimination program of the Jewish labor committee, United States and Canada*. March. MG 28, V 75, vol. 50, Library and Archives Canada.

Johnson, L. 2005. "One community's total war against prejudice": Citizenship for democracy in Springfield, Massachusetts, 1939-1945. Paper presented at the American Educational Research Association meeting, 11-15 April, Montreal.

Joppke, C. 2004. The retreat of multiculturalism in the liberal state: Theory and policy. *British Journal of Sociology* 55(2): 237-57.

Joshee, R. 1995. An historical approach to understanding Canadian multicultural policy. In *Multicultural education in a changing global economy: Canada and the Netherlands*, ed. T. Wotherspoon and P. Jungbluth, 23-41. New York: Waxmann Munster.

–. 2004. Citizenship and multicultural education in Canada: From assimilation to social cohesion. In *Diversity and citizenship education: Global perspectives*, ed. J.A. Banks, 127-56. San Francisco: Jossey-Bass.

Joshee, R., and L. Johnson. 2005. Multicultural education in the United States and Canada: The importance of national policies. In *International handbook of educational policy*, ed. N. Bascia, A. Cummings, A. Datnow, K. Leithwood, and D. Livingstone, 53-74. Dordrecht, Netherlands: Kluwer Academic Publishing.

Kelley, N., and M. Trebilcock. 1998. *The making of the mosaic: A history of Canadian immigration policy*. Toronto: University of Toronto Press.

Kidd, J.R. 1947. The Canadian Citizenship Council. PhD diss., Columbia University.

McGuinty, D. 2003. Character education: A key part of the Ontario Liberal plan. *Orbit* 33(2): 15.

McKeown, R. 1945. Our servicemen become Canadians. *Canadians All* 18(summer): 58.

Martin, P. 1946. *House of Commons debates: Official report. Canadian citizenship*. MG 28, I 179, vol. 25, Library and Archives Canada.

Minutes of the conference on citizenship training and naturalization. 1944. 9 December. MG 28, I 85, vol. 45, Library and Archives Canada.

Mossberger, K., and H. Wolman. 2003. Policy transfer as a form of prospective policy evaluation: Challenges and recommendations. *Public Administration Review* 63(4): 428-40.

Phillips, D., and K. Ochs. 2003. Processes of policy borrowing in education: Some explanatory and analytical devices. *Comparative Education* 39(4): 451-61.

Reitz, J.G., and R. Breton. 1994. *The illusion of difference: Realities of ethnicity in Canada and the United States*. Toronto: C.D. Howe Institute.

Selman, G. 1991. *Citizenship and the adult education movement in Canada*. Vancouver: Centre for Continuing Education, University of British Columbia.

Stone, D. 2004. Transfer agents and global networks in the "transnationalization" of policy. *Journal of European Public Policy* 11(3): 545-66.

Taylor, S., and M. Henry. 2003. Social justice in a global context: Education Queensland's 2010 strategy. *International Journal of Inclusive Education* 7(4): 337-55.

Toronto Civil Liberties Association. 1946. Update to members. MG 31, K 9, vol. 8, Library and Archives Canada.

Walker, J.W. St. G. 1997. *"Race," rights and the law in the Supreme Court of Canada*. Waterloo, ON: Osgoode Society and Wilfrid Laurier University Press.

Welland Public Library. 1946. Preface. *A Programme of Citizenship. Experimental edition*. N.p.: Welland Public Library.

Winton, S. 2004. *Character education: Help or hindrance in the preparation of students for active citizenship?* Paper presented at the annual conference of the Canadian Society for Studies in Education, 29 May-1 June, Winnipeg.

2

Diversity Policies in American Schools: A Legacy of Progressive School Leadership and Community Activism

Lauri Johnson

For American educators, the present policy context appears bleak for the promotion of educational opportunity and multicultural curriculum in local school districts. A push toward "educational accountability" over the last decade has resulted in largely top-down educational policy-making processes that have mandated high-stakes assessments for students, centralized decision making, narrowed curriculum offerings, and employed punitive sanctions for teachers, administrators, and schools that fail to meet the arbitrary benchmarks imposed by state and federal officials. In this high-risk, low-trust environment (Blackmore 2002), affirmative action programs are being revamped, bilingual education policies rolled back, and the racial achievement gap widens (Gay 2001; Noguera 2005).

Although today's "chilly" climate provides few examples, we might draw on the rich (and largely forgotten) historical legacy of community activism and school district leadership for socially just policy making. This chapter traces the development of diversity policies in three urban school districts during the 1930s and 1940s. In particular, I ask: What is the role of historical context and the importance of advocacy and activism by school officials and community groups in the development of US educational policies that promote diversity? And what might we learn from history as we strive to advocate for socially just policies and keep multiculturalism on the educational agenda? This approach situates multicultural policy development within historical, social, and political contexts and provides an American voice in a cross-border conversation that argues for a renewed emphasis on diversity policies and policy-making processes that embody democratic, inclusive, and equitable principles.

Policy analyses often date America's response to racial and cultural diversity in the schools from the 1954 Supreme Court decision in *Brown* v. *Board of Education of Topeka*, which declared "separate but equal" education for African American students to be unconstitutional (see, for example, Gollnick 1995). Yet policy efforts to address issues of cultural pluralism in

US school districts began at least twenty years before the *Brown* decision. Scholarship, public discourse, and community activism that deconstructed and reconstructed prevailing notions of race and ethnicity were evident in several US school districts throughout the 1930s and 1940s (Johnson 2003). Known as intercultural or intergroup education, this precursor to multicultural education contrasted America's stated democratic ideals of freedom and equality of opportunity with the reality of ongoing racism and discrimination, in an effort to "make democracy real" for those diverse groups who were disenfranchised and marginalized from the school system. This discursive strategy of evoking the promise of America's democratic principles and foundational documents in order to highlight groups who have been excluded from that vision has been used effectively by rights advocates throughout US history.[1]

Efforts to formulate diversity policies in local US school districts have often been reactive and crisis-oriented, generally arising in response to racial, ethnic, or religious conflict (Placier, Hall, and Davis 1997). On the one hand, multicultural and diversity policies have been used by school district officials to demonstrate that they have "taken action" on the conflict and to symbolically reassert America's democratic ideals. On the other hand, the development and advocacy of multicultural policies has served as a significant organizing tool in the "politics of recognition" and the empowerment of community groups who have been disenfranchised and marginalized by the school system. The development of diversity policies and intercultural curricula in New York City, Detroit, and Pittsburgh during the 1930s and 1940s illustrates this process.

Educating for Democracy in New York City

The onset of the Second World War brought America's racial and ethnic inequities to the forefront of public consciousness. The rise of Nazism in Europe in the late 1930s and subsequent anti-Semitic rallies in cities like New York City and Boston, the internment of over 110,000 Japanese Americans on the west coast, increased tensions concerning the treatment of segregated Black soldiers, and the failure to employ Black workers in southern defence plants challenged America's image as the "arsenal of democracy"[2] (Takaki 2000).

In response to anti-Semitism abroad and racial and religious conflicts at home, several urban school districts enacted local policies and developed curriculum to promote diversity. One of the first recorded multicultural policies was in the New York City schools. On 14 December 1938, after a report of anti-Semitic incidents near several high schools, New York City Board of Education member Johanna M. Lindlof, a former classroom teacher, union leader, and an ardent defender of democratic education, introduced a resolution that mandated "tolerance" assemblies in the schools:[3]

Resolved: That in every public school in the city of New York assemblies be devoted to the promulgation of American ideals of democracy, tolerance, and freedom for all men; that these assemblies be devoted to making the children of our nation aware of the contributions of all races and nationalities to the growth and development of American democracy; that the programs for all these assemblies be based on the social and political history of the United States; and that these programs present the contributions of all races and nationalities in a way such as to develop esteem, respect, good will, and tolerance among students and teachers in all the schools. (New York City Board 1938)

An important impetus for this policy was the work of Rachel Davis DuBois, a Quaker and founder of the Service Bureau for Intercultural Education who offered in-service classes on racial and ethnic tolerance to New York City teachers in the late 1930s. DuBois developed year-long school assembly programs, intercultural curriculum materials, and a national weekly radio program on CBS called *Americans All, Immigrants All* that focused on the history, achievements, and contributions of specific (mainly European) ethnic groups (C.A.M. Banks 2004).

To implement its policy, the New York City superintendent's office issued a circular advising all principals to plan school assemblies to teach tolerance and promoted *Americans All, Immigrants All* by ordering several sets of the recordings and curriculum materials for use in New York City high schools.[4] Over thirty New York City teachers, many of whom had attended DuBois' workshops, developed their own curriculum projects in intercultural education that were chronicled in *High Points*, a journal for teachers published by the Board of Education (Schaffer 1996).

By 1943 racial and ethnic tensions in New York City had reached a crisis stage. The contradiction between fighting for democracy abroad and Jim Crow racial segregation at home weighed heavily on Black New Yorkers. When a Black enlisted man on leave was slightly wounded by the police as he interceded during an arrest, rumours spread throughout the streets of Harlem that a Black soldier had been killed by a White police officer. The Harlem riot of August 1943 followed on the heels of racial conflicts in Detroit and Los Angeles, and resulted in six deaths, four hundred injuries, and an estimated $5 million worth of damage to Harlem stores. Of the five hundred Harlemites arrested for looting, the majority were teenagers (Johnson 2001).

That winter a series of anti-Semitic attacks on Jewish children on the west side of Manhattan and in central Brooklyn were recounted daily in the liberal press. After a string of incidents in which Jewish children were beaten up by roaming gangs of Irish youth, the American Jewish Congress called for a meeting with the principals of the nine public schools in the Flatbush area of Brooklyn to request that assembly programs and essay contests be

sponsored by the schools based on "living the democratic ideals of tolerance" (Johnson 2001).

School Superintendent John Wade responded to these conflicts with a
special *Brotherhood Week* circular issued on 21 February 1944 that included
a "Charter for Intercultural Education" and was distributed to all assistant
superintendents and principals. This informal policy affirmed that "our
democracy is both a form of government and a philosophy for group living
... founded on the moral principle of the brotherhood of man ... (and that
justice is a right and not a privilege)." This statement linking democratic
ideals with racial and religious tolerance was later reprinted in an intercultural
curriculum guide entitled "Unity through Understanding" developed by
members of the Superintendent's Advisory Committee on Human Relations
(New York City Board 1945).

During the war years a network of progressive scholars, teachers union
activists, and community advocacy groups promoted intercultural education
and agitated for school reform throughout New York City, particularly in the
Harlem schools. In 1935 Lucile Spence, one of the first African American
teachers at Wadleigh High School and the secretary of the Teachers Union
of New York City, formed the union's Harlem Committee along with parents
and community members. The purpose was to lobby the mayor for new
school buildings and Black representation on the school board. The committee later sponsored in-service courses on Black history and race relations,
staged a human relations film series, and developed a collection of African
American children's literature available on loan to teachers for classroom use
(Johnson 2002).

In 1941 another community-based coalition, the City-Wide Citizens'
Committee on Harlem (CWCCH), assembled key progressive leaders in the
African American and White communities to promote African American his-
tory and race relations, adopting many of the Harlem Committee's goals. This
consciously interracial organization included prominent African American
political and labour leaders such as Adam Clayton Powell Jr. and A. Phillip
Randolph, Black intellectuals such as Lawrence Dunbar Reddick, director of
the Schomburg Collection at the 135th Street branch of the New York Public
Library, and White liberals such as Algernon Black of the Ethical Culture
Society and Frank E. Karelsen, Jr., of the Public Education Association. With
the belief that "there must be a constant re-educating of the white population
of the city in respect to the Negro and his rights, privileges, achievement, and
background" (CWCCH 1945, 6), the committee advocated for school building
improvements, reduced class size, additional guidance counsellors, in-service
teacher courses on intercultural education, and African American representation on the New York City Board of Education. They funded a human relations
counsellor in a racially divided section of Washington Heights, sponsored an
intercultural education course on "The Negro in America," worked to establish

community schools (known as all-neighbourhood schools) and nursery school programs, and agitated for additional recreational facilities and playgrounds for Harlem children. Through an effective public education campaign of book lists, public forums, and radio programs, the CWCCH worked to "educate for democracy" and change the racial conceptions of New Yorkers by portraying the "problems presented by America's Harlems" as a test for democracy, charging that "if we fail in the solution, we will fail to make democracy work" (CWCCH 1943, 4).

Efforts to promote intercultural education in New York City continued into the late 1940s but lost school district support by 1948, when intercultural courses were criticized as "subversive and un-American." Several union leaders and scholars who were frequent guest speakers at in-service workshops on intercultural education were subject to red-baiting during the Cold War era (Johnson 2002).

"Never Again": Detroit's Intercultural Code

During the week of 20 June 1943 Detroit experienced one of the most violent racial conflicts in US history when armed White mobs attacked African American residents, resulting in thirty-four deaths, 676 injured, and more than $2 million in property damage (Lee and Humphrey 1968). The Detroit riot became a symbol to cities across the country that summer – a stark reminder of the true state of race relations in the United States and how far the nation was from resolving the "American dilemma."[5]

The Second World War had transformed Detroit, as Black and White workers from the South poured into the city to work in automobile factories converted for the war effort. As an "arsenal of democracy," Detroit became the largest producer of military equipment in the country during the war years. The African American population of Detroit more than doubled during the 1940s, from 149,119, about 9 percent of the population, to 303,721, more than 16 percent. As the new migrants settled into predominantly White or Black neighbourhoods, the city (and its schools) became increasingly segregated (Mirel 1993).

Commentators on the riot point to a number of contributing factors, including overcrowded and inadequate housing, the Jim Crow attitudes of recent southern White migrants, strikes and friction in war plants, and the racist speeches and broadcasts of demagogues such as Father Charles Coughlin and Gerald L.K. Smith, who fanned the flames of prejudice (Lee and Humphrey 1968). In the aftermath, the Detroit schools, along with other local institutions, were implicated in the city's racial tensions. One local newspaper columnist described "racist teachers" in the Detroit schools as part of the problem. A week after the 1943 riot, the Detroit chapter of the National Association for the Advancement of Colored People (NAACP) called on school leaders to hire more Black teachers and counsellors, to end the policy of assigning African American teachers only to schools with predominantly Black enrolment, and to elect an African American to the Board of Education (Mirel 1993).

In the fall of 1943 School Superintendent Dr. Warren Bow appointed a group of teachers and administrators to form the Administrative Committee on Intercultural and Interracial Relations (later known as the Coordinating Committee for Democratic Human Relations) to work with community groups to develop a districtwide curriculum and provide ongoing staff development in intercultural education. This committee arranged teacher visits to other school districts, such as Chicago; Springfield, Massachusetts; and New York City, to examine their intercultural education programs. In 1944 it initiated what became a five-year relationship with Dr. H.H. Giles and the Bureau for Intercultural Education (Rachel DuBois' former organization) to provide ongoing technical assistance to the district in human relations. The bureau surveyed interracial practices, disseminated curriculum materials, funded summer institutes for teachers, and developed an intercultural curriculum guide entitled *Building One Nation, Indivisible* (Detroit Public Schools 1944) that was distributed to all Detroit schools. For several years the Bureau for Intercultural Education also compiled exemplary intercultural curriculum approaches from local schools. The resulting publication, *Promising Practices in Intergroup Education* (Edmon and Collins 1947), outlined eleven approaches to intercultural education, ranging from the "cultural contributions" approach, to the study of prejudice, to providing vicarious experiences of discrimination, to community participation in democratic decision making. The practices outlined in this book, distributed nationally by the bureau during the 1940s, are strikingly similar to many current approaches to multicultural education in US schools.

The school board's administrative committee, along with religious and community leaders, also campaigned for months for the adoption of a far-ranging intercultural policy for the schools that would send a message to the rest of the country that Detroit was dealing aggressively with its racial problems. On 9 January 1945 the board unanimously approved the Detroit Intercultural Code, which was modelled on a policy that Detroit social service agencies had adopted.

The policy stated: "The school has responsibility for treating all people fairly regardless of race, creed, national origin, or economic status." Detroit's policy prohibited racial discrimination in the hiring and promotion of employees, prevented out-of-district transfers based on race in an effort to curb "White flight," mandated staff development and teacher education in "sound intercultural concepts" and the "understanding of minority groups," and advocated that the curriculum "provide for each pupil the educational experiences best suited to meet his needs and abilities" (Harrison 1953). In his ten-year study of intercultural efforts in the Detroit schools, Harrison

(1953) identifies the Intercultural Code as the most significant accomplishment of the administrative committee. He notes that as result of the policy the district discontinued support for racially segregated summer camp programs and High Y activities, and that school administrators even boycotted a local segregated golf club. Personnel policies of the Detroit schools were also reviewed and aligned to the provisions of the Intercultural Code, illustrating how the enactment of a diversity policy influences other school district policies.

Intercultural education activity in the Detroit schools abated in the early 1950s, as the district ended its relationship with the Bureau for Intercultural Education and the activists in the African American community increasingly turned their attention to issues of school desegregation and the neglect of schools in predominately Black neighbourhoods.

Promoting Intercultural Education in Pittsburgh

As Pittsburgh developed into a major industrial centre in the early twentieth century, it became home to the world. Between 1880 and 1930, the city's population tripled, from 235,000 to 670,000, largely due to an influx of Italian, Polish, German, Austrian, and Czechoslovakian immigrants (including a substantial Jewish population), and southern Blacks who had followed the great migration north in search of economic opportunity in Pittsburgh's factories. By 1940 foreign-born immigrants, their children, and African American migrants from the South constituted a majority of the residents of Pittsburgh and surrounding Allegheny County (Faires 1989).

Yet Pittsburgh's Black population and many of these "new Americans" failed to reap the full benefits of democratic citizenship. A series of Depression-era social surveys revealed that "poverty is rampant, unemployment extensive, living conditions disgraceful and dangerous, local government inefficient, inadequate and expensive, and the dominant class of English, Scotch, and Irish snub the foreign born and Negroes" (Klein 1938, 239). The inequities in housing, employment, social services, and schooling revealed in these studies became the catalyst for social change by Pittsburgh's community advocacy groups. For example, a Pittsburgh Urban League study noted that of the ten largest cities in the country, Pittsburgh stood out as the only one that did not employ Black teachers (Reid 1930, 289). Throughout the 1930s the Urban League agitated for the hiring of Black teachers and Black representation on the Pittsburgh School Board. Proposals included a one-day strike by Black schoolchildren and a boycott of school taxes in order to "dramatize the fight for Negro teachers in the Pittsburgh schools" (Pittsburgh Urban League 1932). Homer Brown, a prominent African American lawyer, state legislator, and president of the Pittsburgh chapter of the NAACP, took up the fight and organized a series of highly publicized legislative hearings into the matter. When the state legislature issued a finding of discrimination against the

Pittsburgh Public Schools in 1937, the district hired its first African American teacher, Lawrence Peeler, to teach music in the Hill district. In 1943 Homer Brown became the first African American appointed to the Pittsburgh School Board, where he continued to advocate for more Black teachers and culturally responsive curriculum (*Philadelphia Tribune* 1943).[6]

For Pittsburgh's immigrant population, Phillip Klein's influential survey documented the lack of social services and concluded that the social problems of first- and second-generation immigrants were "mainly those of ethnic, cultural, and economic assimilation" and "mutual distrust and lack of understanding between old and new Americans." Instead of traditional social services, he recommended "long-range educational programs" for Pittsburgh's immigrants that would "advance mutual understanding and minimize destructive prejudices" (Klein 1938, 909).

In response, the American Service Institute of Allegheny County was created in 1941 to reduce racial and ethnic prejudice and serve as a resource to other agencies and organizations in the "development of programs for integrating individuals and groups of diverse ethnic, social, racial, and religious backgrounds into the total community life" (Green 1945). Utilizing social work graduate students' from the University of Pittsburgh, the agency conducted ongoing training in group work and prejudice reduction techniques for Pittsburgh teachers and leaders of youth organizations. They also provided classes and technical assistance to immigrants who were applying for American citizenship.

The American Service Institute's most unique contribution to intercultural education was two series of highly successful radio programs. The first series, modelled after Rachel Davis DuBois' *Americans All, Immigrants All* radio program, featured historical vignettes and ethnic groups specific to western Pennsylvania and utilized well-known citizens of Pittsburgh as amateur actors (American Service Institute 1942a). The next radio series, entitled *You Are an American*, was broadcast live from the Salvation Army studio throughout 1942. The first episode, "The Negroes in the Making of Our Democracy," was staged before a packed audience that included prominent African American leaders, city officials, and the media. The program opened with the Urban League's Community Choir singing "Lift Every Voice and Sing" and included historical features on well-known African Americans of achievement, as well as local Black leaders such as Martin Delaney, a doctor and the first Black field officer in the US Army, Homer Brown, and Robert Vann, founder of the *Pittsburgh Courier* (American Service Institute 1942b).

Key Pittsburgh school district leaders and board members also promoted intercultural education, particularly after the 1943 race riots in Detroit, Los Angeles, and Harlem. Mrs. F.B. Chalfant, a school board member since 1927 from a prominent local family, travelled to Springfield, Massachusetts, and spent three days visiting classes and talking with teachers, administrators, and parents to observe their communitywide intercultural education program (National Conference of Christians and Jews 1945). She was so impressed with the Springfield Plan (Chatto and Halligan 1945) that she urged the Pittsburgh School Board to adopt a similar approach to intercultural education at a public meeting sponsored by the American Service Institute. Arguing that the recent Detroit riots exemplified people "thinking with their spinal cords and not with their heads," Chalfant urged the school board to adopt a districtwide curriculum focused on "democratic citizenship" to help Pittsburgh avoid racial conflicts (*Pittsburgh Courier* 1943). Clyde Miller, from the National Conference of Christians and Jews (NCCJ), and Alice Halligan, from the Springfield Public Schools, came to present staff development workshops for Pittsburgh administrators and teachers on the Springfield curriculum (see Chapter 1 for a discussion of how this program was adapted in Ontario).

In August 1943 the Pittsburgh School Board authorized and funded a series of curriculum bulletins in all subject areas (including physical education and industrial arts) loosely modelled on the Springfield Plan's approach (Pittsburgh Board of Education 1944). At the urging of the local branch of the NCCJ and with the backing of school board members Chalfant and Brown, the school district produced its own radio series on KDKA, entitled *Loom of Life,* which dramatized incidents of racial and cultural misunderstanding and conflict and then "pointed out the need for intercultural education and understanding among groups" (Pittsburgh Council on Intercultural Education 1945, 2).

Through scholarships from the NCCJ and local foundations, about fifty Pittsburgh teachers attended summer institutes on intercultural education at the University of Chicago, Teachers College, and Harvard University. The lesson plans developed at these institutes were subsequently published in the *Pittsburgh Schools,* the district's yearly journal (Pittsburgh Board of Education 1946).

Intercultural education efforts in Pittsburgh had tapered off by the mid-1950s, with a shift in organizing efforts following the *Brown* v. *Board of Education of Topeka* decision. As the Pittsburgh schools became increasingly Black and segregated, local African American advocacy groups, much like Detroit's activists, focused on school desegregation and improving the academic achievement of Black students (Glasco 1989).

Lessons from History: Leadership, Networks, and Innovation

Carey McWilliams (1964), former editor of *The Nation* and an early civil rights advocate, contends that more happened in the field of race relations in the United States from 1943 to 1950 than during the previous eighty years. One compelling explanation for the proliferation of diversity policies and multicultural curriculum in the late 1930s and early 1940s is that increasing racial and ethnic diversity in urban areas and the resulting conflicts served as a catalyst to develop school programs (Johnson and Pak 1995).

Clearly the larger political and social context of global war, social disloca-
tion, and an international ideology of racial and ethnic superiority served
as a lever to develop diversity policies and prejudice reduction programs.
But some school districts without overt racial and ethnic tensions (such as
Pittsburgh) developed extensive intercultural education programs, while
other cities that experienced racial and ethnic conflicts (such as Beaumont,
Texas) did not. Why? An analysis of these cases highlights three key features
that I believe served to promote diversity policies in the schools: advocacy by
school leaders, interracial networks, and local innovation in curriculum and
staff development.

Many school leaders who promoted these diversity efforts adopted a leadership style that was proactive in the creation of responsive learning environments for students from diverse backgrounds and their families. Johanna
Lindlof was a tireless advocate on the New York City Board of Education
for teachers' rights and the creation of child-centred "schools of tolerance."
Harlem educators, such as Lucile Spence from the Harlem Committee of the
Teachers Union, adopted an activist stance toward systematic school reform
that entailed working with community and parent organizations to address
issues of inequality. Other school district leaders, such as Pittsburgh's Homer
Brown, made the recruitment of a diverse teaching force a priority and
took legislative action to make it happen. This advocacy by school leaders
was critical in efforts to develop, promote, and implement progressive diversity policies.

The individual school district leaders who served as diversity advocates
in the 1930s and 1940s did not work alone. Interracial networks of school
board members, principals, university scholars, teachers union activists,
and broad-based community organizations were common throughout this
period. In some cities they collectively produced innovative child-centred
curriculum, ongoing staff development programs, and school district policies that promoted diversity. These networks, often funded and nurtured by
advocacy groups like the Bureau for Intercultural Education, the National
Conference of Christians and Jews, and the antidiscrimination committees
of labour unions such as the United Auto Workers, extended across the
country and into Canada. They facilitated the development of national
summer institutes for teachers and the production and dissemination of
films, radio shows, and other curriculum materials, and provided individual
school districts with the material resources necessary to develop and sustain
intercultural programs (see Chapter 1). The importance of these networks
cannot be underestimated. Siddle Walker (2004) has suggested that the current absence of these types of regional and national networks, particularly
among African American educators, signals a critical difference between past
successful organizing and advances for African American students and current inactivity in many school districts regarding diversity issues.

Finally, intercultural advocates in the late 1930s and 1940s assumed that in order to refashion the beliefs and behaviour of teachers and administrators, new curriculum materials and pedagogical approaches were required. Developing a curriculum guide to implement diversity policies was a common strategy across school districts. While some intercultural education programs in the 1940s utilized nationally produced curriculum materials and staff development approaches, many tailored classroom curricula, audiovisual materials, and staff development programs to their local context. Intercultural curriculum approaches varied in their conceptual sophistication and systematic approach to inequality, as multicultural education programs do today. Some, like the American Service Institute's curriculum guides and radio programs, focused on local cultural and ethnic groups and embodied a "cultural contributions" approach. Others, like the Springfield Plan, attempted to refashion citizenship curriculum as racial and religious tolerance and rewrite an inclusive (if idealized) vision of American democracy where all citizens had a voice and the responsibility to exercise it. Most intercultural education curriculum ignored institutionalized racism and discrimination, although the stance of activists like Lucile Spence and the Teachers Union of New York City came closest to challenging racism and structural inequalities.

Conclusion

The historical development of diversity efforts in US school districts does not reflect a steady progression of ever more inclusive policies. Many of the diversity issues debated in the 1930s and 1940s, for example, remain on the multicultural agenda. Those issues include the need for more teachers of colour, increased parent and community involvement in school decision making, culturally responsive curricula that reflect the history, values, and cultural knowledge of students from diverse backgrounds, and teacher education that prepares educators to "teach for diversity." Community organizations and school district advocates have historically used the media, school board meetings, the courts, and the streets to promote their issues and debate their concerns in the public arena. This symbolic function of the policy-making process as a catalyst and discursive space for community debate about diversity issues has been largely ignored in both the multicultural and policy analysis literature.

Yet this historical advocacy and debate about diversity policies appears to have had little lasting effect on the power relationships in local school districts or the dominant discourses about whose history and culture "counts" in the school curriculum. Thus, each subsequent generation of school advocates and community activists has needed to continue to press its concerns to keep diversity issues on the educational agenda. But while US diversity policies in local school districts may be primarily symbolic and are seldom fully implemented, I believe (to paraphrase Catherine Cornbleth in Chapter 17) that they can provide space – and language, leverage, and legitimation – to challenge inequities in schools and society for those who care to use them.

Notes

1 Three examples come to mind. The "Declaration of Sentiments," a version of the Declaration of Independence rewritten by Elizabeth Cady Stanton to include women, launched the women's rights movement in Seneca Falls, New York, in 1848. Dr. Martin Luther King Jr. evoked the phrase "we hold these truths to be self-evident – that all men are created equal" and the promise of "life, liberty, and the pursuit of happiness" for Black Americans in his "I Have a Dream" speech during the 1963 March on Washington. And the Black Panther Party used the preamble to the Declaration of Independence and the Bill of Rights in the late 1960s to bolster its call to bear arms and abolish any government that no longer "derived its just powers from the consent of the governed."

2 In Franklin Delano Roosevelt's radio address to the nation on 29 December 1940, he coined the term "arsenal for democracy" and linked America's production of war goods with preserving democratic institutions in the Western world (see US Department of State 1943, 598-607).

3 Known as the Swedish Fightingale, during her term on the New York City school board (1936-43) Lindlof also advocated for moveable furniture in classrooms, sabbaticals and maternity leaves for teachers, a summer camp for city children, and a progressive, student-centred curriculum. See New York Teachers Guild, *Guild Bulletin*, 20 May 1943, 3.

4 On the 15 January 1939 episode of *Americans All, Immigrants All,* the announcer commended the New York City Board of Education for its policy to promote "tolerance and freedom for all men." See Mail plug, "Germans in America" episode. IHRC 114, box 25, FF2, Immigration History Research Center Archives, University of Minnesota.

5 Gunnar Myrdal's book *An American Dilemma: The Negro Problem and Modern Democracy* (1944), which documented the social and economic conditions of African Americans during the first half of the twentieth century, became emblematic of the gap between the democratic promise of the American creed and the lived reality for most African Americans.

6 Glasco (1989) notes that Pittsburgh did not hire large numbers of African American teachers until the late 1940s.

References

American Service Institute. 1942a. *Americans all script*. Pittsburgh: American Service Institute.

–. 1942b. *You are an American: The Negro, series 2*. Pittsburgh: American Service Institute.

Banks, C.A.M. 2004. Intercultural and intergroup education, 1929-1959: Linking schools and communities. In *Handbook of research on multicultural education*, 2nd ed., ed. J.A. Banks and C.A.M. Banks, 753-69. San Francisco: Jossey-Bass.

Blackmore, J. 2002. Leadership for socially just schooling: More substance and less style in high-risk, low-trust times? *Journal of School Leadership* 12(2): 198-222.

Chatto, C.I., and A.L. Halligan. 1945. *The story of the Springfield Plan*. New York: Barnes and Noble.

CWCCH (City-Wide Citizens' Committee on Harlem). 1943. *Does this light reach Harlem?* Frank Crosswaith Papers, Microfiche SC 001,286, Schomburg Center for Research in Black Culture, New York Public Library.

–. 1945. *Origins, gains, and goals*. Brochure. Microfiche SC 000,995, Schomburg Center for Research in Black Culture, New York Public Library.

Detroit Public Schools. 1944. *Building one nation indivisible: A bulletin on intercultural education*. Detroit: Detroit Public Schools.

Edmon, M., and L.B. Collins. 1947. *Promising practices in intergroup education*. New York: Bureau for Intercultural Education.

Faires, N. 1989. Immigrants and industry: Peopling the "Iron City." In *City at the point: Essays on the social history of Pittsburgh*, ed. S. Hays, 3-31. Pittsburgh: University of Pittsburgh Press.

Gay, G. 2001. Educational equity for students of color. In *Multicultural education: Issues and perspectives*, ed. J.A. Banks and C.A.M. Banks, 195-228. New York: John Wiley and Sons.

Glasco, L. 1989. Double burden: The Black experience in Pittsburgh. In *City at the point: Essays on the social history of Pittsburgh*, ed. S. Hays, 69-109. Pittsburgh: University of Pittsburgh Press.

Gollnick, D.M. 1995. National and state initiatives for multicultural education. In *Handbook of research on multicultural education*, ed. J.A. Banks and C.A.M. Banks, 44-64. New York: Macmillan.

Green, H.D. 1945. *A social agency stimulates intergroup education*. Pittsburgh: American Service Institute.

Harrison, H.J. 1953. A study of the work of the Coordinating Committee on Democratic Human Relations in the Detroit Public Schools from September, 1943 to June, 1952. PhD dissertation, Wayne State University.

Johnson, L. 2001. "We declare that teachers need more intercultural education not less": The politics of intercultural education in the New York City schools – 1944-1950. Paper presented at the annual meeting of the History of Education Society, 18-21 October, Yale University, New Haven, CT.

–. 2002. "Making democracy real": Teacher union and community activism to promote diversity in the New York City public schools, 1935-1950. *Urban Education* 37(5): 566-87.

–. 2003. Making a difference: Leadership for social justice in historical perspective. Paper presented at the annual convention of University Council of Educational Administration, 10-13 November, Portland, OR.

–. 2005. "One community's total war against prejudice": Citizenship for democracy in Springfield, Massachusetts, 1939-1945. Paper presented at the American Educational Research Association meeting, 11-15 April, Montreal.

Johnson, L., and Y. Pak. 2005. "There ain't no North any more": Racial conflict and the struggle for intercultural education in the Detroit and Los Angeles schools, 1943-1950. Paper presented at the annual meeting of the History of Education Society, 20-23 October, Baltimore, MD.

Klein, P. 1938. *A social study of Pittsburgh: Community problems and social services of Allegheny County*. New York: Columbia University Press.

Lee, A.M., and N.D. Humphrey. 1968. *Race riot (Detroit, 1943)*. New York: Octagon Books.

McWilliams, C. 1964. *Brothers under the skin*. Boston: Little, Brown and Company.

Mirel, J. 1993. *The rise and fall of an urban school system: Detroit, 1907-1981*. Ann Arbor: University of Michigan Press.

Myrdal, G. 1944. *An American dilemma: The Negro problem and modern democracy*. New York: Harper.

National Conference of Christians and Jews. 1945. *Education for democracy in Springfield public schools*. New York: National Conference of Christians and Jews.

New York City Board of Education. 1938. *City of New York Board of Education Journal* 2: 2705.

–. 1945. Unity through understanding. *Curriculum Bulletin* 4: 1-3.

Noguera, P. 2005. The racial achievement gap: How can we assure an equity of outcomes? In *Urban education with an attitude*, ed. L. Johnson, M.E. Finn, and R. Lewis, 7-15. Albany: State University of New York Press.

Philadelphia Tribune. 1943. Pitt attorney named to Board of Education, 6 November, 1.

Pittsburgh Board of Education. 1944. *The Board of Public Education minutes*, 22 August. University of Pittsburgh Library.

–. 1946. *Pittsburgh Schools* 20: 2-3.

Pittsburgh Council on Intercultural Education. 1945. *Publicity committee minutes*, 2.

Pittsburgh Courier. 1943. Democracy to be taught in local schools, 25 September, 2.

Pittsburgh Urban League. 1932. *Conference on public school situation in Pittsburgh*, 1 October 1934.

Placier, M., M. Hall, and B.J. Davis. 1997. Making multicultural education policy: The transformation of intentions. In *Race, ethnicity, and multiculturalism: Policy and practice,* ed. M. Hall, 169-201. New York: Garland.

Reid, I.D.A. 1930. *The social conditions of the Negro in the Hill district of Pittsburgh.* Pittsburgh: General Committee on the Hill Survey.

Schaffer, R. 1996. Multicultural education in New York City during World War II. *New York History 77*(3): 301-32.

Siddle Walker, V. 2004. African American perspectives on *Brown* v. *Topeka Board of Education:* Teacher activism, cultural consciousness, curriculum theorizing, and citizenship preparation. Symposium presented at the annual meeting of the American Educational Research Association, 12-16 April, San Diego, CA.

Takaki, R. 2000. *Double victory: A multicultural history of America in World War II.* Boston: Little Brown.

US Department of State. 1943. *Peace and War: United States Foreign Policy, 1931-41.* Publication 1983. Washington, DC: US Government Printing Office.

3
We Are Already Multicultural: Why Policy and Leadership Matter
Yoon K. Pak

The philosopher Hans Georg Gadamer (1993) once wrote that we are already related. Extending that thought, I question how our perceptions of the world and each other might be different if we presupposed that our current relations were built upon a well-established multicultural past. In other words, what if we came from the position that we are already multicultural? Historians of the American West have certainly written about this notion and how the accounts of its past have neglected to weave the intricate relationships of various racial, religious, and ethnic groups into a complex narrative. They argue that we need to view society "through its complex, varied, paradoxical history rather than as a collage of stereotypes," for our nation has been the home of "Indians, Hispanics, Asians, blacks, and Anglos ... who share the same region and its history, but wait to be introduced" (Patricia Limerick quoted in Taylor 1998, 315). To be sure, the Joshee and Winton chapter and Johnson's narrative bring us closer to that reality. These chapters provide a much-needed analysis of the development of a Canadian multicultural policy coupled with the parallel rise of diversity policies in select American schools. Given the geographical proximity, is it not plausible that ideas focused on the building of democratic human relations were shared across borders? Joshee and Winton provide ample evidence of how the United States influenced Canadian policies, but Americans were less willing to admit that we needed assistance from foreign countries to help establish democratic relations in the schools. Our American arrogance notwithstanding, I focus this discussion on why policies and leadership matter, particularly in the development of intercultural relationships: precisely because our societies have yet to embrace the intricate web of pre-existing multicultural relations.

As a precursor to this discussion, I also argue that citizenship education featured prominently in complicating matters of policy and leadership. How could policy and theoretical directives to educate citizens and students for equal membership in society work for those denied full participatory citizenship? What does it mean to be an American? A Canadian? For people without the full legal rights of citizenship, this question always lingers. Positioned literally and figuratively on the outskirts of society, disenfranchised people sought to expose the hypocrisy of the nation's democratic rhetoric. For people situated among the comforts of mainstream society, the idea of equality and the reality that their privileged status would have to be shared posed a threat. So while the vision of equality stated in multicultural policies may not have been anything new to those on the margins, it approached a reversal of relations for others.

Intercultural educators carefully toed the line by providing educational aims that would appease the majority while recognizing the rights of the minority. One example of this method is the CBS radio series entitled *Americans All, Immigrants All,* nationally broadcast in 1938-39. It was the brainchild of the progressive educator Rachel Davis DuBois, who brought a cultural contributions approach, the first of its kind, to the discussion of America as a mélange of cultures.[1] The *Americans All, Immigrants All* series featured a different racial or ethnic group each Sunday afternoon and worked to dispel certain myths about these groups while creating and reinscribing others. The twenty-six half-hour episodes in the series spotlighted the contributions of various cultural groups to the economic, social, and political development of the United States. The programs were presented by the US Office of Education and the Columbia Broadcasting System with the cooperation of the Service Bureau for Intercultural Education and the Works Progress Administration (Orientals 1939, para. 1). Groups featured included Hispanics, Jews, Scotch-Irish, Italians, English, Orientals,[2] and Negroes. Predicated on the immigrant model, each episode dealt with some of the obstacles each group had overcome to "make it" in American society. Even African Americans, who were forced into slavery, and Native Americans, who were already in the United States, fit into the immigrant paradigm. Sidestepping the issues of slavery (by framing it as the "importation of Africans") and the removal of indigenous people from their ancestral homelands made it easier for the average radio listener to adopt an immigrant model for all. Furthermore, the representation of immigrants, such as the Chinese and Japanese, in the radio programs allowed for the early development of what I deem the "model minority other."

Even though the phrase *model minority* is typically associated in the United States with the Chinese and Japanese during the 1950s and 1960s, especially as a deliberate strategy to wage unfair comparisons with African Americans and Latinos during the civil rights era, I assert that such racialized categorizations began much earlier.[3] Model minority may seem an innocuous moniker, perhaps even one to which racial and ethnic groups should aspire. Yet such idealizations portray a form of model citizenship outside the norms and boundaries of regular citizenship – a hypercitizen, if you will. The contradiction, however, centres on how this mode of citizenship for Asians does not truly exist.

For too long, Asian Americans have remained on the periphery of the social, political, and historical discourses. In what the legal scholar Angelo Ancheta (2000) terms "outsider racialization,"[4] such normative views of Asian-Pacific Americans as perpetual foreigners have made citizenship central in the formation of Asian American histories. Specifically, anti-Asian sentiment manifested itself in segregation and discriminatory laws that dictated the social, political, and moral precepts of everyday life. Since the late nineteenth century, anti-Asian laws included: "1) federal naturalization laws that imposed a racial barrier on Asian immigrants seeking United States citizenship; 2) federal immigration laws limiting migration from Asian and Pacific Island countries; and 3) state and local laws discriminating against Asians, often based on their ineligibility for citizenship" (22). Resident Asians could not become naturalized citizens until after the Second World War. As such, the model minority myth represents one end of the yellow peril continuum that has plagued Asian immigrants in the United States and Canada. It has stood as a hegemonic device to pit one racial group against another (Lee 1996). The contrast between the ideal and the reality of life for Asian immigrants still has troubling ramifications when devising educational policies supposedly based on equal opportunities.[5] While I won't delve into such complicated matters here, I do want to examine how the radio series *Americans All, Immigrants All,* while quite progressive for its time, fell short of broaching the unequal citizenship status of Asians.

"Orientals in the United States" was the sixteenth of the twenty-six episodes of the *Americans All* series. The broadcast of the program was preceded by extensive discussion of how the early Japanese and Chinese immigrants should be portrayed. Much to DuBois' credit, she made genuine efforts to gather accurate information on the cultural contributions of various groups. She consulted with the directors of the Chinese and Japanese Institutes to provide the mainstream American audience with an experience designed to develop sympathetic attitudes. However, compromises ensued. For example, the opening scene used a distorted adaptation of Chinese opera, because traditional Chinese and Japanese music might have appeared too strange to the average listener. Without giving listeners an opportunity to decide for themselves, the music was westernized.

Another compromise in representation, raised by a Japanese consultant, was the White actors' use of accents.[6] As the minutes of the script meeting detail, "In the case of the accents (said one of the Japanese) there is a standard Oriental accent which is certainly not the way either of these Orientals speak."[7] When asked by DuBois if the Asian advisors could "easily teach" the White actors the proper use of accents, they replied that it would be a rather difficult task. With time working against them, the program developers went with what they had. The program would feature Asian immigrants with distorted accents, but portray voices of the second generation with no accent at all. Or so it was agreed.

The broadcast radio program featured the contributions of lesser-known Chinese and Japanese scientists who made significant advancements in agriculture[8] and medicine, as well as a final story depicting the model citizen of Chinese heritage. The narrative about the early Chinese immigrants dealt primarily with how they came as cheap labour, ready and eager to contribute to the welfare of a growing nation through the building of railroads. A recurrent theme throughout the program was overwhelming gratitude that the US government had opened its arms to welcome Asians. Allusions to immigration and other exclusionary policies were virtually nonexistent, as that story would rupture the idealized picture of how individual contributions, and especially hard work, *can* make a difference in America. Individual sacrifice, even death, as in the case of Japanese medical scientist Hideyo Noguchi, who worked on the serum for yellow fever, were well worth the exchange for living in America.

The final story of the program is worth exploring here because the appeal of the Chinese as possessing honour, humility and reverence for authority speaks to the representation of the Chinese as model citizen other. The scene fades to New York's Chinatown, where twelve-year-old Eddie Wu, a second-generation Chinese, is brought to Children's Court for truancy for a week's absence from school. Ashamed by his son's delinquency, Mr. Wu appeals to the court in broken English: "I humbly apologize to the United States Government for my son's heinous offence. I am completely ashamed." When asked by the judge why he ran away from school, Eddie replies in the same broken English as his father (although there was to be no accent used), "Please, sir – teacher said that we are all naughty boys in class. She said, 'You cause me great pain. You are very bad.' So not to make her feel sad and suffer, I didn't go to school." Oblivious to the fact that the judge had already considered the case moot, Mr. Wu states further, "Honourable sir – before you pass sentence upon my great criminal of a son, may I make a statement? ... Upon my own ill-mannered self is the blame for his misdeeds. I have not properly instructed him in the virtues of scholarship. Therefore kindly sentence *me* to prison in place of my unknowing son" (Orientals 1939, 17-18). Feeling that the Wu family has "lost much face" in the court and society, Eddie's father promises to punish his son by forbidding him to go anywhere but his regular day school and the Chinese language school afterwards. Additionally, all of his toys would be taken away and Mr. Wu would not speak to his son for two months. The judge seems to play the role of a benevolent paternal figure, declaring that Mr. Wu is being too hard on his son. But Mr. Wu insists that his son's actions must be treated immediately so as to avoid any future disgrace to his family, his Chinese community, and to the country. Mr. Wu wins the admiration of the judge at that point and further sustains the belief that the Chinese were never delinquent. The omniscient voice of the narrator concludes the program with the following characterization of Asians in the United States:

The wisdom of the Orient, expressed in daily life or in art or science or thoughts of the philosophers, must be the great contribution of the Japanese and the Chinese to American life. Coming here originally as manual workers – and doing their work well – they are now limited in numbers and it is hard for them to enter completely into many phases of American life. But in a country dedicated to freedom of the individual, the oriental immigrant makes us understand that people with different habits of mind can live harmoniously side by side. We have seen how the patient labor of Chinese and Japanese has reclaimed land from the desert, created new crops, made vital discoveries in medical science and how the oriental habit of life, dignified, formal, and humane, can bring something of the highest value to our own lives. (19)

Even though other groups of Asians such as Filipinos, Koreans, and Indians lived in the United States at the time, the broadcast portrayed Chinese and Japanese as representing the whole of Asian immigration. And while there is the allusion (the phrase "now limited in numbers" in the quotation above) to structural exclusionary practices, the idea of rugged individualism, coupled with the Protestant work ethic, reigns supreme. With hard work, anyone can succeed.

In the 1940s, Canada followed this example with a series of radio programs titled *Canadians All*. The series focused similarly on various immigrant groups to reflect on Canada's cultural mosaic. For the "Asiatic Canadians," the model minority myth also prevailed:

In Canada, especially on the West Coast, we have 23,000 Japanese, 46,000 Chinese, and a few hundred Hindus. Our Japanese show a lower crime rate (1931 census) than any other group in Canada. Their young people recently won first place for comedy in the greater Vancouver Young People's Drama Festival, and Miss Aki Hyodo has captured for two years in succession the Best Actress Trophy donated by Percy Gomery. In spite of restrictions in the franchise, the younger generation in particular thinks of itself as Canadian, has excelled in our Canadian schools, and is today warmly supporting Canada in its time of need. (Kirkconnell 1941, 25)

The irony of this myth of the model Asian immigrant in the United States and Canada is exposed by the incarceration of Japanese Americans and Canadians along the west coast during the Second World War. In both countries, where the idea of multiculturality reigned, the reality of racialized exclusionary policies, based on racist myths of the Oriental other, remained.

To overcome one myth with another rarely proves useful. In this case, intercultural educators' genuine attempts to embark on a form of social democracy through *Americans All, Immigrants All* and *Canadians All* were built on both fact and fiction. While trying to disprove the narrow vision of what constituted "American" and "Canadian," they invented a new myth of Asians that has continued to deny equal opportunities. Policies in employment and education delimit the full participatory powers of Asians because, as a homogenous model minority, they have reached the pinnacle of success and are thereby fully incorporated into the fabric of society. We have yet to realize the vast multiracial identities and experiences of Asians in the United States and Canada.

As the previous two chapters reveal, achieving multicultural policies in both Canadian and US contexts requires us to view our existing multicultural relationships as realistically as possible. The gap further challenges current educators to seek a leadership model that works to enhance, not detract from, diversity.

Notes

1 Additional information on the role of DuBois in the formation of intercultural education curriculum can be found in Pak 2004.
2 The term *Oriental* is not readily used today. Its historical context established the Orient as the oppositional – weak and feminine – dichotomy to the strong and masculine Occident. An extensive description of this can be found in the seminal work of Edward Said (1978).
3 The two newspaper articles that fuelled the image of Chinese and Japanese Americans as the model minority were William Petersen, Success story: Japanese-American style, *New York Times Magazine*, 9 January 1966, 20-43; and Success story of one minority group in U.S., *U.S. News and World Report*, 26 December 1966, 73-76. It was no coincidence that these appeared shortly after the passage of the 1964 Civil Rights Act and 1965 Voting Rights Act.
4 According to Ancheta (2000, 44), "The racialization of Asian Americans has taken on two primary forms: racialization as non-Americans and racialization as the model minority," most often perceived as foreign-born outsiders.
5 The continuing debate over affirmative action and how Asian Americans are often excluded from such policies, because of our overwhelming "success," is but one example.
6 White actors typically portrayed the characters in the series, with the exception of the program dedicated to African Americans, where northern Blacks played southern Blacks.
7 Notes on Reading of Oriental Script, 16 February 1939. Rachel Davis DuBois Papers, no. 114, box 23, FF5, Immigration History and Research Center, University of Minnesota.
8 Lue Gim Gong developed a type of orange that was extremely hardy and resistant to diseases. The Lue Gim Gong variety orange received the prestigious Wilder Medal from the American Pomological Society around 1911-12.

References

Ancheta, A.N. 2000. *Race, rights, and the Asian American experience*. New Brunswick, NJ: Rutgers University Press.
Gadamer, H.G. 1993. *Truth and method*. New York: Continuum.
Kirkconnell, W. 1941. *Canadians all: A primer on Canadian unity*. Ottawa: Minister of National War Services.
Lee, S. 1996. *Unraveling the "model minority" stereotype: Listening to Asian American youth*. New York: Teachers College Press.
Orientals in the United States. 1939. Script 1 6, *Americans All, Immigrants All*. University of Iowa Libraries.

Pak, Yoon K. 2004. Teaching for intercultural understanding in the social studies: A teacher's perspective in the 1940s. In *Social education in the twentieth century: Curriculum and context for citizenship,* ed. C. Woyshner, J. Watras, and M.S. Crocco, 57-75. New York: Peter Lang.

Said, E. 1978. *Orientalism.* New York: Pantheon Books.

Taylor, Q. 1998. *In search of the racial frontier: African Americans in the American West, 1528-1990.* New York: W.W. Norton.

Part 2:
First Nations and
Native American Education

4

First Nations Education Policy in Canada: Building Capacity for Change and Control

Jan Hare

For generations now, Aboriginal communities in Canada have called for change in the policies that affect the education of their children.[1] Reports and working groups over time have consistently articulated the need for improved educational design and delivery of programs for Aboriginal children and youth[1]. These programs would give Aboriginal children opportunities for educational success consistent with their non-Aboriginal counterparts. As a national working group reported to the minister of Indian affairs and northern development in December 2002, "First Nations education is in a crisis. With some outstanding exceptions, there is no education system, no education accountability, no goals or objectives and First Nations parents, elders and educational leaders lack the authority and the means to remedy the crisis as administered by the federal and provincial territorial governments" (Canada, DIAND, Minister's Working Group 2002, 2). One need only learn of the 50 percent high school dropout rate among Aboriginal students to appreciate the extent of the crisis and the urgent need for educational reforms in both policy and practice (Canada, DIAND 2002). Yet more than achievement levels is at issue here.

Historical and Contemporary Context

For so long, Aboriginal languages, traditions, and cultures have been undermined by Canadian educational policy and practice, yet sustained against this erosion by the strength of our communities through the beliefs and values of their members. Our languages, traditions, and cultures remain critical components of educational attainment in Aboriginal people's aspirations for their children, as well as fostering children's positive sense of identity. The retention and strengthening of cultural identity, in particular, has been on the table since 1967, when H.B. Hawthorn was commissioned to report on the social, educational, and economic conditions of Aboriginal people in Canada. The Hawthorn Report revealed that Indian people consistently experienced substandard living conditions resulting from the unequal distribution of power, wealth, and rights between Aboriginal and non-Aboriginal society (Graham, Dittburner, and Abele 1996). What Hawthorn articulated in 1967 with regard to Aboriginal education remains salient today:

> It is difficult to imagine how an Indian child attending an ordinary public school could develop anything but a negative self-image. First, there is nothing from his culture represented in the school or valued by it. Second, the Indian child often gains the impression that nothing he or other Indians do is right when compared to what non-Indian children are doing. Third, in both segregated and integrated schools, one of the main aims of teachers expressed with reference to Indians is "to help them improve their standard of living, or their general lot, or themselves," which is another way of saying that what they are and have now is not good enough: they must do and be other things. (Hawthorn 1967, 142)

Subsequent policy reports on Aboriginal education have made similar observations regarding schooling trends, concluding that any vision of education for our children must ensure that "strong cultural identity and equally strong individual academic performance will create First Nations citizens who walk with ease and confidence in two worlds" (Canada, DIAND, Minister's Working Group 2002, 1).

To better understand how Aboriginal people's vision of education can be fully realized, this chapter begins by examining the shifts in Aboriginal educational policy in Canada, which have been marked by the state's focus on themes of civilization, assimilation, integration, and, finally, local control. The state's underlying assumption, at least until the current concern with local control, has been that Aboriginal people lack the capacity to participate in the schooling of their own children. Until the 1960s, Aboriginal education policy was directed by non-Aboriginal people with outsider agendas in mind, part of a larger colonial enterprise intended to dispossess Aboriginal people of their lands, resources, and identities to accommodate the exploitation and expansion of Canada by newcomers. The British North America Act (1867) gave the government exclusive jurisdiction over Indians and land reserved for Indians. Subsequent legislation such as the Act for the Gradual Enfranchisement of Indians (1869) imposed a Canadian political ideal of elected local government on Indian bands to lead Aboriginal people away from what was thought of as an inferior political system (Tobias 1991). Full political domination of Aboriginal people was achieved through the Indian Act (1876), which even today controls every aspect of Indian people's lives, including education, which came under federal control.

Education was one of the principal vehicles for the domination and assimilation of Aboriginal people in Canada, ensuring that the process of schooling would lead to the demise of First Nations' cultures and languages. Having been marginalized in the formal educational process, Aboriginal families, communities, and governance structures have been left to struggle to acquire the experience and capacity to manage our own educational affairs and assert for ourselves any kind of involvement in the education of our children and youth against the backdrop of government control. Despite the gains we have made, the control is widely recognized to lie elsewhere: "Aboriginal education continues to be influenced by the external voices of the state and the educational community. Aboriginal parents and communities, as the core group of stakeholders, continue to be marginalized in the decision making process" (British Columbia Human Rights Commission 2001, 17).

Aboriginal responses to educational policy since the 1960s have focused on achieving local control, resulting in improvements in Aboriginal education in Canada. Numerous recommendations for greater Aboriginal control over education have been concerned with issues of jurisdiction, infrastructure, and finance. One question has been subsumed in reports and policy documents concerned with local control of Aboriginal education and needs to be brought to the forefront in the development of educational policies and recommendations: how might local control best be achieved so that Aboriginal families, organizations, and communities are equipped with the means to overcome the challenges of implementing their own vision of education? This chapter focuses on the need to expand discussions of local control to take into account mechanisms that will provide for the development of the relevant knowledge, skills, and confidence necessary to assume ownership of our own education.

Capacity building for self-governance in areas such as education is the most pressing issue in Aboriginal communities today. Capacity building is the vehicle for achieving effective and sustainable social, economic, cultural, and educational self-determination. It will move Aboriginal parents and communities from the periphery to the very heart of educational processes and decision making. The latter part of this chapter suggests ways educational institutions can contribute to the development of capacity for Aboriginal people and bridge the divide between policy and the ability to bring policy to fruition. Building the capacity of Aboriginal communities to manage our own affairs offers the most potential for improving the poor social conditions endemic in Aboriginal communities and for achieving a vision of education that assumes accountability, leadership, and our inherent right to exercise jurisdiction over Aboriginal education.

It is Aboriginal treaty rights, negotiated between sovereign entities (however unfairly settled), that set Aboriginal peoples apart from other groups in Canadian society. The unique position of Aboriginal peoples within the larger Canadian society dates back to the Royal Proclamation of 1763, which declared that the role of the British government was to protect Aboriginal lands from non-Aboriginal interference and to negotiate land surrenders through treaties on a nation-to-nation basis. The Constitution Act, 1982 recognized existing Aboriginal and treaty rights, upholding our rights as different from those of other Canadians. For unique historical, political, geographic and legal reasons, Aboriginal peoples have set themselves apart from multiculturalism policies, which do not recognize historical and legal contractual obligations. "Applying the concept of multiculturalism creates a situation in which Aboriginal peoples' needs and aspirations are deemed to be the same as those of everyone else, thus avoiding the need to confront the history of colonialism" (British Columbia Human Rights Commission 2001, 8). This is the context in which our right to self-determination in education is situated.

Shifts in Aboriginal Education Policy

Assimilation

The shifts in Aboriginal education policy over time have, to a great extent, been determined by the nature of the relationship between Aboriginal people and non-Aboriginal people. Among the Europeans who began taking Canada's land as their own in the sixteenth century, missionaries first took up the task of providing formal schooling for Aboriginal children, always with an eye toward converting them to Christianity and "civilizing" them based on newcomer ways. Schooling arrangements for Aboriginal children across Canada played out differently, depending on the location of missionary settlements, the kinds of relations missionaries were able to establish with either Aboriginal groups or incoming settlers, and of course, federal government policy developed toward Aboriginal people.[2]

The first known boarding-school arrangement for Aboriginal youth in Canada began in 1620 under the direction of the Recollects, who took young boys into their seminary with the agenda of "civilizing" the Indian to a sedentary lifestyle and Christian values (Miller 1996). Alliances between missionaries and Aboriginal groups formed a model of formal schooling. Keen to convert Aboriginal groups, missionaries would learn the local language while setting up a mission and building a school. Aboriginal teachers would translate sermons and teachings into the Native language for the congregation. In some instances, Aboriginal groups requested missionaries to come to our territories, knowing that the practice of studying the Bible, which entailed reading and writing, would give us access to schooling and participation in the newcomers' world. A school would then be close to the community, allowing children, youth, and adults to acquire new forms of knowledge to complement their existing understandings of the world. Although "civilizing" the children remained the policy of mission schools, Aboriginal parents recognized the importance of learning about newcomers' ways. To ensure our survival in a changing world, Aboriginal parents chose to send their children to day and industrial schools, knowing they would return home daily or weekly.

When it became apparent to government officials that the missionary influence on Aboriginal children was limited, plans for civilizing were intensified: "In the view of politicians and civil servants in Ottawa whose gaze was fixed upon the horizon of national development, Aboriginal knowledge and skills were neither necessary nor desirable in a land that was to be dominated by European industry and, therefore, by Europeans and their culture" (Milloy 1999, 4-5). The government's response was to make assimilation of Aboriginal people its official goal. The publicly declared intent of this policy was nothing less than, in the words of Sir John A. Macdonald, Canada's first prime minister, "to do away with the tribal system and assimilate the Indian people in all respects with the inhabitants of the Dominion, as speedily as they are fit to change" (Macdonald in 1887, quoted in Milloy 1999, 6). Assimilation through education gained momentum following Nicholas Davin's review of segregated residential Indian institutions in the United States: "Davin was much taken by the American schools, which he regarded as an especially successful aspect of the American policy of 'aggressive civilization' that had been implemented by the Grant administration in 1869" (Miller 1996, 101). Day schools were ineffective tools of assimilation, as the "influence of the wigwam was stronger than the influence of the school" (Davin quoted in Milloy 1999, 24). Assimilation could best be achieved if children were removed from the influences of their family and community, so day schools and boarding schools were collapsed into a larger category known as residential schools. These totalizing institutions, in which attendance was required by law, proved to be the most destructive force on Aboriginal cultures, traditions, and languages.

Church-run residential schools were centralized in deliberate attempts to isolate children from the socializing structures of their lives. The schools' character became increasingly regulated in policy and practices. Children dressed in uniforms, were given a number aligned to their Christian name, and assumed a rigorous schedule of prayer, school, and labour. Though the government provided limited funding for the schools' maintenance, the church relied on the children to sustain the daily operation of the school, which limited their time in the classroom and academic opportunities. Personal testimonies provide a damning portrait of child labour and partial education: "We spent very little time in the classroom. We were in the classroom from nine o'clock in the morning until noon. Another shift [of children] came into the classroom at one o'clock in the afternoon and stayed there until three" (Manuel and Posluns 1974, 64). The schools' curriculum emphasized vocational skills and religious training. Boys learned farming, blacksmithing, and carpentry, while girls learned sewing, cooking, and household chores. As Canadian historian Jean Barman (2003) suggests,

Aboriginal children were schooled for inequality, permitting their entry into mainstream society only at the lowest rungs.

Policies and practices at the schools were systematically aimed at eradicating Aboriginal culture and language. If not banned outright, both were so disparaged in school that they were among its casualties. "We couldn't speak our own language ... We weren't allowed to speak our own language. We'd get a strappin' or something," remembers Ramona Gus, a Tsishiaa-aksup, who spent fifteen years in a residential school in British Columbia (Nuu-chah-nulth Tribal Council 1996, 50). The constant threat of punishment or humiliation for any expression of their language or culture loomed daily. A student attending Kamloops Indian Residential School, in the interior of British Columbia, reported: "We were not allowed to speak our language; we weren't allowed to dance, sing because they told us it was evil. It was evil for us to practice any of our cultural ways ... Some of the girls would get some Indian food ... They'd take it away from us and just to be mean they'd destroy it right in front of us" (quoted in Haig-Brown 1988, 58). The personal narratives of those who attended residential school, and those who have family who attended the schools, tell similar stories. Their recollections reveal a dehumanizing experience marked by isolation, hunger, hypocrisy, and the demise of Indian culture, all carried out through spiritual, emotional, physical, and mental abuse.

Aboriginal families and communities suffered greatly by being forced to send our children to residential schools by law. The intimate connection between families and children was broken. Janice Acoose, an Aboriginal woman of Anishinaabe and Métis-Nehiowak descent, recalled her arrival at the Cowessess Indian Residential School in Saskatchewan: "From the day my mother walked my brother, sisters, and I up to that ominously looming structure, I began to understand the depth of those black-robe's power and influence. Almost immediately, my mother's authority was undermined and subverted by a nun who authoritatively pushed her out the door" (Acoose in Jaine 1993, 4). Residential school accounts report similar experiences of families unable to visit and children unable to return home. Children were socialized in environments devoid of the nurturing that our families and communities provided. Children were wards of the government and parental rights were extinguished; parents were not consulted in any decisions regarding the lives of their children. Basil Johnston, Anishinaabe writer and former student, recalls in his book *Indian School Days* (1988, 8), "The mothers and grandmothers cried and wept, as mine did, in helplessness and heartache. There was nothing, absolutely nothing, that they could do, as women and as Indians, to reverse the decision of 'the Department.'" Residential schools predominated in the lives of Aboriginal children and families until the 1950s.

Integration

Educational policy for Aboriginal peoples shifted from assimilation toward integration in response to pressure from Aboriginal parents (Kirkness and Bowman 1992). In hearings on the Indian Act by the Special Joint Committee of the Senate and House of Commons between 1946 and 1948, Aboriginal communities and organizations submitted that federally sponsored vocational education did not prepare Indians for pursuing higher levels of education, preventing them from achieving economic parity with their non-Aboriginal counterparts. Among the recommendations made by the committee was the education of Indian children with non-Indian children. Revisions to the Indian Act in 1951 resulted in the federal government entering into joint agreements with provincial governments or charitable and religious groups to provide education for Indian children. In his review of Indian policy in Canada, John Tobias (1991, 140) states, "In essence, the joint committee approved the goal of Canada's previous Indian policy – assimilation – but disapproved some of the earlier methods to achieve it."

Beginning in the early 1950s, residential schools were slowly phased out, and Aboriginal children began to attend schools within the provincial system alongside their non-Aboriginal counterparts or schools on reserves where provincial school curriculum was the norm. The policy of integration did not prove to be educationally advantageous for many Aboriginal children. Increasing numbers of Aboriginal children had new schooling options from which to choose. However, school systems were not prepared to create intellectual space for Aboriginal knowledge, culture, and languages, resulting in lags in age-grade placement, streaming for special education, high dropout rates, and the consequent lack of economic opportunities. In his soliloquy "A Talk to Teachers," the late Chief Dan George made this point: "Can we talk of integration until there is social integration? ... Unless there is integration of hearts and minds you have only a physical presence ... and the walls are as high as the mountain range" (quoted in Kirkness and Bowman 1992, 14). Although integration was the basis for educational policy, the practices of schooling remained assimilative as attempts persisted to absorb Aboriginal children into the dominant culture.

Even given increased educational choices, Aboriginal communities and families had little opportunity to participate in the education of their children. They were underrepresented in the schools and on the school boards that administered education to their children, and were not consulted in the terms of joint agreements between federal and provincial bodies. In his inspiring book *The Unjust Society: The Tragedy of Canada's Indians*, Cree tribal leader Harold Cardinal (1969, 51) suggests that the systematic exclusion of Indian and Métis people from the governance of Canadian school systems served to expropriate any control Aboriginal parents and communities might have in the process of schooling: "No educational program can be successful

... where the people most directly concerned and affected have no voice whatever in their own education." Unsatisfied with the integration of their children in schools in which they had no voice, some Aboriginal parents and communities began to protest that joint agreements negotiated between federal and provincial bodies were unacceptable (Kirkness and Bowman 1992; Richardson and Richardson 1986).

Toward Indian Control of Indian Education

The findings of the Hawthorn Report (1967) recognized the challenges posed by integration policy, but recommended its continuation and, further, provided the federal government with a new agenda for dealing with Aboriginal peoples: total assimilation by removing any distinctions between Indian and non-Indian people in Canada. The Indian Act was to be abolished and control of all matters pertaining to Indian people relegated to the provinces. The policy White Paper that proposed this formalization of total assimilation did not sit well with Aboriginal communities and organizations. Politically organized, Aboriginal groups rejected the White Paper, responding formally with the document *Citizens Plus* (Indian Association of Alberta 1970), also known as the Red Paper. The preservation of an Indian identity remained at the core of discussions, with assimilation and integration rejected outright. "It was [only] with the growth of organized aboriginal self-determination, both in Canada and more generally across the world, that assimilation through education ceased to be official government policy. Shortly after Indian opposition forced the withdrawal of a 1969 federal White Paper ... the Indian rights organization, the National Indian Brotherhood, issued a position paper entitled 'Indian Control of Indian Education'" (Barman, Hebert, and McCaskill 1987, 1-2). Deemed a landmark in Aboriginal education policy, *Indian Control of Indian Education* (ICIE) was adopted in principle by the federal government in 1972. It advocated local control and parental involvement in Aboriginal education. In this way, Aboriginal identity could be reinforced, even as Aboriginal children would be prepared for making a living in modern society (National Indian Brotherhood 1972). While emphasizing jurisdictional control of education, *Indian Control of Indian Education* highlighted the need for relevant programs, teacher training, and improved educational facilities and services.

Aboriginal response to educational policy development continued with *Tradition and Education: Towards a Vision of Our Future* (Assembly of First Nations 1988). This three-volume report spanned four years of consultation and review of First Nations education in Canada on issues of jurisdiction, quality, management, and resourcing of First Nations education. Though the report identifies policy development needs and makes recommendations, its most significant contribution has been that it centres changes in thinking about First Nations education on the concept of self-government: "Education is an inherent right which must be respected by all levels of government. In particular, First Nations governments must assure that children, teachers of their children, and community members understand fully that the concepts of self-government and self-sufficiency are related" (3: 27). While recommendations advance the discussion of Aboriginal educational policy beyond ICIE, giving Aboriginal parents and communities new opportunities for control and authority in the education of their children, these same groups are left to make appropriate connections between policy and practical implementation of recommendations.

The *Report of the Royal Commission on Aboriginal Peoples* (RCAP 1996) represents a significant turning point in Aboriginal and non-Aboriginal relations, and made possible important contributions to advancing First Nations education. The mandate of the commission was to investigate the evolution of the relationship between Aboriginal peoples, the federal government, and Canadian society, examining all issues relevant to Aboriginal people. The RCAP report concludes with nearly 150 recommendations aimed at restructuring the relationship of Aboriginal people and Canada. The commission examined education in terms of two sets of relationships. The first set of relationships involved the connection between learning and the life cycle, reviewing education from early childhood through adult education. The second set of relationships was examined holistically, connecting learning to spiritual, emotional, physical, and cognitive development. This conceptualization reflects the values of First Nations education, where learning is a lifelong process aimed at nurturing the whole individual. Key concerns identified by RCAP resonate with previous policy documents that emphasize the need for culturally based curriculum and language programming, parental involvement, and self-governance in education. RCAP's recommendations open the door to fundamental changes in the practice of education that can be implemented within current jurisdictional arrangements, shifts to self-governments, or by self-governing First Nations. The range of responses available to parents, communities, and governments make this document a valuable resource for moving Aboriginal education in Canada forward.

Abele, Dittburner, and Graham (2000) review major policy discourse from 1966 to 1996 to determine the extent of progress toward a mutual understanding of Aboriginal and non-Aboriginal perspectives on Aboriginal educational policy. Their analysis finds that the provincial and federal governments have responded differently in the development of Aboriginal educational policy. While Aboriginal groups and the federal government have focused on education within the context of governance, provincial governments have paid more attention to multiculturalism and human rights in Aboriginal education policy. They further find that despite the progress in consultation with Aboriginal groups, notions of control, differing discourses on policy, essential power relationships, and lack of commitment to funding hinder the achievement of a common vision in Aboriginal education.

Since the inception of Indian control of Indian education as a policy stance, reports and consultations with Aboriginal groups have consistently made the indictment that paternalistic definitions of control and funding arrangements leave the Department of Indian Affairs in charge of fundamental issues underlying ICIE, hindering the policy's implementation in relevant and effectual ways. Dianne Longboat (1987) provides one of the best critiques of ICIE, identifying the legislative, relational, structural, and administrative impediments that prevent a full and meaningful transfer of control. Her analysis of the Indian Act demonstrates that none of the changes to the act that followed ICIE give any leverage to communities to take systematic and well-organized charge of their own education. The federal government retains total control over the determination and allocation of resources needed to establish, maintain, and operate First Nations schools. She notes the apparent contradiction: "The institutional structure of the Department of Indian Affairs was not designed to operate or administer schools. It is hampered in its operation by federal fiscal guidelines and regulations and by a budgetary system that is out of step with the school year" (35). Similar arguments continue to support her appraisal (Abele, Dittburner, and Graham 2000; Assembly of First Nations 1988; British Columbia Human Rights Commission 2001; Canada, DIAND 2002; Kirkness and Bowman 1992; Kirkness 1998; McCue 1999; RCAP 1996).

The most recent stand on Aboriginal education has come from the Minister's National Working Group on Education (Canada, DIAND, Minister's Working Group 2002), commissioned by the Department of Indian Affairs and Northern Development to provide strategies and measures to foster excellence in First Nations elementary and secondary education and to reduce the gap in academic achievement between First Nations students and other Canadians. The working group asserted the need for three immediate actions: transferring the jurisdiction for education to First Nations, creating a First Nations education infrastructure with supporting mechanisms, and revising educational budgets to reflect the reality of First Nations educational renewal and reform. The underlying agenda of its recommendations for the development, implementation, and evaluation of educational policy is First Nations ownership of education. The working group identified nine important facets that must be addressed to enhance the quality of First Nations education, making clear that although any reform will require the participation of the Department of Indian Affairs and other federal officials, it must be led and driven by First Nations. The report concludes that "First Nations education is extremely complex and will require a sustained commitment from all to support the recommendations and to ensure that ownership and responsibility rests with First Nations parents, elders and communities" (39).

From Policy to Capacity

Changes to Indian education policy have brought about some positive results in the last decade. The number of community-controlled schools is growing. As of 1998, there were 466 schools under First Nations management and only eight federal schools managed by the Department of Indian Affairs (Canada, Auditor General 2000). The proportion of children attending First Nations community-controlled schools increased from 44 percent in 1990-91 to 61 percent in 2000-01, with the number of children enrolling in provincial/private and federal schools declining (Canada, DIAND 2001). There has also been an increase in the number of registered status Indians attending postsecondary institutions. Exciting curriculum initiatives and relevant programming are finding their way into schools attended by Aboriginal children.

Yet we still have significant gains to make. Aboriginal youth are significantly more likely to drop out of school and less likely to complete high school than their non-Aboriginal counterparts. The auditor general of Canada (2000, 1) noted, "Indian and Northern Affairs Canada cannot demonstrate that it meets its stated objective to assist First Nations students living on reserves in achieving their educational needs and aspirations. For example, the Department does not have the necessary assurance that First Nations students are receiving culturally appropriate education. Moreover, the progress in closing the education gap for Indian students living on reserves has been unacceptably slow. At the current rate of progress, it will take over 20 years for them to reach parity in academic achievement with other Canadians." First Nations education in Canada has been identified as being in a state of crisis (Canada, DIAND, Minister's Working Group 2002). As Martineau (2002, 13) suggests, "Another study is not required, but an adjustment in attitude on the part of the government, First Nations and all Canadians is necessary in order to put into use all of the work that has been done over the last century to effect a much needed revolution in Canada's approach to First Nations education. The responsibilities of everyone must be defined and declared, adequate funding must be in place, and a policy vision based on the *educational needs and aims* of First Nations people and on *sound, relevant educational theory* must be developed and implemented in order for change to occur."

Past policies of schooling aimed at civilization, assimilation, and integration undermined the responsibility Aboriginal families and communities once assumed in their children's education. The capacity that has been lost over the generations needs to be restored, so Aboriginal families and communities can reassert their rightful place in educating their children and in Canadian society. Current educational trends that have input from Aboriginal peoples offer encouraging solutions for transformation. But just as this loss took place over generations, so will it take generations to regain this capacity.

After being formalized as policy in 1972, Indian control of Indian education came into effect quickly, with little opportunity for Aboriginal communities to acquire the knowledge, skills, and confidence needed to design, deliver, and participate in relevant educational programming. Leading First Nations educator Verna Kirkness (1998, 11-12) suggests one of the factors hindering the implementation of ICIE was "our own peoples' insecurity in taking control and failing to design an education that would be based on our culture, our way of life, and, most important, our world view. For many of our communities ... time has been lost either emulating the federal or public school systems or merely Band-Aiding, adapting, supplementing when they should have been creating a unique and meaningful education. At the base of this attitude is the difficulty of overcoming colonial domination." With the fundamental control of education for First Nations children resting with governments, Aboriginal families and communities have been marginalized in the educational process and deprived of participation and decision making in parenting, the administration of education, the design of programs, involvement in educational experiences, and the responsibility and authority of educating their children based on their own vision of education.

Government attempts to transfer control have been superficial at best, as the federal government remains in the position of ultimate authority, and Aboriginal, provincial, and federal groups differ in their approaches to the development and implementation of educational policy. It has been far too convenient for provincial and federal governments to say they have transferred control through band-operated (tribal) schooling, or make claims of space for Aboriginal participation and representation on school boards and parent advisory committees, and then quickly blame Aboriginal groups for failing to achieve a vision of education consistent with their aspirations or needs. In some provinces, legislation provides for community representation on school boards via trustees, with representation written into the conditions of tuition agreements between the federal government and local authorities. Often Aboriginal representatives from the community find themselves not listened to in meetings if they are representing only registered status Indian children, or find that they may speak only for elementary education enrolment. In frustration, Aboriginal parents and community representatives stop attending meetings (Common and Frost 1994). The federal government assumes there is dissent or confusion in the Indian community when there is no clear "Indian" position on education, which proves difficult given the diversity of perspectives in the many First Nations across Canada (Pauls 1996).

The quick transfer of control that followed ICIE also left Aboriginal communities to develop expertise in managing finances on a large scale: "The government's decision to give Aboriginal communities the authority to determine their own expenditures was done without giving them any training in economic management. The lack of foresight by governments and communities has resulted in the mismanagement of funds, which in turn has led to cutbacks in educational programming for some communities, with implications for the quality of education for Aboriginal children" (Hare and Barman 2000, 352). Aboriginal communities are blamed for mismanagement, although the government transferred control to communities with no opportunities for specific training in management skills for financial or educational responsibility.

Defining Capacity
The key to the successful transfer of control, or First Nations ownership in education, is building leadership and organizational capacity within Aboriginal communities and organizations. The major reports by Aboriginal groups outlined above express the need for capacity building, whether through the development of infrastructure, training of Aboriginal teachers, inclusion of parents and community members in education, or design of innovative curriculum. But the recommendations put forward need to expand on the concept. Earlier reports, such as *Indian Control of Indian Education* (National Indian Brotherhood 1972), did not specify the kinds of training, skills, or knowledge needed to build competency in areas where Aboriginal people have lacked opportunities to gain these experiences in the past. More recent reports by RCAP (1996) and the Minister's Working Group on Education (Canada, DIAND, Minister's Working Group 2002) provide specific direction for First Nations educational policy, detailing examples and making concrete recommendations that demonstrate how capacity might be restored to Aboriginal parents, family, and community members. For example, RCAP suggests that much can be learned from the highly innovative Akwesasne Science and Math Curriculum project and the process followed to develop and implement it. The characteristics of this project include Mohawk knowledge, values, and beliefs forming the foundation of the curriculum; bridging Western and Aboriginal concepts of math and science; holistic approaches to curriculum development; experiential opportunities for learning; community involvement; elder participation; non-Aboriginal collaboration; and evaluation of the programming.

Specific discussions of educational issues give rise to a variety of responses aimed at fulfilling Aboriginal peoples' vision of education. Suggesting that governments take immediate steps to ensure full participation of Aboriginal people in the decision-making processes that affect the education of their children, RCAP (1996) recommends legislation to guarantee Aboriginal representation on school boards, recognition of Aboriginal control of schools, establishing Aboriginal-governed schools affiliated with school districts, and the creation of Aboriginal advisory committees to school boards. The potential of RCAP to change the lives of Aboriginal peoples has been diminished, however, by a lack of legitimacy. RCAP has yet to be viewed in the same political context as other royal commissions, such as the 1963 Royal Commission on Bilingualism and Biculturalism, which did so much to advance the legislated status of Canada's official languages of French and English and provided the basis for the multiculturalism policy.

The final report of the Minister's Working Group on Education makes further attempts to move forward First Nations educational policy by addressing at length what constitutes First Nations ownership of education and raising significant topics in First Nations education today. The recommendations that follow topic discussions are much like those of the RCAP in that they are aimed at achieving final goals. In the area of early childhood education, the report recommends that "First Nations, with the support of the federal government, develop community-based strategies to address the full spectrum of early childhood services based on Indigenous principles and benchmarks. This should include the development of early identification strategies, a process for communication and integration of findings into the program development" (Canada, DIAND, Minister's Working Group 2002, 22). While such a recommendation may prepare young children to meet the challenges of schooling and empower families and communities to provide meaningful early childhood experiences, neither the extent of support for these measures nor the means by which programs might achieve these goals is clear. What financial or training resources would permit Aboriginal people to take advantage of community-based early childhood education (ECE) strategies? What significant changes to ECE training are required so that Aboriginal ECE caregivers might assist the programs in which they work to develop Aboriginal standards? Without the means for change, communities continue to reinvent the wheel or learn as they go along. Worse yet, they continue to apply non-Aboriginal standards and models to their curricula.

Clearly, the recommendations being put forward are excellent starting points, but more work remains to be done regarding the means by which we can achieve these ends. Relevant policy guidelines need to support and develop initiatives that make explicit how recommendations in Aboriginal education policy can be achieved. They must identify possible opportunities for the development of capacity to attain such goals, whether through mentorship prospects, specific training programs and workshops, visits to exemplary programs, or the development of resources and strategic Aboriginal-directed collaborations. The development and reclaiming of this capacity needs to be seen not as a precondition to the transfer of power and control, as in the past when Aboriginal people had to demonstrate a capacity for managing the transfer of power before it could take place. Rather, capacity building needs to be seen as a critical component in the exercise of power, with the direction and responsibility for it falling to Aboriginal communities and organizations. Efforts to rethink First Nations educational policy will require new strategies and partnerships, whereby Aboriginal families and communities, once kept to the sidelines of their children's education, can initiate and control the development of capacity from within our own communities, ensuring the patronized aspects of capacity building are not repeated in this process.

The Role of Postsecondary Education in Capacity Building
A significant site for capacity building in Aboriginal education has been postsecondary institutions. Across Canada, several Native Indian teacher education programs have taken the lead in bringing First Nations teachers to Aboriginal classrooms. Social work and law are other areas of study in which Aboriginal people have made great strides in attaining training that will enhance the quality of life for First Nations people, and new opportunities in academia are emerging for Aboriginal students.

Exemplary Aboriginal programs need to be seen as sources for sharing knowledge and wisdom across First Nations communities. Evidence of such programming can be seen in the postsecondary education program known as Ts"kel, a graduate program initiated in the Faculty of Education at the University of British Columbia in 1984 to prepare First Nations people for the field of educational administration. The program provided for research in issues directly related to First Nations schooling, particularly administration, and assisted First Nations educators to become principals, education directors in their communities, and leaders for First Nations education organizations and governments. Since its inception, Ts"kel has fostered research in a wide range of topics related to First Nations education. The program now offers master's and doctoral degrees, expanding opportunities beyond administration for First Nations graduate students and contributing to the research capacities of First Nations communities.

The challenge falls to institutions to respond to the needs articulated by First Nations communities, rather than to take the easy road of simply marketing existing programs to First Nations students. A good example of an Aboriginal initiative in capacity development that could be assisted by postsecondary institutions can be seen in the Nisga'a Treaty. The Nisga'a have asserted their right to develop processes to manage heritage sites on Nisga'a lands in order to preserve the heritage values associated with those sites from proposed land and resource activities (Canada, British Columbia, and Nisga'a Nation 1998). The Nisga'a are clearly looking to build capacity, and this initiative is part of their treaty. They seek not to simply control the preservation of their heritage, but to establish management processes as a way of building the capacity to ensure the future of their heritage. Within these processes, the Nisga'a will begin to formulate their needs and ask specific questions, at which point postsecondary institutions could make available relevant programming based on consultation and collaboration.

Still, treaty negotiations should not be needed to change the power relations between postsecondary institutions and Aboriginal communities.

When communities set out to determine their own needs and initiate relations with such institutions, they have already begun to demonstrate the capacity to shape their own destiny. This instance may represent something of an ideal future in community/postsecondary relations, but places Aboriginal people in control of their own education processes; at this point, institutions can demonstrate their commitment and responsiveness to First Nations educational programming.

Conclusion

What does it mean to include capacity building as a component of policies aimed at power transfer? It can take many forms, of course, with two common elements: the allocation of resources, and the identification of specific strategies and processes to foster skills and knowledge among the Aboriginal population that would enable the development of self-determination in educational programming, the creation of culturally sensitive curricula, and the exercise of leadership in implementing these changes, as well as in evaluating them. Aboriginal communities need to be placed in a position to engage a new generation of potential contributors to the advancement of Aboriginal education. New programs and existing collaborations must demonstrate how they are developing a sustainable capacity for self-determination both within the specific project and also as a model for other Aboriginal communities. Our young people need to see opportunities to participate in formal and informal educational initiatives, both within and outside their communities, that are aimed at giving them the experience needed to take a greater leadership role, with an eye to being responsive, accountable, and confident in serving the larger educational cause of self-determination in the governance of education and the structure of the curriculum. The restoration of self-governance among Aboriginal people is being fostered by developing capacities for leadership, initiative, and responsibility. The ongoing development of these capacities has always been implicit in education, but these capacities are only beginning to be acknowledged as part of the development of educational policy that needs to be carried into every educational meeting and planning session to provide focus and strength in undertaking the work that will see us into *our* future.

Notes

1   *Aboriginal* and *First Nations* refer in this chapter to Native peoples in Canada. The term *First Nations* is generally used in Canada to refer to various groups of indigenous peoples except for Métis and Inuit. In the United States the terms *American Indian/Alaskan Native (AI/AN), Indian,* and *Native Americans* are all used interchangeably. Other cross-border language differences include *band* (Canada) and *tribe* (United States), and *reserve* (Canada) and *reservation* (United States).

2   Many of the formal schooling options for Aboriginal people in Canada are described in Barman, Hebert, and McCaskill 1986. The book analyzes the history of Indian education

in Canada, focusing on specific regions and periods through case studies of various schooling options.

References

Abele, F., C. Dittburner, and K. Graham. 2000. Towards a shared understanding in the policy discussion about Aboriginal education. In *Aboriginal education: Fulfilling the promise*, ed. M.B. Catellano, L. David, and L. Lahache, 3-24. Vancouver: UBC Press.

Assembly of First Nations. 1988. *Tradition and education: Towards a vision of our future*. 3 vol. Ottawa: Assembly of First Nations.

Barman, J. 2003. Schooled for inequality: The education of British Columbia Aboriginal children. In *Children, teachers and schools in the history of British Columbia*, 2nd ed., ed. J. Barman and M. Gleason, 55-79. Calgary: Detselig Enterprises.

Barman, J., Y. Hebert, and D. McCaskill. 1986. *Indian education in Canada*. Vol. 1: *The legacy*. Vancouver: UBC Press.

–. 1987. The challenge of Indian education: An overview. In *Indian education in Canada*, vol. 2: *The challenge*, ed. J. Barman, Y. Hebert, and D. McCaskill, 1-21. Vancouver: UBC Press.

British Columbia Human Rights Commission. 2001. *Barriers to equal education for Aboriginal learners: A review of the literature*. Vancouver: British Columbia Human Rights Commission.

Canada. Auditor General. 2000. *Report of the auditor general of Canada to the House of Commons. Chapter 4: Indian and Northern Affairs Canada – Elementary and Secondary Education*. Ottawa: Minister of Public Works and Government Services.

Canada, British Columbia, Nisga'a Nation. 1998. *Nisga'a final agreement*. Ottawa: Queen's Printer for Canada.

Canada. DIAND (Department of Indian Affairs and Northern Development). 2001. *Aboriginal Labour Force Characteristics from the 1996 Census*. Ottawa: First Nations and Northern Statistics, Information Management Branch.

–. 2002. *Basic departmental data*. Ottawa: DIAND.

–. Minister's Working Group on Education. 2002. *Our children – Keepers of the sacred knowledge*. Final report. Ottawa: DIAND.

Cardinal, H. 1969. *The unjust society: The tragedy of Canada's Indians*. Vancouver: Douglas and McIntyre.

Common, R., and L. Frost. 1994. *Teaching wigwams. A modern vision of Native education*. Muncey, ON: Anishinaabe Kendaaswin Publishing.

Graham, K.A., C. Dittburner, and F. Abele. 1996. *Soliloquy and dialogue: Overview of major trends in public policy relating to Aboriginal peoples*. Ottawa: Canada Communication Group Publishing.

Haig-Brown, C. 1988. *Resistance and renewal: Surviving the Indian residential school*. Vancouver: Tillicum.

Hare, J., and J. Barman. 2000. Aboriginal education: Is there a way ahead? In *Visions of the heart: Canadian Aboriginal issues*, 2nd ed., ed. D. Long and O. Dickason, 331-59. Toronto: Harcourt Canada.

Hawthorn, H.B. 1967. *Survey of contemporary Indians of Canada*, vol. 2. Ottawa: Queen's Printer.

Indian Association of Alberta. 1970. *Citizens plus*. Edmonton: Author.

Jaine, L., ed. 1993. *Residential schools: The stolen years*. Saskatoon: Extension University Press, University of Saskatchewan.

Johnston, B. 1988. *Indian school days*. Toronto: Key Porter Books.

Kirkness, V. 1998. Our peoples' education: Cut the shackles; cut the crap; cut the mustard. *Canadian Journal of Native Education* 22(1): 10-15.

Kirkness, V., and S.S. Bowman. 1992. *First Nations and schools: Triumphs and struggles*. Toronto: Canadian Educational Association.

Longboat, D. 1987. First Nations control of education: A path to our survival as Nations. In *Indian education in Canada*, vol. 2: *The challenge*, ed. J. Barman, Y. Hebert, and D. McCaskill, 22-42. Vancouver: UBC Press.

McCue, H. 1999. An analytical review of First Nations elementary-secondary education. Paper prepared for the Assembly of First Nations by Harvey McCue Associates. Available at Turtle Island Native Network, http://www.turtleisland.org/education/afn.doc.

Manuel, G., and M. Posluns. 1974. *The fourth world: An Indian reality.* Toronto: Collier Macmillan.

Martineau, C. 2002. Issues of control, appropriateness and efficacy in Band-controlled First Nations schools: Too many chiefs? http://www.ucalgary.ca.

Miller, J.R. 1996. *Shingwauk's vision. A history of a Native residential school.* Toronto: University of Toronto Press.

Milloy, J. 1999. *A national crime. The Canadian government and the residential school system, 1879 to 1986.* Winnipeg: University of Manitoba Press.

National Indian Brotherhood. 1972. *Indian control of Indian education.* Ottawa: National Indian Brotherhood.

Nuu-chah-nulth Tribal Council. 1996. *Indian residential schools: The Nuu-chah-nulth experience.* Port Alberni, BC: Nuu-chah-nulth Tribal Council.

Pauls, S. 1996. An examination of the relationship between First Nations schools and Departments of Education in Alberta, Saskatchewan, and Manitoba. PhD diss., University of Alberta.

RCAP (Royal Commission on Aboriginal Peoples). 1996. *Report of the Royal Commission on Aboriginal Peoples.* 5 vols. Ottawa: Canada Communication Group Publishing.

Richardson, D.T., and Z. Richardson. 1986. Changes and parental involvement in Indian education. *Canadian Journal of Native Education* 13(6): 21-25.

Tobias, J. 1991. Protection, civilization, assimilation: An outline history of Canada's Indian policy. In *Sweet promises: A reader on Indian-White relations in Canada*, ed. J.R. Miller, 127-44. Toronto: University of Toronto Press.

5

Policy Issues in the Education of American Indians and Alaska Natives

John W. Tippeconnic III and Sabrina Redwing Saunders

The intent of this chapter is to identify and briefly discuss policy issues concerning the education of American Indians and Alaska Natives (AI/AN)[1] in schools, with a focus on the current and future status of Indian education. Contemporary Indian education policies have been shaped by the past policies and practice of Indian education, Indian affairs in general, and the overall history of the United States. We hope that an ongoing dialogue among scholars and practitioners will further refine and develop the issues identified so that educational policy and research will support improved Indian education in America, especially greater student success in schools.

As background, we discuss some key historical developments in educational policy regarding Native students. Then we give demographic information about Indian education and describe the environment in which the education of AI/AN students takes place. Next we identify and discuss the implementation of current policy issues, including the No Child Left Behind Act of 2001, and conclude with some key questions to consider as we look toward the future of Indian education.

The History of Educational Policy for Native Students

The term *policy* has a number of different meanings in education (for a fuller discussion see Chapter 13). Fowler (2004, 9) discusses definitions of policy in and outside of education and arrives at the following: "Public policy is the dynamic and value laden process through which a political system handles a public problem. It includes a government's expressed intentions and official enactments as well as its consistent patterns of activity and inactivity." Tyler (1973, 1-2) defines Indian policy as "a course of action pursued by any government and adopted as expedient by that government in its relations with any of the Indians of [the] Americas. By expedient, we mean action that is considered by government to be advantageous or advisable under the particular circumstances or during a specific time span."

The current Indian policy of the federal government is tribal self-determination, which means that tribes control their own affairs. The policy evolved from termination to self-determination in the 1960s and 1970s, in notable part because Indian tribes and tribal members fought against termination and for treaty rights, and raised important historical and awareness issues during the civil rights era.

A series of national policies form the backdrop for Indian education today. From the beginning of European presence on this continent, there has been influence on the education of Indians. Although contact and the colonization process occurred centuries ago, the resulting devastating impact on Indian tribes and communities is still felt. Congress did not establish the Bureau of Indian Affairs until 1834, but a government agency or task force designed to deal with the Indian problem has always existed.

In 1863, the first American reservation was established in Connecticut. Through a series of treaties from 1778 to 1871, the government gained control of the education of Indian children. In 1879, the first off-reservation boarding or residential school for the education of the Indian was established in Carlisle, Pennsylvania. By 1887, merely eight years later, nearly fifteen thousand Indian students were attending 167 boarding schools across the country. As Skinner (1999, 4) states, "It became obvious to policy makers that education was a powerful tool for subjugating and controlling the destinies of Native people."

Educational philosophies about Native education began to shift in 1928 when the federal government released the report titled *The Problem of Indian Administration* (Meriam 1928), which became known as the Meriam Report. The Meriam Report discussed cultural considerations within school curricula in the opening paragraph of its chapter on education:

> The most fundamental need in Indian education is a change in a point of view. Whatever may have been the official governmental attitude, education for the Indian in the past had proceeded largely on the theory that it is necessary to remove the Indian child as far as possible from his home environment; whereas the modern point of view in education and social work lays stress on upbringing in the natural setting of home and family life. The Indian education enterprise is peculiarly in need of the kind of approach that recognizes this principle; that is, less concerned with a conventional school system and more with the understanding of human beings. (346)

The 1969 Senate report *Indian Education: A National Tragedy – A National Challenge*, known as the Kennedy Report, recommended against the termination of federal responsibilities in education and for "maximum participation and control by Indians in establishing Indian education programs" (US Senate Subcommittee 1969, 106). The adoption of this approach to educate

Native students within their communities was premised on the understanding that minimal changes had occurred over the forty years since the Meriam Report (DeJong 1993, 197-201).

On 8 July 1970 President Richard Nixon presented a special message to Congress on Indian affairs. He declared that the policy of forced termination was "wrong" and that "Indian policies of the federal government [need to] begin to recognize and build the capacities and insights of the Indian people" (Nixon 1970, 2). In Indian education, Nixon acknowledged the Indian control efforts at Rough Rock and Black Water, Arizona, and Ramah Navajo, New Mexico, stating, "Every Indian community wishing to do so should be able to control its own Indian schools" (6).

The Indian Education Act of 1972 created changes in the direction of Indian policy. The 1975 Indian Self-Determination and Education Assistance Act resulted in further changes, such as giving tribal governments authority to contract and operate federal programs. Following from this legislation, by the 1980s the federal government was encouraging public schools to accept Native students by providing subsidies (Tippeconnic 1991). School districts were required to have parent committees as a way to increase parent involvement, and discretionary funds were made available to tribes, Indian organizations, and Indian institutions to provide educational services to tribal members. Fellowships were also made available to individuals to attend colleges and universities.

Authors such as DeJong (1993) and Reyhner (1994) note the lack of change in Native education despite more recent legislation such as the Indian Education Act (1988) and the Native American Languages Act (1990). Reyhner, in his commentary on the Self-Determination Act and the 1990-91 Indian Nations at Risk Task Force, concludes: "Many Native students still attend schools with an unfriendly school climate that fails to promote appropriate academic, social, cultural, and spiritual development among many Native students. Such schools also tended to exhibit a Eurocentric curriculum, low teacher expectations, a lack of Native educators as role models and overt and subtle racism. These factors contribute to Native students having the highest high school dropout rate (36 percent) of any minority group in the United States" (16).

Reyhner (1994, 17) endorsed the over sixty recommendations made by the task force and offered four key points for school improvement:

1 promoting students' Native language and culture as a responsibility of the school
2 training Native people to be teachers
3 school administrators and educators bringing the cultural perspectives of the students (cultural, historical and contemporary) into the school

4 expanding all curricula to include a wide range of multicultural components
   in order to promote understanding and eliminate racism.

These recommendations were made in the context of a strategic framework
for reforming schools to improve student learning.

In addition, the 1998 Executive Order 13096 on American Indian and
Alaska Native Education spelled out six priorities or goals that should be
attained to develop Native education:

1 improve reading and mathematics
2 increase high school completion and postsecondary attendance rates
3 reduce the influence of long-standing factors that impede educational performance, such as poverty and substance abuse
4 create strong, safe, and drug-free school environments
5 improve science education
6 expand the use of educational technology. (Northwest Regional Educational
   Laboratory 1999)

Neither this executive order nor its updated 2004 version defines any new
problems or solutions, and neither creates a means of resolving the issues
facing American Indian and Alaskan Native students. As a result, little
progress has been made in meeting these goals, and without significant new
funding, attainment will remain lower than mainstream standards. Similarly,
the new Indian education purpose (from the No Child Left Behind Act of
2001) is to "support the efforts of local education agencies, Indian tribes
and organizations, postsecondary institutions, and other entities" so that the
Native students can have the same level of accomplishments and "meet the
same challenging State student academic achievement standards as all other
students are expected to meet" (s. 7102).

Although the 1928 Meriam Report recommended significant changes in
the ways Indian students should be educated, over seventy-five years later
the US federal and state governments still have not provided a culturally relevant education. Often the students themselves are blamed for cultural and
academic failure rather than the educational systems they attend. McDonald
(1978) notes that those who leave the reservation setting to attend university
are often considered to be choosing to reject traditional ways and may not be
supported. He notes that "many Indian students who have completed their
degrees find it extremely difficult to return to their reservation to work" and
that "there is a mistrust toward an Indian who has obtained an education"
(83). He compares this attitude to the pride and family support given to
non-Native students.

Indian Education Today

The 2000 census reports that the US population is 281.4 million (US Census Bureau 2002). Of that number, 2.5 million or 0.9 percent self-identify as solely American Indian/Alaska Natives. An additional 1.6 million or 0.6 percent reported AI/AN as well as one or more other races in their heritage. The total of 4.1 million American Indian/Alaska Natives represents 1.5 percent of the population of the United States.

Over 670,000 AI/AN are attending schools at all levels of education. Among K-12 students, approximately 90 percent, or 473,000, attend public schools. Approximately 9 percent, or 48,000, attend schools in the federal system administered by the Bureau of Indian Affairs, under the US Department of the Interior. A smaller number attend private and charter schools; there are a growing number of AI/AN charter schools around the country. Approximately 145,000 AI/AN students attend colleges and universities, including over 25,000 at more than thirty tribal colleges and universities (US Census Bureau 2002).

AI/AN as a group have the lowest educational attainment rates and the highest high school dropout rates of any group in the United States – only 6 percent of the approximately 90,000 Natives who attended college in 1988 received a degree at the end of four years (Lin, LaCounte, and Eder 1988). By 2000 these numbers had increased slightly, but Native Americans still accounted for only 1.1 percent of the total of all students enrolled in undergraduate programs (Babco 2003). The Indian Nations at Risk (1991) report noted a high school dropout rate of 36 percent, although the numbers may be higher depending on the statistics used. Cummins (1992, 3), discussing the effects of colonialism on the educational attainment of marginalized peoples, notes that those with "a long history of subjugation and overt racism at the hands of the dominant white society" have the highest rates of academic failure and the lowest attainment. As a societal norm, educational attainment is directly correlated to future income and the quality of life of individuals.

Policy Makers and Indian Education

Indian education policy has been and is currently driven by political and economic forces rather than educational considerations. Because the historical relationship between Indian nations and the federal government is based on treaties, court decisions, acts of Congress, legislation, and executive orders, the major policy players in Indian education represent the federal government. The federal government – the president, members of Congress, and the courts – has the power to determine policy, implement policy, assess policy, and change policy, and has done so in spite of the tribal sovereignty of Indian nations and the stated policy of tribal self-determination. In a political environment, the closer one is to federal representatives, agencies, and decision-making processes, the more one can influence policy development and implementation.

In our experience, there is a misconception in "Indian country" that the people in the two top Indian education jobs in Washington, DC, have the authority to make and change policy and practice to meet local needs. The director of the Office of Indian Education in the US Department of Education and the director of the Office of Indian Education Programs in the Bureau of Indian Affairs, US Department of the Interior, actually implement policy under specific directions from the president. While the two Indian education directors can influence how policy is implemented, the Office of Management and Budget has more authority to make policy. Various secretaries in the executive branch also have authority to determine policy.

One of the interesting dilemmas in Indian education is that Indian educators have been more involved in policy development and implementation than have Indian tribal leadership, in spite of the government-to-government relationship between tribal governments and the federal government. Indian educators have found more success in working directly with Congress during the reauthorizing of legislation or the determination of appropriations. Vine Deloria (1985, 3) made a statement over twenty years ago that holds true today: "Even the most astute of scholars has a difficult time discerning how policies were formulated and put into effect. Change and happenstance are more often the determinative factors in our lives than we would be willing to admit."

Policy Implementation and Indian Education

The education of AI/AN students does not take place in isolation from the rest of the education world. Because of the political nature of education, Indian education is often isolated, forgotten, and a low priority in the bigger picture. Currently, for example, the No Child Left Behind Act (NCLB) is at centre stage and controls what is going on in Indian education at the K-12 levels. Unless there are changes in NCLB, the "Indian" in Indian education will continue to take a back seat to what is happening in US education more generally. Unfortunately, Indian education is often also a low priority at the tribal level. At times it is difficult to get tribal leadership to provide strong and continual support for Indian education. This is understandable given their priorities of economic development, national resources, protecting tribal sovereignty, and building tribal infrastructures.

The federal policy of self-determination is followed closely where the federal government is involved in education. Because the states control them, public schools do not adhere to tribal self-determination. Yet some tribes have achieved greater involvement and control over public schools, especially schools located on their lands. One such effort is by the Rosebud Sioux Tribe, which, in collaboration with the Native American Rights Fund, developed a tribal education code that applies to all schools and educational programs on their reservation. The implementation of the code gave the tribe greater authority and influence to hold schools accountable for their actions.

Several factors inhibit policy implementation in Indian education. The first is the lack of voice of Indian people in decisions that impact Indian education. While some attempts are made to involve parents and community leaders in education, lack of agreement on issues often results in none of the perspectives being included. Another factor that constrains policy implementation is the lack of adequate resources, both human and fiscal. For example, tribal colleges and universities are authorized by federal law to receive $6,000 per Indian student, but they have never received the authorized amount through Congressional appropriations. This indicates that the key policy makers are the appropriation committees in Congress; budget decisions determine what can be done in practice.

A third factor is conflicting policies. For example, the policy of self-determination conflicts with NCLB. Indian control means local decisions based on tribal and community needs, whereas NCLB is a top-down directive that is viewed as a barrier or threat to Indian education, especially where tribal languages and cultures are part of the school curriculum. The lack of flexibility in NCLB to meet local needs is being challenged today, not just in Indian education but also by states that have significant numbers of schools that are small, rural, and located in isolated areas.

Leadership is a fourth factor in policy implementation. Educational leaders, especially school principals, superintendents, and school board members, must be better prepared to understand and navigate change and deal with resistance in the complex world of Indian education, so that more students can be successful in schools. More leaders are needed in Indian education who have a vision, focus on teaching and learning, and take risks to improve Indian education.

American Indian Identities and Indian Education

For the most part, formal education in the United States has not been relevant to the needs of American Indian/Alaska Native students, with the "deficit model" leading to cultural discontinuity in the delivery of teaching and learning. In 2007, we are still struggling with the integration of Native languages and cultures into the school curriculum. We are not where we want to be; however, progress is being made. The tribal colleges and universities and Indian studies programs are good examples of utilizing Indian content in the curriculum at the higher education level. The struggle continues to be at the K-12 levels, especially in public schools, where Indian students are often in the minority and where there is a lack of AI/AN teachers, administrators, counsellors, and other certified school personnel.

The problem becomes more complex as the number of fluent Native language speakers decreases and languages are lost. AI/AN languages and cultures are threatened by the factors associated with living in urban environments; however, loss is also being experienced in many rural and reservation settings. Loss of language and culture is also associated with exposure to the larger US economy and lifestyles that promote the English language (for a fuller discussion see Chapters 8 and 9).

One of the more fundamental policy issues in Indian education is the role of education or schools in promoting, developing, and revitalizing AI/AN languages and cultures. What role should schools play in identity development? Can certain sacred aspects of tribal cultures be taught in classrooms? What role should tribes and parents play? How do we deal with schools, usually in urban areas, where numerous tribes are represented in their student bodies? Perhaps a more important question is how an "American Indian" will be defined twenty, forty, or eighty years from now. Will we turn to multitribal "Indian values," as some urban schools are doing, rather than focusing on specific tribal languages and cultures?

Policy Initiatives of the Twenty-first Century

The No Child Left Behind Act was released in 2001 and passed into law on 8 January 2002. A major initiative of the George W. Bush administration and the largest educational reform in decades, its three main goals are achievement, accountability, and quality educators, with ten distinct categories of implementation. The first goal, achievement, refers to the need to ensure that all students in a school, including those from low-income families, from minority populations, with limited English proficiency, and with disabilities, perform at par in the areas of reading and mathematics. The heightened use of high-stakes testing, such as high school exit exams, has begun to show that more and more schools are passing functionally illiterate students (Hursh 2005). Accountability holds schools responsible if children are not at or above grade level. Despite tremendous flexibility from state to state on what the testing parameters and set grade levels will be, NCLB forces states to become responsible for districts and individual schools or lose federal funding. The third explicit goal of NCLB is that there be highly qualified teachers in each classroom across the country. The Education Trust (2003) estimates one-fourth of public middle and high schools in the United States employ teachers untrained in the subject areas in which they are working. This phenomenon is more evident in classrooms with high percentages of "disadvantaged" children.

Native Implications of NCLB

Like the rest of the country, "Indian country" has been split as to the ramifications and implications of NCLB. NCLB is divided into ten main categories, or titles. Relevant to the AI/AN student are Title I, Improving the Academic Achievement of the Disadvantaged; Title VI, Flexibility and Accountability; Title VII, Indian, Native Hawaiian, and Alaska Native Education; and Title VIII, Impact Aid Program.

The goal of Title I to close the achievement gap for both disadvantaged schools and disadvantaged students speaks to the on- and off-reservation schools that service many Indian students. Schools on reservations that are within the public system are categorized as Title I. Additionally, given the low socioeconomic status of many off-reservation students, Indian students living in urban settings are often enrolled in Title I schools.

Title VI does not directly discuss the flexibility and accountability issues of Native education, even though Title VII explicitly states that Native American students should be enabled to meet the same standards as all other students. Thus, Title VI has caused community concern.

One such concern is in the flexibility of the standards of elementary schools on the reservation run by the Bureau of Indian Affairs (BIA), compared to those of the off-reservation elementary schools in adjacent communities. Both sets of students will eventually be enrolled in the same high school and therefore will have to attain the same level. When considering all of the (cross-border) feeder school situations of on-reservation elementary students attending off-reservation high schools across the country, standardization for the BIA schools is problematic. Accountability is also of concern in the BIA-run school. A school district is normally accountable to its community, and officials of the district have the potential of being fired or voted out of office. To whom is the BIA accountable? With no direct line to community and student needs, a generalized agenda and generic implementation of change will occur across territories. The BIA district is federal and therefore has a more generalized understanding of standards and needs, even with boards of education or local advisory groups.

Further, on-reservation schools that have curricula outside of the state or federal norm have regularly registered themselves as charter schools. Although these charter schools are subject to NCLB, the reporting of standards and attainment to state and federal bodies is conducted infrequently, which reduces the immediacy of flexibility and accountability. As well, the loss of per student and school funding from state and federal education bodies has little impact on the private and charter schools, which, if publicly owned, would be put into third-party receivership or closed.

Title VII (Indian, Native Hawaiian, and Alaska Native Education) contains approximately forty pages of legal jargon addressing AI/AN and Native Hawaiian education. Part A speaks to the relationship and responsibility set through treaty law to educate Indian peoples for elementary, secondary and postsecondary levels (s. 7101).

Title VIII refers to schools whose student population includes AI/AN and children of military parents. NCLB states, "During the 1999 school year, more than 50,000 children attended 185 Native American schools in 23 states. The majority of these schools managed by the Bureau of Indian Affairs (BIA) are concentrated in Arizona, New Mexico, North Dakota, South Dakota, and Washington State. Enrolment in BIA schools is growing, having increased by 25 percent since 1987. While more children are attending BIA schools, they are doing so in physical environments that are among the worst in the nation" (Bush 2001). NCLB offers hope that construction dollars will be released for upgrading and rebuilding Native schools through both the Impact Aid Program and the Bureau of Indian Affairs.

Although the act could in theory bring new dollars to improve the substandard systems and infrastructure often found in predominately Native schools, the main benefit of NCLB appears to be highlighting the current disparities in the attainment of Native students for state and federal officials. Other than increasing awareness, the act has little power to improve schooling on the reservation. Community members have been concerned that student failure under NCLB could force the relocation of entire districts of students. Forced relocation of Indian students at the behest of another government education mandate would be taken in the spirit of the former residential schools.

The Reality of NCLB

As researchers and educators, we feel it is prudent to have severe "reservations" regarding the practicality of NCLB and the ability to implement it. At a series of meetings held at Montana State University-Billings about the implications of NCLB for Native American students, Fitzgerald (2003) noted, "The need is desperate. According to statistics provided Tuesday, 81 percent of Native American fourth-graders are not proficient in science; 83 percent were not proficient in reading and 86 percent were not proficient in math. By the 12th grade, 90 percent were not proficient in math and 91 percent were not proficient in science."

With Native students already at the lower end of attainment and comprising a significant portion of the US dropout rate, it is unrealistic to assume that a model based on high-stakes testing will improve the current situation without increasing the dropout rate. We also suspect that language and cultural curriculum content will be forced out of the school day in order to focus more energy on end-of-year test preparation. If that happens, what will be achieved? Students would be better able to regurgitate test responses – something which has not been shown to improve a student's knowledge base – to the detriment of the newly expanding cultural and language literacy initiatives that have been implemented in recent years.

A Way Forward

Indigenous or Native paradigms have been described as "a way of both decolonizing Indigenous minds by 'recentering' Indigenous values and cultural practices and placing Indigenous peoples and their issues into dominant, mainstream discourses which until now have relegated Indigenous peoples to marginal positions" (Kuikkanen 2000, 411).

We believe an understanding of indigenous knowledge is imperative to conducting research involving Native peoples. Battiste and Henderson (2000) note that researchers must respect the knowledge that is inherent and sacred to Native peoples, and that Native researchers have the right to protect indigenous knowledge while producing research and publications that support the needs of their communities. Most Native researchers agree that extraordinary ethics are needed in order to protect Native communities and their knowledge bases, but there is little consensus as to how that protection should occur. Still others have cloaked themselves in the blanket of indigenous knowledge in order to conduct research without having to fully answer to mainstream research standards and methodologies. Since what constitutes indigenous knowledge is based on the perspective of the individual community or institution, the definition can change depending on who is creating it. Battiste (1998, 21), one of the first researchers to formally discuss this topic, writes, "In effect, Eurocentric knowledge, drawn from a limited patriarchal sample remains as distant today to women, Indigenous peoples, and cultural minorities as did the assimilation curricula of the boarding school days. For Indigenous peoples, our invisibility continues, while Eurocentric education perpetuates our psychic disequilibrium."

Indigenous knowledge should not be defined by the mere fact that a Native person holds the knowledge. As Native authors, for example, we have in our possession a range of diverse knowledge ranging from trigonometry to counselling theories to Greek architecture. In the same light, indigenous knowledge of ceremonies and traditional teachings cannot be owned by any one person or group (including the elected tribal council or university) as only one's own actions and original thoughts can be owned, sold, and copyrighted. The words and thoughts of the ancestors, the enlightened ones, and the Creator do not fit within this definition, as they have always been present and have been passed on through the generations.

This unwritten policy sphere is where discussions about indigenous knowledge become heated in many non-Native and Native academic institutions, as well as within Native reservations and communities that are subject to a bombardment of requests for approval to do research. As Native researchers and authors working in primarily Eurocentric academic settings, we realize that we are often at odds with ourselves. We see that traditional approaches to policy research have not yielded results and we believe that research based on indigenous knowledge could prove more productive. We need to explore Native ways of thinking about policy and education as a starting point.

Conclusion

Today we are at a critical juncture for the education of AI/ANs in America. Policy, practice, and leadership in this country over the next few years will affect not only the future direction of Indian education but, more importantly, the future of a strong Indian identity. The federal government's policies of forced assimilation and assimilation disguised as self-determination have resulted in difficult situations for most American Indian students and the schools they attend. The federal No Child Left Behind Act of 2001 places unrealistic expectations on Indian schools and students by focusing on student academic achievement test scores as the single most important measure of student success. It does not seem realistic to expect that all AI/AN students will be "proficient" in math, reading, science, and other basic content areas in twelve years, when over two hundred years of federal and public school failure and neglect have led us where we are today: a situation where too many students lack success in schools as measured by standardized test scores, dropout rates, and attendance rates.

The federal policy of tribal self-determination has resulted in more Indian involvement and more Indian control of Indian education programs (see Tippeconnic 2000 for a discussion of the challenges and successes of Indian control of education). But the unique government-to-government relationship based on treaties between tribes and the US government has not resulted in total tribal control of education. Historical, economic, social, health, and political factors continue to influence what happens in Indian education. At times confusion arises about the roles and responsibilities of tribes, states, and the federal government, and what the purpose of Indian education should be for tribal youth and adults. This is especially so given the federal BIA school system, public, private, and charter schools Indian students attend in rural and urban areas. There are some success stories, with tribal colleges and universities being the best example of Indian control of Indian education. In addition, many young AI/ANs are doing well in school and demonstrating leadership that gives us hope for a positive Indian future. Another hopeful sign is that more AI/ANs are conducting and taking greater control of educational research. Tribes are developing research protocols that control access to data and how data and research findings are to be used.

Given the above, the education of AI/ANs in America remains complex and often difficult to understand. Adding to the complexity is the language and cultural diversity among the over five hundred federal and state recognized tribes, and the differences among the fifty state public school systems. This complexity presents a formidable challenge for policy makers, educational leaders, and others trying to improve the condition of education for AI/ANs in the United States. It is in this context that educational policy and practice take place. The challenge is to build on the substantial policy issues and to be proactive rather than symbolic in efforts to improve Indian education.

The Indian education policy arena offers a lot to think about and do. It is imperative to be knowledgeable about policy issues and address them proactively. If not, we will continue to be in a reactive mode with very little progress to show for our efforts. Now is the time for increased thinking, questioning, and action to improve the condition of Indian education in the future.

Notes

1 The terms *American Indian/Alaskan Native, AI/AN, Indian* and *Native* are all used interchangeably throughout this chapter. The names have changed throughout time, but the meanings have remained the same. These terms do not differentiate between on-reservation or off-reservation in the United States. In Canada the terms Aboriginal and First Nations are more commonly used to refer to Native peoples. Other cross-border differences include *band* (Canada) and *tribe* (United States), and *reserve* (Canada) and *reservation* (United States).

References

Babco, E.L. 2003. Trends in African American and Native American Participation in STEM Higher Education. Washington, DC: Commission on Professionals in Science and Technology. http://www.cpst.org/STEM.pdf.

Battiste, M. 1998. Enabling the autumn seed: Toward a decolonized approach to Aboriginal knowledge, language and education. *Canadian Journal of Native Education* 22(1): 16-27.

Battiste, M., and J.Y. Henderson. 2000. *Protecting Indigenous knowledge and heritage: A global challenge.* Saskatoon: Purich Publishers.

Bush, G.W. 2001. Foreword to *No Child Left Behind.* http://www.whitehouse.gov/news.

Cummins, J. 1992. The empowerment of Indian students. In *Teaching American Indian students,* ed. J. Reyhner, 3-12. Norman: University of Oklahoma Press.

DeJong, D. 1993. *Promises of the past: A history of Indian education in the United States.* Golden, CO: North American Press.

Deloria, V. Jr., ed. 1985. *American Indian policy in the twentieth century.* Norman: University of Oklahoma Press.

Education Trust. 2003. *Telling the whole truth (or not) about highly qualified teachers: New state data.* http://www2.edtrust.org.

Fitzgerald, J. 2003. Native Americans study No Child Left Behind Act. *Billings Gazette,* 24 September. http://www.billingsgazette.net/archive.

Fowler, F.C. 2004. *Policy studies for educational leaders: An introduction.* Upper Saddle River, NJ: Pearson Education.

Hursh, D. 2005. The rise of high-stakes testing, accountability and education markets and the decline in educational equality. *British Educational Research Journal* 31(5): 605-22.

Indian Nations at Risk Task Force. 1991. Indian nations at risk: An educational strategy for action. Washington, DC: US Department of Education.

Kuikkanen, R. 2000. Towards an Indigenous paradigm: From a Sami perspective. *Canadian Journal of Native Studies* 20(2): 411-36.

Lin, R., D. LaCounte, and J. Eder. 1988. A study of Native American students in a predominantly white college. *Journal of American Indian Education* 27(3): 8-15.

McDonald, A. 1978. Why do Indian students drop out of college? In *The schooling of Native America,* ed. T. Thompson, 72-85. Washington, DC: American Association of Colleges for Teacher Education.

Meriam, L. 1928. *The problem of Indian administration*. Baltimore: Johns Hopkins Press.

National Center for Educational Statistics. 2002. Scholastic Assessment Test (SAT) score averages (Table 134), *2001 digest of educational statistics*. http://nces.ed.gov/programs/digest/d01/dt134.asp.

Nixon, R.M. 1970. *Special message on Indian affairs, July 8, 1970*. Available at US House of Representatives Committee on Resources, Office of Native American and Insular Affairs, http://resourcescommittee.house.gov/subcommittees/naia.

The No Child Left Behind Act of 2001. Public Law 107-110, *US Statutes at Large* 115 (2002): 1425. Available at http://www.ed.gov/policy/elsec/leg/esea02/index.html.

Northwest Regional Education Laboratory. 1999. *Catalogue of school reform models*. Portland, OR: Author.

Reyhner, J. 1994. *Fastback: American Indian/Alaskan Native education*. Bloomington, IN: Phi Delta Kappa Educational Foundation.

Skinner, L. 1999. Teaching through traditions: Incorporating language and culture into curricula. In *Next steps: Research and practice to advance Indian education*, ed. K.G. Swisher and J.W. Tippeconnic III, 107-34. Charleston, WV: Appalachian Educational Laboratory.

Tippeconnic, J.W. 1991. The education of American Indians: Policy, practice and future direction. In *American Indians: Social justice and public policy*, ed. D.E. Green and T.V. Tonnesen, 180-207. Madison: Board of Regents, University of Wisconsin.

–. 2000. Towards educational self-determination: The challenge for Indian control of Indian schools. *Native Americas: Hemisphere Journal of Indigenous Issues* 12(4): 42-49.

Tyler, S.L. 1973. *A history of Indian policy*. Washington, DC: Bureau of Indian Affairs, US Department of Interior.

US Census Bureau. 2002. *The American Indian and Alaska Native population: 2000. Census 2000 Brief*. Washington, DC: US Department of Commerce.

US Senate. Special Subcommittee on Indian Education. 1969. *Indian Education: A national tragedy – a national challenge*. 91st Cong., 1st sess., S. Rep. no. 91-501.

6

What We Know about Native Participation in Higher Education

Augustine McCaffery

The characterization of the history of Native education as the "battle for power" (Lomawaima 2000, 2) aptly describes the experiences of American Indians and Aboriginal peoples in Canada outlined in the preceding chapters by Hare and Tippeconnic and Saunders. Native people in both countries have long fought for the right to control and determine the nature of their education. Recent Native research on education reveals the parallels in education policy and lived experiences in the two countries both historically and, in certain respects, in the contemporary context.

Historically, the political agendas of the United States and Canada determined the nature of education policies and practices for Native Americans and Aboriginal people. As national political climates shifted, these changes were reflected in Indian education policies. In the United States, Indian education policy was driven by the federal government's desire to acquire tribal lands (Adams 1995). Manifest destiny, or the desire to create empire, underlay governmental initiatives. In Canada, similar ideologies led to the imposition of political and social systems on Aboriginal peoples. Education was considered the ideal mechanism to achieve government goals. While mission schools and day schools were also used, the US and Canadian governments considered residential boarding schools to be the best education model. As Hare notes, residential schools were seen as the most effective means of achieving assimilation, based in the belief that disrupting tribal communities and systems, and altering identities embedded in tribal cultures, would effect assimilation. Thus, during the nineteenth century, Native youth in the United States and Canada were removed from their families and communities and placed in residential schools to undergo identity transformation, extinguish the image others had of them as savages, and integrate into mainstream "civilized" societies (Kirkness 1999). In the United States, the off-reservation boarding school system flourished with extensive federal funding. By 1902, twenty-five schools were established, primarily in the western United States (Adams 1995). It was a "dark period in the history of Indian education" (Kirkness 1999, 4) for both American Indians and Aboriginal people in Canada.

The education provided in these institutions failed students in several ways: the vocational curricula did not prepare students academically for higher education; students were unable to utilize the vocational skills when they returned to the reservations; and students were not prepared to seek employment in off-reservation communities, except as menial labourers or domestics (Adams 1995; Szasz 1999). Critical theorists have argued that educational systems "provide different classes and social groups with forms of knowledge, skills and culture that not only legitimate the dominant culture but also teach students into a labor force differentiated by gender, racial and class considerations" (Quinnan 1997, 47). This analysis is borne out by the results of Indian education policies. The education provided in federally funded and operated boarding schools relegated Indian people to the lowest status within the American social and economic system (Hoxie 1984). Succeeding generations of Indian people suffered the consequences, not only socially and economically, but politically as well. In the United States, particularly, the current low level of American Indian participation and achievement in undergraduate and graduate education is evidence of the long-term impact of federal Indian education policies.

Indian Education Reform

In contemporary education reform initiatives, the history of education policy remains a driving force for Native people at both the local and national levels. For American Indian tribes, sovereignty and the right to self-determination are at the core of education reform initiatives (Lomawaima 2000). Native Americans and Aboriginal people in Canada seek the ability to create educational systems they perceive to be best for their children – systems designed to be culturally relevant, to strengthen cultural identity, and thereby to strengthen tribal societies.

Dramatic changes occurred in the 1960s in mainstream and Indian education in the United States. As Hare has noted, similar developments also occurred in Canada. There was a "shift in the balance of power" (Lomawaima 2000) in both countries with the enactment of federal legislation, tribal initiatives, and numerous policy projects. Two major pieces of education legislation passed by Congress benefited American Indian tribes: the Economic Opportunity Act gave tribes control over education programs, and the Elementary and Secondary Education Act provided funding to improve the education of Native children (US Senate Subcommittee 1969).

Changes in the national political climate during this period created opportunities for American Indians and Alaska Natives to pursue self-determination, particularly in higher education. This goal was central to the tribal college movement in the late 1960s. The Navajo Community College created in

1968, known now as Diné College, was a model for tribally governed higher-education institutions. Thirty-four culturally and community-based tribal colleges now exist throughout the United States (American Indian Higher Education 2005). The establishment and success of tribal colleges is a significant element of tribal self-determination in education. These institutions are instrumental in educating many tribal and non-tribal members, and their growth nationally is evidence of the need in American Indian communities for culturally relevant institutions. The value of tribal colleges goes beyond increasing educational opportunities for American Indian communities, however, as they also improve social and economic conditions in these communities.

Access to Higher Education
Compared to the US population as a whole, Native American families are more likely to have lower social and economic status, to live at the poverty level, and have a lower rate of educational attainment (Fries 1987; O'Brien 1992; Pavel et al. 1999). Native American students remain the most under-represented minority group in undergraduate education at both public and private institutions, with the exception of the reservation-based tribal colleges and a few colleges and universities located in states with large Native American populations. More glaring is the underrepresentation of Native Americans in graduate education, even in states with high concentrations of Indian people.

Results of a two-year study on undergraduate education revealed that for every hundred Native American students matriculating to the ninth grade, sixty will attain a high school diploma, twenty will attend a four-year institution, and approximately three students will receive a bachelor's degree (Tierney 1992). The low attainment of baccalaureate degrees necessarily results in low participation at the graduate level, and thus low attainment of master's and doctoral degrees for Native Americans. The National Center for Education Statistics data for 1993-94 indicate that 134 doctorates were awarded to Native Americans (Pavel et al. 1999). In 1999-2000, 155 doctorates were awarded to Native Americans (Knapp et al. 2003). Both sets of data represented 0.3 percent of the doctorate degrees awarded nationally during those years. The number of graduate degrees awarded continues to be disproportionate to the total Native American population.

Although access to educational opportunity and achievement in higher education remains a major concern for Native Americans, initiatives by public and private institutions to increase diversity have made some progress in this area. College-level preparatory outreach programs target minority populations that historically have been underrepresented in higher education. College and university undergraduate programs provide support services geared to retain enrolled minority student populations, which include American Indian and Alaska Native students. Major philanthropic organizations also have launched national initiatives to strengthen tribally based higher education institutions and Native nonprofit educational organizations, and to promote partnerships with mainstream colleges and universities.

Research Challenges

The dearth of literature on American Indian and Alaska Native participation in graduate education indicates that few scholars have examined this area of higher education (O'Brien 1992; Williamson 1994). Blackwell (1992, 123) observed Native Americans to be the "forgotten minority" in higher education research, due to their small numbers. Many major national organizations, such as the Council of Graduate Schools and the Western Association of Graduate Schools, have not included Native American student participation, retention, or degree attainment in their research studies. The American Council on Education, which conducts periodic studies on minority participation and degree attainment in higher education, usually includes some education data on Native Americans (Harvey 2002). O'Brien (1992) conducted a comprehensive study on American Indian participation in higher education that included public and private colleges and tribal colleges. In 1998, the National Center for Education Statistics sponsored a major study by Native American scholars that focused on participation in higher education and included data on graduate education (Pavel et al. 1998). Although large-scale population studies for American Indians and Alaska Natives in higher education may be problematic due to their small numbers, more qualitative studies are needed to better understand how to increase access and success in graduate education for Native populations.

Why is the participation of Native Americans in graduate education understudied in academia? One reason may be found in the need for the kind of capacity building that Hare advocates: seemingly, until Native Americans and Aboriginal people in Canada develop the capacity to conduct research that is relevant to their own communities and interests, it simply will not be done.

One challenge to conducting research on the participation of American Indians in higher education is that the small Native population means a small sample size in studies (Astin 1982; O'Brien 1992; Tierney 1993; Pavel et al. 1998). As of 2000, American Indians and Alaska Natives constituted only 0.9 percent of the total population (US Census Bureau 2002). Small sample sizes in national survey data tend to produce "high standard errors" that reduce the statistical significance of data. In addition, the small sample size presents a confidentiality issue for participants involved in national survey studies. Maintaining confidentiality in studies with small sample sizes may require researchers to merge categories of study data (Pavel et al. 1998, xxxii).

As well, it was only in the 1980s that American Indians and Alaska Natives were identified as a discrete group in studies. Prior to that, studies labelled Native populations as "other or combined them with other racial/ethnic groups" (Pavel et al. 1998, xxxii).

Another issue that arises in Native population studies regards identity, specifically the reliability and instability of self-identification. In recent decades there has been an increase of people of mixed race or ethnic background. Accuracy in data gathering is questionable for this variable – in terms of both the formulation of and the answers to questions about identity. The quality of this exchange determines whether people of mixed race/ethnicity identify as American Indian or Alaska Native or another race/ethnicity. Ethnic fraud by students who self-identify as American Indian or Alaska Native is also problematic in the United States and remains a major concern (Fries 1987; O'Brien 1992; Pavel et al. 1998). American Indians and Alaska Natives maintain the sovereign right to determine membership within the tribe, band, corporation, or village. In recent years increasing numbers of people have been self-identifying as American Indian or Alaska Native in order to benefit from employment and educational opportunities or scholarships (Pavel et al. 1998). Most institutions or agencies do not require documentation to validate tribal affiliation. Fraudulent self-identification of students at higher education institutions results in inaccurate data on Native student representation in undergraduate, graduate, and professional education. The seriousness of this issue prompted the national organization of American Indian and Alaska Native faculty to develop a policy statement urging institutions to require documentation.

The final issue associated with identity is that American Indian and Alaska Native quantitative data are usually combined and rarely disaggregated according to tribe. There are 510 American Indian tribes and each differs culturally from the others (O'Brien 1992). The US Census Bureau is the only agency that segregates data for the twenty-five largest Indian tribes. O'Brien and Zudak (1998) argue that the diversity of tribes creates difficulty in identifying needs and conditions through either quantitative or qualitative research approaches.

Retention Issues
In recent years, minority student retention has become an area of study for minority scholars, but only a few studies in the 1990s focused on American Indian and Alaska Native student retention or were authored by Native scholars (see, for example, Tierney 1992; O'Brien 1992). New paradigms are needed to better understand Native student persistence in higher education because the prevailing theoretical models on student retention may not adequately capture cultural nuances of Native student populations (Pavel 1999; Tierney 1992; Rendon, Jalomo, and Nora 2000). Swisher (1996, 86) argues, "It takes

American Indians and Alaska Natives themselves to understand the depth of meaning incorporated in Indian education, to ask appropriate questions and to find appropriate answers." This takes us back to Hare's argument for capacity building in Chapter 4. Swisher's argument, like Hare's, does not negate the value of research and scholarship by non-Native scholars, but is a challenge to Native scholars regarding the importance and need for research on Native populations to reflect Native perspectives. Representation of Native perspectives alters the dominant framework by helping to define and reframe the complexity of issues and to seek solutions (Kidwell 1980; Smith 1999). Native perspectives locate tribal sovereignty and self-determination as the basis from which to examine the realities of Native education in contemporary American society (Swisher 1996; Lomawaima 2000).

Parallel to the gains Tippeconnic and Saunders note for American Indians and Alaska Natives in K-12 education have been incremental gains in access to educational opportunity and achievement in higher education. But parity has yet to be achieved in degree attainment at either the undergraduate or graduate levels. Personal, academic, and institutional factors still hinder access to and achievement in higher education for Native students. Addressing and determining solutions to these factors requires involvement beyond American Indian, Alaska Native, and Aboriginal communities, and a policy context in both the United States and Canada that supports Native students in higher education. Collectively we must work to strengthen areas in which progress has been made and to improve those areas that remain problematic.

References

Adams, D.W. 1995. *Education for extinction: American Indians and the boarding school experience*. Lawrence: University Press of Kansas.

American Indian Higher Education Consortium. 2005. *Current roster of the tribal colleges.* http://www.aihec.org/tribal_college_roster.cfm.

Astin, A.W. 1982. *Minorities in higher education*. San Francisco: Jossey-Bass.

Blackwell, J.S. 1992. Cowboys and Indians: Perceptions of Western films among American Indians and Anglos. *American Sociological Review* 57: 725-34.

Fries, J. 1987. *The American Indian in higher education: 1975-76 to 1984-85*. Report no. CS87-321; ERIC no. ED281693. Washington, DC: Center for Education Statistics.

Harvey, W.B. 2002. *Minorities in higher education 2001-2002: Nineteenth annual status report*. Washington, DC: American Council on Education.

Hoxie, F.E. 1984. *A final promise: The campaign to assimilate the Indians, 1880-1920*. Lincoln: University of Nebraska.

Kidwell, C.S. 1980. The status of Native American women in higher education. In *Conference on the Educational and Occupational Needs of American Indian Women, 12-13 October 1976*, ed. National Institute of Education, 83-89. Washington, DC: US Department of Education, Office of Educational Research and Improvement.

Kirkness, V.K. 1999. Aboriginal education in Canada: A retrospective and a prospective. *Journal of American Indian Education* 39(1): 14-30.

Knapp, L.G., J.E. Kelly, R.W. Whitmore, S. Wu, L.M. Gallego, and E. Grau. 2003. Postsecondary institutions in the United States: Fall 2000 and degrees and other awards conferred: 1999-2000. *Education Statistics Quarterly* 4(4). http://nces.ed.gov/pubsearch.

Lomawaima, T.K. 2000. Tribal sovereigns: Reframing research in American Indian education. *Harvard Educational Review* 70(1): 1-21.

O'Brien, E.M. 1992. American Indians in higher education. *Research Briefs* (American Council on Education) 3(3): 1-16.

O'Brien, E.M., and C. Zudak. 1998. Minority-serving institutions: An overview. *New Directions for Higher Education* 102: 5-15.

Pavel, M.D. 1999. American Indians in higher education: Promoting access and achievement. In *Next steps: Research and practice to advance Indian education*, ed. K.G. Swisher and J.W. Tippeconnic III, 239-58. Charleston, WV: Appalachian Educational Laboratory.

Pavel, M.D., R.R. Skinner, E. Farris, M. Cahalan, J. Tippeconnic, and W. Stein. 1998. *American Indians and Alaska Natives in postsecondary education: Report for the National Center for Education Statistics.* Washington, DC: US Department of Education.

–. 1999. American Indians and Alaska Natives in postsecondary education. *Education Statistics Quarterly* 1(1): 67-74. http://nces.ed.gov/pubsearch.

Quinnan, T.W. 1997. *Adult students "at risk": Culture bias in higher education.* Westport, CT: Bergin and Garvey.

Rendon, L., R. Jalomo, and A. Nora. 2000. Theoretical considerations in the study of minority student retention in higher education. In *Reworking the student departure puzzle*, ed. J. Braxton, 127-56. Nashville, TN: Vanderbilt University Press.

Smith, L.T. 1999. *Decolonizing methodologies: Research and indigenous peoples.* New York: Zed Books.

Swisher, K.G. 1996. Why Indian people should be the ones to write about Indian education. *American Indian Quarterly* 20(1): 83-90.

Szasz, M.C. 1999. *Education and the American Indian: The road to self-determination since 1928.* 3rd ed. Albuquerque: University of New Mexico Press.

Tierney, W. 1992. *Official encouragement, institutional discouragement: Minorities in academe – the Native American experience.* Norwood, NJ: Ablex Publishers.

–. 1993. The college experience of Native Americans: A critical analysis. In *Beyond silenced voices*, ed. L. Weis and M. Fine, 309-24. Albany: State University of New York Press.

US Census Bureau. 2002. *American Indian and Alaska Native data and links.* http://factfinder. census.gov/home/aian/index.html.

US Senate. Special Subcommittee on Indian Education. 1969. *The education of American Indians: A compendium of federal boarding school evaluations.* 91st Cong., 1st sess.

Williamson, M.J. 1994. Strengthening the seamless web: Fostering minority doctoral success with Mexican American and American Indian students in doctoral programs. Paper presented at the annual meeting of the American Education Research Association, 13-17 April, New Orleans.

Part 3:
Immigrant and Language Education

7
Canadian Policies on Immigrant Language Education
Tracey M. Derwing and Murray J. Munro

Canadian policies on immigrant language education are relatively recent, but Canada's historical development has had a significant and lasting impact on its response to immigrant language needs. To understand why language policies have developed as they have, it is necessary to consider both immigration policies and the cultural and linguistic context in which they were implemented.

Immigration Policies

Canada's population is small, about 32 million people, approximately one-tenth the size of the United States. Like the United States, Canada was colonized by Europeans, principally the British and the French. Canada's immigration records are available from 1860, when 6,276 newcomers arrived in the country. At that time, most migrants came from northern Europe, looking for economic opportunities. The peak period of immigration occurred between 1910 and 1913, when the country was actively seeking immigrants to support population growth and to settle its western regions. However, immigration abruptly declined with the start of the First World War, a pattern observed again during the Great Depression of the 1930s and during the Second World War, when immigration was restricted for economic and social reasons. After the Second World War, the government again began to actively promote immigration to support the economy. Although they varied with the strength of the economy, immigration levels remained reasonably high throughout the rest of the twentieth century. In recent years, the federal government has set annual goals of 200,000-225,000 immigrants. In 2001, 226,039 newcomers arrived in Canada (Dolin and Young 2002).

What is not evident in these numbers is the change in newcomers' source countries. In the earliest days of Canadian immigration there were no restrictions, but by 1885 the government established a head tax to severely limit Chinese immigration. White Americans and Europeans were preferred, and northern Europeans were preferred over those from eastern and southern Europe. Canada later implemented further discriminatory immigration policies favouring Whites from Europe and the United States. In 1910 an Immigration Act was introduced that gave the cabinet the right to refuse "immigrants belonging to any race deemed unsuited to the climate or requirements of Canada" (Canada 1910, s. 38, para. c). In 1923, Canada formally divided source countries into preferred and nonpreferred categories: immigrants from Britain, the United States, the Irish Free State, Newfoundland, Australia, New Zealand, and South Africa faced no restrictions, while immigrants from the nonpreferred countries had to meet certain conditions, depending on their country of origin (Green and Green 1996). Essentially, the federal government was answerable to no one with regard to immigration decisions.

These discriminatory policies were in place until 1962, when the federal government began to reform immigration law. In 1978, a new Immigration Act was passed. This act, in effect until 2002, stated Canada's objectives for immigration: to meet the country's demographic, social, economic, and cultural goals in a nondiscriminatory fashion and to meet humanitarian goals by facilitating family reunification and refugee resettlement in Canada. Over the last forty years, then, visible minorities from a variety of ethnocultural backgrounds have made up the majority of immigrants to Canada. As can be seen in Table 7.1, the current top ten source countries include only two of the countries favoured before the early 1960s (the United Kingdom and the United States).

Table 7.1

Top ten source countries for Canadian immigrants, 2001

Country	Total immigrants	
	Percentage	Number
China	16.10	40,306
India	11.11	27,813
Pakistan	6.13	15,346
Philippines	5.15	12,893
Republic of Korea	3.84	9,613
United States of America	2.35	5,883
Iran	2.29	5,732
Romania	2.23	5,583
Sri Lanka	2.20	5,508
United Kingdom	2.14	5,357
Total top ten countries	53.54	134,028
Total other countries	46.46	116,318
Total immigration, all countries	100.00	250,346

Source: Citizenship and Immigration Canada 2002.

Immigrants enter Canada in one of three main classes: independent (economic), family, and refugee. More than half the people who currently immigrate to Canada are in the independent category – skilled workers, entrepreneurs, and provincial nominees.[1] There are also significant numbers in the family class category; these individuals are sponsored by family members who already live in Canada or by church or ethnocultural groups. A small number of people enter through other categories, primarily as guest workers who can apply for landed immigrant status after two years, such as nannies, and, increasingly, caregivers for old people. In addition, refugees make up approximately a tenth of each year's intake. In total, Canada admitted about 0.75 percent of the current population of the country in 2001.

Although the federal government makes family class and refugee determinations for Quebec, that province controls the selection of independent immigrants. Because of language considerations, its source countries are somewhat different; France, for example, is in the top ten list in Quebec. The federal government makes nearly all other immigrant determinations in the country.

Approximately one-fifth of the people living in Canada today are first-generation Canadians. When they arrive, they go overwhelmingly to large cities. Areas with high concentrations of newcomers make more resources available to immigrants, particularly linguistic support (Abu-Laban et al. 1999). For the last several decades, many of the immigrants who have come either do not speak an official language or do not speak one well enough to obtain employment.

The federal government is trying to attract immigrants for demographic and economic reasons: baby boomers are approaching retirement age, and the birth rate in Canada is very low. In fact, for the last fifteen years, immigration "has accounted for approximately 50 percent of Canada's population growth" (Canada, Office of the Commissioner 2002, 1). Former citizenship and immigration minister Denis Coderre indicated that by 2011, all growth in the labour force in Canada will stem from immigration (Kunz 2003). Thus, Canada's long-standing tradition of immigration is likely to continue.

Canadian Linguistic Context
At the time of Confederation in 1867, when Canada became a country, the government made English and French the official languages, ignoring Aboriginal languages altogether, both at the federal level and in the province of Quebec. Later, when it joined Confederation, Manitoba gave French official language status as well, but in most parts of Canada French eventually began to lose ground. Manitoba rescinded its French language policy; Ontario abolished French schools in 1912; and other provinces put restrictions on the use of French. Most immigrants learned English, especially in the western parts of Canada. According to the Office of the Commissioner of Official Languages, "language policy in Canada is designed to influence the

relative use of the various languages in whatever ways are currently judged to serve the general interest. As those perceptions change over time, so does the consensus about what constitutes linguistic justice. Language policy is not a fixed law, but an evolving accommodation to changing linguistic circumstances and the social and political climate" (Canada, Office of the Commissioner 1988, 1175).

Eventually, the decline of French became important to the political climate. In 1963, the Royal Commission on Bilingualism and Biculturalism was established. This commission resulted in the Official Languages Act of 1969, which gave English and French equal status in Parliament and throughout the federal public service (in addition, the province of New Brunswick became officially bilingual that year). The bilingualism and biculturalism commission also heard a great deal from ethnic groups of non-French or non-English heritage, particularly Ukrainians; in response, it recommended that their contribution to Canada be officially recognized. In 1971, the federal multiculturalism policy was adopted. That year the province of Alberta made it legal to use any language as the medium of instruction in publicly funded schools and, two years later, Ukrainian-English bilingual programs were established. Manitoba and Saskatchewan developed similar programs not long afterwards.

The implementation of the Charter of Rights and Freedoms in 1982 further guaranteed the preservation and enhancement of multiculturalism in Canada. The Charter also introduced a clause "guaranteeing the right of children of Canadian citizens who find themselves in an official language minority situation" (such as a francophone in western Canada, or an anglophone in Quebec) "to an education in their own language wherever numbers warrant it" (s. 23). In other words, there generally need to be enough students to form a class in order for a school curriculum to be offered in a minority language. Multiculturalism received more federal support in 1988 with the passage of the Canadian Multiculturalism Act. The act specifically mentioned the government's responsibility to preserve and enhance the use of languages other than English and French, while strengthening the status and use of the official languages of Canada. It also promised to advance multiculturalism throughout Canada in harmony with the national commitment to the official languages of Canada. That is to say, the two official languages, English and French, must take precedence over heritage languages in schools. This is not just in recognition of the most important groups who helped to establish the country – if that were the case, the languages of Aboriginal people would have similar status. It is a political matter. The federal government has been concerned since the early 1960s that Quebec will separate from the rest of Canada. In a 1995 referendum in the province of Quebec, in which over 93 percent of eligible voters cast a ballot, only 50.6 percent voted against separation. The federal government has been working on strengthening the role of French-language and francophone communities in the rest of Canada ever since.

To try to assuage Quebec, since 2001 Speeches from the Throne (which set the agenda for Parliament at the opening of each session) have routinely reiterated the federal commitment to the two official languages. "Canada's linguistic duality is fundamental to our Canadian identity and is a key element of our vibrant society. The protection and promotion of our two official languages is a priority of the Government – from coast to coast. The Government reaffirms its commitment to support sustainable official language minority communities and a strong French culture and language. And it will mobilize efforts to ensure that all Canadians can interact with the Government of Canada in either official language" (Speech from the Throne 2001). The following year brought the statement: "Linguistic duality is at the heart of our collective identity. The government will implement an action plan on official languages that will focus on minority-language and second-language education, including the goal of doubling within ten years the number of high school graduates with a working knowledge of both English and French" (Speech from the Throne 2002).

According to Canada's division of political powers, education is a provincial responsibility. Soon after the Official Languages Act was passed in 1969, most provinces instituted second-language programs, and immersion for majority language students became extremely popular. The government of Quebec felt that French was still under enormous threat, despite the act, and there-fore passed Bill 22 in 1974 to protect the status of French in the province. Children of immigrants were required to attend French-only schools. Bill 101 in 1977 went even further: French became the only official language of Quebec. The only children allowed to study the school curriculum in English were the sons and daughters of anglophones who themselves had attended school in English in Quebec – all other children were required to study in French. A program called *bain linguistique* is in place for some francophone students whose parents want them to learn English – the students study the entire year's curriculum in French in one semester, then study noncurricular subjects in English in the other semester in order to avoid breaking the law. In April 2003, the Supreme Court announced that it would hear a case challenging Bill 101 instigated by French-speaking parents in Quebec who want the right to send their francophone and allophone children (whose first language is neither French nor English) to English schools (Thompson 2003). The Supreme Court ruled to uphold Bill 101.

This, then, is the context immigrants encounter – they come to a country where English and French have priority and where federal resources are heavily invested in sustaining minority official language communities. So, for instance, in many cities there are both French immersion programs for non-francophone children and francophone schools for the minority children whose first language is French. All of these programs receive federal funding, even though education is strictly a provincial responsibility.

Language Instruction Policies for Immigrants

Two separate government jurisdictions determine language instruction policies for immigrants. K-12 education is a provincial responsibility, but language and citizenship training for adult immigrants is the responsibility of the federal government.

Language Education for Adults

Prior to 1992, much of the adult second-language education for immigrants was designed for those who wanted to enter the labour market (Thomson and Derwing 2004). Priority was given to the principal breadwinner in a household, which normally meant men. Immigrants who identified the men in their families as the breadwinners often had no idea when they first arrived in Canada that the women would end up being the principal wage earners, yet they would be ineligible for language training. A very small program called the Settlement Language Program was developed for people who were not working, but few resources went into SLP. There was also a small fund that supported citizenship instruction to prepare adult immigrants for their citizenship hearing. SLP and citizenship funding were both eliminated with the advent in 1992 of Language Instruction for Newcomers to Canada (LINC).

LINC is an English as a second language (ESL) program that was introduced by the federal government across English-speaking Canada. Quebec established its own program of francophonization, which is similar to LINC in that it is aimed at low proficiency French-as-a-second-language learners. The curriculum is essentially survival language French, with a heavy emphasis on citizenship – that is, becoming a citizen of Quebec. In the other provinces, LINC is meant to be available to adult immigrants until they become citizens, that is, within the first three years of arrival, but it is really designed for people who are in their first year in Canada. The program is intended for individuals who have little or no English on arrival, under the assumption that they will be able to continue language learning on their own within the community. LINC was introduced for the following reasons:

· to provide more immigrants with access to language training
· to foster greater consistency of access and quality
· to maximize the cost-effectiveness of language training
· to provide greater flexibility within programs to meet varied needs of clients
· to develop greater cooperation and coordination among governments, nongovernmental organizations, the private sector, and other partners

· to incorporate information on Canadian values into training programs. (Employment and Immigration Canada 1991, 3)

The last objective was initially very controversial and also had major implications for curriculum development. One enduring feature of Canadian identity is its indefinability. Canada has often been accused of being a nation of navel gazers, asking "Who are we?," so the notion that ESL teachers could neatly distil Canadian values and present them to people who speak very rudimentary English was naive at best. When LINC was first introduced, Employment and Immigration Canada contracted a company to develop a publication entitled *Canada: A Source Book for Orientation, Language and Settlement Workers* (Arcturus Productions 1991) with information on Canadian culture and values to help teachers with this task. It was roundly criticized by workers in settlement agencies and ethnocultural groups as patronizing and unrepresentative of Canadian behaviour. The book was replete with statements under the headings "Canadians do this" and "Canadians do not do that." It was quickly withdrawn, although much of the material found its way onto the Citizenship and Immigration website. The controversy, however, was a flash in the pan. A recent survey of LINC programs across Canada found that, in fact, most teachers who address values talk about issues such as respect for diversity, legal rights, gender equality, and so on. A sizeable proportion of teachers (22 percent) indicated that they do not teach about values at all, but simply concentrate on survival English (Thomson and Derwing 2004).

Interestingly, despite the fact that LINC is a federal program, there are regional inequities in the amount of language training available. Students in Manitoba can access LINC for as long as they wish. Students in Ontario can study up to LINC level 5, which is an intermediate proficiency, while students in Alberta can attend only up to level 4. Students in British Columbia, Newfoundland, and Nova Scotia are limited to level 3 (the original level proposed by the federal government). The lower the level allowed, the less likely teachers are to address values; they are still busy covering such topics as basic health matters and simple telephone conversations.

Quality of instruction is also a major issue. Although there are increasingly more professional preparation programs in Canada in teaching English as a second language – and more emphasis in provincial ESL teachers' associations on the importance of teachers' skills – the federal government's choice to contract LINC programming to private providers and nongovernmental organizations, as well as colleges, has resulted in competition and undercutting. The federal government does not concern itself with the qualifications of instructors, claiming this is a provincial responsibility. In the meantime, some funders appear to have no criteria other than cost efficiency for judging the merits of competing programs. On the whole, however, there is now greater access to ESL than in the past, and some good programs with committed and talented teachers exist in most parts of the country.

It has been argued that LINC "is a hegemonic force that operates to manage linguistic, and hence, ethnic difference in a monolingual/bilingual nation-state that is threatened by linguistic (and 'other') diversity ... The path that leads to 'integration' through ESL instruction is littered with issues of identity, race and ethnicity, and assimilation that makes becoming 'integrated' a much more complicated journey" (Cleghorn 2000). Indeed, the government does use language proficiency as a measure of integration, and it is not a perfect measure. One can have a good grasp of English without being integrated – language is a necessary but insufficient requirement for that. As well, Canada is not free from racism and neither are LINC programs. ESL students, however, are unlikely to agree that LINC is assimilationist in nature: these adult immigrants, most of whom are well-educated, are perfectly capable in their first language, and, for the most part, have made an explicit choice to come to an English-speaking part of Canada to start a new life. In a survey of a thousand former LINC students, Hart and Cumming (1997) found that their principal complaints about LINC concern the quality of instruction and the limited time they have access to LINC. They want more language instruction, not less.

Despite its problems, LINC provides adult immigrants with a starting point in all parts of English-speaking Canada, and some provincial governments offer further ESL instruction. In Alberta, for example, adults can receive Student Finance Board funding for both tuition and a living allowance for up to two years in order to take higher levels of ESL or other education. Clearly, considerable support from the federal government and some of the provinces is available for adults. ESL provision for immigrant children in kindergarten to grade 12 is a different matter.

Language Policies for Minors

Every school board in Canada works with immigrant and Canadian-born ESL populations differently. Most provinces have ESL policies, all of which essentially promise the same things, the primary difference being the length of time students receive support. Most provinces emphasize mainstreaming students into English classrooms as soon as possible. The range of options for how this is accomplished varies, depending in part on the number of students in the system. However, all provinces acknowledge, at least on paper, that first language maintenance is important and that second language proficiency takes several years to develop.

There appears to be a general consensus across governments that the limited funding dedicated to ESL should be concentrated in the higher grades, since several provinces offer less ESL at the elementary level (see Van Ngo 2002). The rationale is that elementary school subjects are fairly concrete and are presented in ways that are as appropriate for second language learners as for native English speakers. Schools that choose to offer more must rely on discretionary funds or volunteers.

At the junior high and high school levels several models exist. In the Vancouver public school system, for instance, all ESL students go first to a reception centre to have their first language skills assessed, as well as their English-language knowledge. In addition, parents are given information in their first language about the schools and the nature of the instruction their children will be receiving. A child's scores are then sent to the classroom teacher before the child arrives at his or her neighbourhood school, where the child is placed in one of three models: reception, transition, or integration (McGivern and Eddy 1999). The reception model organizes groups of up to twenty ESL students "in a fully supported ESL class, where they spend most or all their time becoming socially and academically prepared for integration"; alternatively, they "receive full-time support from English-language support teachers in subject/grade classes, or, whenever possible, from trained ESL teachers in pullout sessions at the English Language Centre, which is a classroom located in the school" (32). In the transition model, students are in at least some regular classes, with additional language and cultural support in the form of ESL classes, transitional subject ESL classes, pullout sessions, and English-language support teachers. The integration model is for students who still have some problems with their academic subject matter or who simply need a little support within the regular classroom. These students may receive language support either from the subject/grade teacher or from an ESL specialist. The ESL models across English-speaking Canada are very similar to Vancouver's, although how schools actually implement them varies widely, depending on resources, the number of ESL students, and the priorities of the school or school board.

Some students arrive in Canada with significant educational gaps in literacy and numeracy. Provisions for these individuals are generally problematic, in part because there is often no more funding for them than for ESL students who come with good educations. The ESL Co-op in Vancouver is an example of a project that was designed to assist such students; rather than carrying on in an academic stream, which they were most unlikely to finish in the time allotted, students were given linguistic support in classes that focused on life and job readiness skills, job searching, employee/employer rights, etc. Many of its students were not happy with the Co-op, however. While they recognized that they were gaining employment skills, they viewed the Co-op as a barrier to graduating from high school (Beynon et al. 1998). Students with educational gaps also experience barriers such as age caps and a lack of appropriate programming. In Alberta, for instance, the year before September first in which a student turns nineteen is the last school year for which he or she can receive high school funding; no specialized programs are in place to help these older ESL students complete their high school educations.

Some immigrant parents choose to place their children in French immersion programs (Dagenais and Day 1998). If they start at the beginning of the program, they are on an even footing linguistically with the other students in the class. In many instances, parents want their children to be achievers recognized for their multilingual status, as opposed to being viewed as deficient because they have limited English on arrival.

Bilingual programs in heritage languages (that is, languages other than French and English) have not been developed extensively except in a few Prairie cities, most notably Edmonton, where for twenty years there have been several successful programs. Currently, students can have subject matter taught 50 percent in English and 50 percent in Arabic, Mandarin, Ukrainian, Polish, German, Hebrew, or Spanish. Most children who attend these schools come from the cultural background represented; some come to school speaking their heritage language, while others arrive with English as their first language. The program is open to any student in the city; some students from other backgrounds enrol because their parents view bilingual programming as an enrichment similar to French immersion. The Vancouver School Board is now experimenting with a bilingual program in Mandarin, but these programs are not yet widespread in Canada. Indeed, in Ontario, the province with by far the largest number of immigrant children, heritage-language classes, although free, are generally taught only after class or on weekends. Bilingual heritage-language programs of the type found in the Prairie provinces do not exist (Cummins and Danesi 1990).

Challenges Facing K-12 Students

In many provinces one of the most serious problems in the provision of education for ESL students is the lack of ESL-trained teachers in the school systems. If a school principal needs a science teacher for a .7 appointment, the remaining .3 of that appointment may end up being ESL, since all teachers speak English. Most provinces have no requirement that ESL be taught by ESL specialists and no requirement that pre-service teachers in teacher training programs take preparation courses in teaching English as a second language. TESL is viewed as an option, as though one could choose to teach classes that have no ESL students in them. A TESL master's program is offered at the University of Alberta, but nearly all the students plan to teach adults. Because a K-12 teaching certificate is not required to teach adults in many institutions, and because there is increasing pressure for teachers of adults to have suitable training, more teachers with professional TESL qualifications are in adult programs than in the school systems.

There is no systemic responsibility for ESL students. The provinces provide limited amounts of money for designated ESL students for different lengths of time – three years in Alberta, two years in Ontario, five years in British

Columbia – but they largely let school boards determine how the money will be spent. Many boards devolve the responsibility to the principals at individual schools. For a school with only a few ESL students, the money is not sufficient to buy an aide's time, much less that of a teacher. According to figures from the Calgary Board of Education for 2001-02, "the qualified ESL teacher per student rating is one ESL teacher to 115 students, more than triple the acceptable teacher/student ratio in Alberta" (Van Ngo 2002, 23). Subject teachers often view ESL students as the ESL teacher's responsibility, not their own. Unless there is strong leadership from the administration in a school, ESL students' needs often go unmet.

Conclusion: What Would Improve the Current Situation?
In adult ESL, federal standards should be in place for LINC programs; these standards should include TESL preparation for teachers at accredited universities. In order to implement such a standard, funding would need to be sufficient to allow programs to hire professional instructors.

Many of the newcomers to Canada are highly skilled and already have some knowledge of English, but their proficiency is insufficient for the labour market. Language support beyond the levels provided in LINC would be most helpful in assisting immigrants in both the settlement and employment processes. Language is not the only barrier facing immigrant professionals (for example, accreditation bodies often do not recognize foreign training), but improved access to higher levels of language programming that is designed to help people re-enter their professions would facilitate what is now a very arduous process. Some advanced language programming should be integrated into workplace settings, thus simultaneously providing Canadian experience and linguistic support, as lack of "Canadian experience" is another major barrier for many immigrants.

In K-12 ESL, requiring TESL as part of teacher preparation in all provinces would be helpful, not just for ESL teachers, but for subject/grade classroom teachers as well. ESL students are no longer limited to certain areas of a city; all teachers should have familiarity with the basic principles of second language acquisition and pedagogical approaches that make content more accessible. Furthermore, all teachers should be culturally sensitive, and efforts should be made to ensure that education faculties attract pre-service teachers who are themselves immigrants. Currently, many ESL children are unlikely to see anyone from their own ethnocultural background at the front of the class (Beynon and Toohey 1995).

Provincial governments and school boards should ensure that appropriate levels of funding are made available for ESL. It is ironic that ESL is viewed as an "extra" when without proficiency in the language of instruction, students' opportunity to learn the curriculum is clearly lost. The US Supreme Court acknowledged this in 1974 in the *Lau* v. *Nichols* case, which recognized the systematic denial of access to public education (Baker 2001; see also Chapters 8 and 9). Many children in Canada are similarly denied an education. ESL should be viewed as the underpinning for all academic subjects (aside from the study of languages other than English). Funding should be provided for all grades. Elementary school children should not be excluded from support on the justification that they will eventually "catch up." Just because catching up to native speaker peers is estimated to take between five and eight years (Cummins 1986), and elementary school-aged children have that time, does not mean these students do not miss the crucial foundational skills normally acquired in the early grades.

More flexibility is required in many school systems; for example, in Alberta, an age cap forces ESL students out of high school before they have had a chance to graduate. Adult ESL programs, which the Department of Education recommends, are unsuitable for these individuals, given that the content in LINC classes is largely settlement-focused. If the students are perceived as too old to be attending high school with the general population, specialized programs with ESL support to allow high school completion should be readily available from the ministries responsible for K-12 education.

The availability of bilingual programs in languages representative of the top ten immigrant source countries would go a long way to promote official language skills and content knowledge in an environment that recognizes and supports first language maintenance. These programs, often labelled "too expensive" (Vancouver School Board, personal communication, 25 April 2003), are in fact no more costly than regular monolingual classrooms (Edmonton Public Schools, personal communication, 25 April 2003). Another model that is closely related to bilingual education and worthy of consideration is dual language education, as advocated by Lindholm-Leary (2001), in which two linguistic groups learn each other's first language in the context of the school curriculum.

The most important recommendation of all is the need for a commitment by all relevant stakeholders to the education of ESL children. Of course committed individuals throughout the country in governments, school boards, schools, universities, and immigrant-serving agencies are making a difference. But because a coordinated effort is lacking in many jurisdictions, it is not clear who has responsibility for ESL – a situation that sometimes results in no one taking responsibility, or, more often, the implementation of Band-Aid efforts that are doomed to fail. We cannot afford to ignore the needs of immigrant children; without equitable access to language and education, they are at risk of becoming an underclass, with all that that entails.

Notes

1 Most provinces in Canada have agreements with the federal government with regard to immigration. Under these agreements they are able to nominate prospective immigrants who fulfil the provincial criteria. Prospective immigrants who wish to become provincial nominees must complete a provincial nomination process before they apply to emigrate to Canada.

References

Abu-Laban, B., T.M. Derwing, H. Krahn, M. Mulder, and L. Wilkinson. 1999. *The settlement experiences of refugees in Alberta,* vol. 1. Edmonton: Prairie Centre of Excellence for Research on Immigration and Integration.

Arcturus Productions. 1991. *Canada: A source book for orientation, language and settlement workers.* Ottawa: Employment and Immigration Canada.

Baker, C. 2001. *Foundations of bilingual education and bilingualism.* 3rd ed. Clevedon, UK: Multilingual Matters.

Beynon, J., and K. Toohey. 1995. Access and aspirations: Careers in teaching as seen by Canadian university students of Chinese and Punjabi-Sikh ancestry. *Alberta Journal of Educational Research* 41: 435-61.

Beynon, J., K. Toohey, L. Laroque, and R. Ilieva. 1998. A critical examination of an ESL cooperative education program. Paper presented at the Metropolis Education Research Forum, Canadian Society for the Study of Education conference, 29 May, Ottawa. http:// Canada.metropolis.net/events/merf/Beynon-MERF.html.

Canada. 1910. *Statutes of Canada.* An Act Respecting Immigration.

Canada. Office of the Commissioner of Official Languages. 1988. Language policy. In *The Canadian encyclopedia,* 2nd ed., 1175-76. Edmonton: Hurtig Publishers.

–. 2002. *Immigration and the vitality of Canada's official language communities: Policy, demography and identity.* Ottawa: Minister of Public Works and Government Services.

Citizenship and Immigration Canada. 2002. *Facts and figures 2001: Immigration overview.* Ottawa: Citizenship and Immigration Canada. http://www.cic.gc.ca/english/pdf/pub/ facts2001.pdf.

Cleghorn, L. 2000. Valuing English: An ethnography of a federal language training program for adult immigrants. MA thesis, Ontario Institute for Studies in Education. Available at Joint Centre of Excellence for Research on Immigration and Settlement, http://ceris. metropolis.net.

Cummins, J. 1986. Empowering minority students: A framework for intervention. *Harvard Educational Review* 56: 18-36.

Cummins, J., and M. Danesi. 1990. *Development and denial of Canada's linguistic resources.* Toronto: Our Schools, Our Selves Educational Foundation and Garamond Press.

Dagenais, D., and E. Day. 1998. Classroom language experiences of trilingual children in French immersion. *Canadian Modern Language Review* 54(3): 376-93.

Dolin, B., and M. Young. 2002. *Canada's immigration policy.* BP-190E. Ottawa: Department of Public Works and Government Services. http://dsp-psd.pwgsc. gc.ca/Collection-R/LoPBdP/BP/bp190-e.htm.

Employment and Immigration Canada. 1991. *Immigrant language training policy framework.* Ottawa: Immigration Policy and Program Development.

Green, A., and D. Green. 1996. *The economic goals of Canada's immigration policy, past and present.* Research on Immigration and Integration in the Metropolis Working Paper 96-04. Vancouver: RIIM.

Hart, D., and A. Cumming. 1997. *A follow-up study of people in Ontario completing Level 3 of the Language Instruction for Newcomers to Canada (LINC) program.* Toronto: Modern Language Centre, OISE/University of Toronto.

Kunz, J.L. 2003. Immigration: Our identity, our business, our choice. Impressions of the Sixth National Metropolis Conference. *Horizons* 6, 2. http://policyresearch.gc.ca.

Lindholm-Leary, K.J. 2001. *Dual language education.* Clevedon, UK: Multilingual Matters.

McGivern, L., and C. Eddy. 1999. Language policy: Vancouver's multicultural mosaic. *TESOL Journal* 8: 29-33.

Speech from the Throne. 2001. Speech from the Throne to open the first session of the 37th Parliament of Canada. 30 January. http://www.pco-bcp.gc.ca.

–. 2002. Speech from the Throne to open the second session of the 37th Parliament of Canada. 30 September. http://www.pco-bcp.gc.ca.

Thompson, E. 2003. Quebec language fight returns to highest court. *Edmonton Journal,* 25 April, A13.

Thomson, R.I., and T.M. Derwing. 2004. Presenting Canadian values in LINC: The role of textbooks and teachers. *TESL Canada Journal* 21(2): 17-33.

Van Ngo, H. 2002. *English as a second language education: Context, current responses and recommendations for new directions.* Calgary: Coalition for Equal Access to Education.

8
Language Education in the Conflicted United States

Carlos J. Ovando and Terrence G. Wiley

This chapter presents both a historical and a contemporary overview of the often conflicted nature of language education in the United States. We use the term *conflicted* because the formation and implementation of educational language policies in the United States have often involved conflicts over the hegemony of English in the nation-building agenda, the best means of promoting instruction in English, the status and utility of languages other than English, and so-called nonstandard varieties of English.

These conflicts derive from a number of common myths that underlie the hegemonic, monolingual English-language ideology at the basis of much of the popular understanding of educational language policies. Among these myths are the following:

· Language diversity in the United States is an abnormal condition that is attributable to immigration.
· Past immigrants quickly and willingly learned English, but recent immigrants resist learning English.
· Language diversity has a disuniting impact on national harmony.
· Language diversity threatens the dominance of English.
· Social and regional varieties of English weaken the purity of "standard" English.
· State- and federally supported bilingual education is a failed program that keeps language minorities from learning English and doing well in school.
· "Foreign" languages – if they are studied at all – should be taught in the higher grades.

(For a more elaborated discussion of this ideology, see Kloss 1971; Macías 1985; Minami and Ovando 2004; Ovando 1990, 1999; Ovando and McLaren 2000; Wiley 2002.)

A US Bilingual Tradition

There "has always been and still is a powerful tradition upholding the merits and desirability of 'one country, one language,' a tradition which has been so much in the foreground that the rival tradition has been well-nigh forgotten, especially during its partial eclipse in the years after World War I" (Kloss 1977/1998, 369). Thus, a brief history of language policies in the United States and their impact on language minorities is needed as a corrective to the popular myths. One of the more prevalent myths is the belief that language diversity is *ab*normal. Although English has been the dominant language throughout US history, language diversity has always been a part of the nation's linguistic tradition. Kloss notes that it "is justified to speak of an American bilingual tradition [but this] must not be understood to imply that it was the prevailing, let alone the, American tradition with regard to language policy" (369). We will elaborate on this tradition below by examining efforts to standardize American English and language issues for Native Americans and African Americans.

Early Efforts to Promote an American English as a National Standard

As in other nations, the early period of American history saw the attempt, most passionately by Noah Webster (1758-1843), to create a unique national character defined by a common *American* English. A staunch Federalist, Webster argued that the country's language, like the government, should be national. Although a few implausible proposals had circulated to make Hebrew or Greek the national language, for Webster the key to linguistic unity was "orthographic independence; by eradicating spelling variations within the United States, he hoped to build Americans' fragile sense of independence" (Lepore 2002, 6). In 1790, at the time of the first census, about 75 percent of the US population – a significantly lower rate than today – spoke English as their native tongue. Out of a population of around 4 million, 600,000 Europeans, 150,000 enslaved Africans, and 150,000 Indians were native speakers of other languages (28). Much like those who denigrate regional and social dialects of English today, Webster was more concerned that northerners spoke differently from southerners: he believed in a uniform, national standard pronunciation that would "demolish those odious distinctions of provincial dialects" (quoted p. 22).

Many of Webster's efforts to regularize English spelling were successful, largely because of his commercial influence as an authority on American English. But his aspiration to eradicate dialects through spelling reform was not to be realized. Lepore (2002, 31) notes, "If spelling does not dictate pronunciation, Webster's entire project – to eradicate dialect by standardizing spelling – makes little sense." Contemporary phonics-only advocates also fail to comprehend this point.

Native Americans: From Enculturation to Symbolic Recognition

For American Indians, scenarios for language education were problematic. Prescribed language policies entailed a mixture of conflict, accommodation, and attempts to deculturalize Native peoples. During the colonial period, there were some efforts to convert Indians to Christianity. German-speakers, among others, attempted to teach their language as they proselytized (Toth 1990). During the early nineteenth century, some of the leaders among the five so-called civilized tribes were bilingual, and some were partly of European ancestry. Given their disadvantaged standing in treaty and legal dealings and their need to retain their ancestral lands, many Native peoples recognized that they must achieve literacy in both their own languages and English if they were to deal effectively with the encroachment of Whites and the threat of forced removal (Ehle 1988; Wiley 2000). Initial attempts at English literacy education were largely unsuccessful. In 1822, however, Sequoyah invented the Cherokee syllabary, making possible the rapid acquisition of Cherokee literacy and the distribution of a weekly bilingual newspaper that became a major voice of opposition to the removal of the Cherokee from Georgia (Weinberg 1995). By 1838, approximately three-fourths of the Cherokee were literate in their own language (Lepore 2002).

To further the goal of removing Native peoples from land Whites wished to occupy, Thomas Jefferson had prescribed that they be required to learn English and domestic skills – an imposition that would force them into economic dependency. Forced English was a means to *domesticate* Indians without economically and politically integrating them (Spring 1994; Wiley 2000). Under the direct administration of the US Bureau of Indian Affairs, beginning in the 1880s Native American children were compelled to attend boarding schools, where they were not allowed to use their own languages. This had the double effect of hampering their efforts to learn English and to retain their own languages (Weinberg 1995; Wiley 2000). Despite the increasing westward migration of Euro-Americans, the Cherokee successfully competed with them, a fact that is widely believed to be linked to Cherokee literacy rates (see, for example, Cherokee Nation n.d.). Because of their success, in 1838 President Andrew Jackson forcibly removed them in one of the largest forced relocations of Native peoples in modern history (Spring 1994; Ehle 1988). After their resettlement in Indian Territory (modern-day Oklahoma), the Cherokee again established their own schools and were successfully competing with White settlers in adjacent areas by the mid-nineteenth century. By the 1930s, efforts at overt deculturalization had relaxed somewhat. By that time, however, considerable language loss was occurring (Spicer 1980). In the late 1960s, with federal support, some promising bilingual education programs were initiated (McCarty and Zepeda 1995). In 1990 the US Congress passed the Native American Languages Preservation Act. While some progress has been made, restoration efforts for many Native languages have proved to be too little too late. The loss of Native languages is occurring at an alarming rate (Schiffman 1996).

The Assault on African American Language and Literacy

Africans were forcibly brought to the British American colonies in 1619, one year before the arrival of the *Mayflower*. From the colonial period to the end of the Civil War in 1865, enslaved people of African origin were not allowed to use their native tongues, and they were prohibited from achieving English literacy through "compulsory ignorance" laws (see Weinberg 1995). The fact that some of the enslaved were literate upon arrival is often ignored in mainstream US history textbooks. Of the 12 million souls wrenched from their homelands during the four centuries in which the Atlantic slave trade ravaged Africa, it is estimated that between 2 million and 3 million were Muslims, literate in Arabic (Lepore 2002). A minority of these people were sent to the English colonies and, subsequently, the southern states. "[The] enslaved Muslims' literacy could be dangerous. Marked as educated, Muslim slaves may have been subject to special persecution and punishment, designed to crush any possibility of rebellion in much the same way that the antebellum slave codes forbade teaching slaves to write in English" (121). Nevertheless, some sought to sustain their level of literacy.

A forced language shift to English was accomplished by mixing together enslaved peoples who spoke many different tongues. English quickly became their common spoken language, even as access to English literacy was denied. Among African Americans, a creolized form of English developed, which has variously been called "African American vernacular English," "Black English," and, most recently, "Ebonics." Although prescriptivists have ridiculed Ebonics as nonstandard, linguists have long since established its rule-governed nature and its existence as a distinct language variety, with some possible West African linguistic influences.

In the 1930s, Woodson (1933/1990, 19) lamented that in "the study of language and schools" African American students were taught to ridicule their own speech rather than to study their own language. A related issue – ongoing to the present – has been the lack of knowledge on the part of many teachers and the public regarding differences in grammar and pronunciation between "standard" English and Ebonics. This problem has been revisited a number of times but was accentuated in 1996, when the Oakland, California, school board endorsed instruction in Ebonics. The board's decision was defended by proponents of applied and sociolinguistics, but it was widely denounced by pundits and the popular media, who saw it as a concession to lower academic standards (Ovando and McLaren 2000; Ovando 2004; Perry and Delpit 1998; Ramírez et al. 2000).

Trends in Foreign Language Education

Despite the dominance of English, schooling in other languages has been prevalent in the United States since the colonial period. Immigrant languages other than English were even carried to indigenous peoples through mission schools established to spread the beliefs of the encroaching Europeans. Germans first arrived in the British colonies in 1683. Among the many languages carried to the colonies and the subsequent United States, German had become the second most prevalent language by 1914 (Toth 1990).

The prominence of German, particularly in education, was severely shaken by the xenophobia and jingoism of the First World War. German Americans were persecuted in many parts of the country in those years. Between 1917 and 1919, thirty-four states passed laws restricting German language instruction. Many universities dropped German language requirements. Despite two Supreme Court decisions that affirmed the right to teach foreign languages in schools, both public (*Meyer* v. *Nebraska* 1923) and private (*Farrington* v. *Tokushige* 1927), the war had ushered in a stronger emphasis on Americanization. Spanish and French made gains at the college level. By 1948, the percentage of high school students studying German had dropped from 25 percent to less than 1 percent (Leibowitz 1971; Wiley 1998).

The Second World War served as the first wake-up call for US inadequacies in foreign language instruction. Because foreign language, math, and science skills were essential for military, international business, and diplomatic endeavours, these subjects became a high priority in the national defence agenda during the Cold War period. As a symbol of the Cold War tensions, the launch of *Sputnik* in 1957 evoked fear among US citizens that the Russians were galloping ahead technologically, thus posing a threat to national security. In response to this threat, the United States developed federal policies in foreign languages, mathematics, and science, which led to the creation of the National Defense Education Act in 1958. The federal government awarded generous NDEA fellowships to promising language teachers to revitalize foreign language programs, and the NDEA promoted much-needed improvement in the teaching of foreign languages at all educational levels.

Today, even elementary schools have an increased emphasis on foreign language programs. At the secondary and higher education levels, enrolments are up in recent years for Chinese, Japanese, Arabic, Portuguese, and Hebrew, as well as for a number of less commonly taught languages. Declines have been noted for Russian, German, French, Italian, ancient Greek, and Latin (Rhodes and Branaman 1999; Brod and Welles 2000). Spanish is in a special class in the United States. With the significant increase in immigration from Spanish-speaking countries, educational enrolments in Spanish language have grown steadily at all levels. Spanish now accounts for more than half of all higher education foreign language enrolments, marking it as the clear second language of choice (Brod and Welles 2000).

Changing Demographics

Although the United States has always been diverse, that diversity was constrained by US immigration policies between 1923 and 1965. Since that time – particularly during the last three decades – US society has again become increasingly both multicultural and multilingual (Ovando 2004). The 1990s, for instance, witnessed a rapid influx of immigrants from Asia and Latin America. A survey conducted by the US Census Bureau (2000) noted that over 13 million immigrants arrived in the United States between 1990 and 2000. Of these, about 10.7 million came from Asia and Latin America. The Census Bureau also increased its estimate of the country's total foreign-born population in 2000, from 28.3 million to approximately 30 million, which roughly corresponds to 11 percent of the nation's 281 million residents (Armas 2001). This change was largely attributable to a higher-than-expected count of Hispanics in the 2000 census; the count of 35.3 million Hispanics nationwide was approximately 2.5 million higher than originally had been estimated. With increased immigration, the number of second- and third-generation Latino and Asian Americans who want to maintain the language of their forebears is also increasing. Absent this factor, maintenance of heritage languages might not be successful (Minami and Ovando 2004).

The Bilingual Education Controversy

From the end of the First World War until the 1960s and 1970s, the majority of language-minority children in the United States were enrolled in "sink or swim" mainstream instruction in English, typically without any specific support. With the rise of federally supported bilingual programs in the late 1960s, some students began to receive accommodation through transitional bilingual education programs. A 1974 decision of the US Supreme Court (*Lau* v. *Nichols*) established the principle that schools were required to teach English to students who did not already speak the language in order to allow them equitable learning of the broader curriculum. The Court left it to the schools to determine how English was to be taught, allowing either bilingual or English as second language programmatic approaches.

The battle against bilingual education began to gain strength during the 1980s, challenging the previous twenty years of program development and research. The politics of language during the Reagan administration provided the context for the anti-bilingual seeds that were sown during the 1980s and continued to develop into the 1990s. For example, reflecting a growing political opposition to education through the home language, Reagan's secretary of education, William Bennett, successfully promoted funding for English-only special alternative instructional programs.

Further weakening bilingual education, the *Lau* compliance standards developed by the Office of Civil Rights were never published as official regulations. And the Reagan administration quickly killed the *Lau* regulations proposal of the Carter administration. It would have mandated bilingual education programs in schools "where at least twenty-five LEP [limited English proficiency] children of the same minority language group were enrolled in two consecutive elementary grades (K-8)" (Crawford 1999, 52).

Beyond Washington, political activists across the nation began to press for a return to the sink-or-swim days and the ideology of the melting pot. Anti-bilingual education pressure groups such as US English, English Only, and English First began to appear on the scene. The war of words sharpened over how long, if at all, the home language should be used before the language-minority student is transferred to an all-English classroom environment. It reached an all-time high when California voters determined in June 1998, through the passage of Proposition 227, that English should be the primary medium of instruction for language-minority students (see PBS Video 1999). This initiative stipulates that English-language learners should remain in a sheltered English immersion program for a period that in most cases should not exceed one year. Even within this program, instruction is to be "over-whelmingly in English," with only limited support in the home language, although parents may request waivers. Upon completion of the sheltered immersion program, students are to be placed in mainstream English-only classrooms (Unz and Tuchman 1997).

While bilingual education has generally been under political siege since the 1980s, it has had support in some circles. For example, in 1999 President Clinton's administration restored funding cutbacks made by the Republican-controlled Congress totalling 38 percent between 1994 and 1996 (Crawford 1997). English Only, US English, English First, and Proposition 227 can be seen collectively as an instrument of the politics of resentment toward massive immigration from developing countries in the 1980s, especially from Asia and Latin America. Proposition 227, for example, is viewed as a harbinger of similar measures in other initiative states, such as Arizona (which passed the similar Proposition 203 in 2000), Colorado, Washington, and Massachusetts.

Given the positive evidence that quality bilingual education programs work (see, for example, Kirk Senesac 2002), why is there continued resis-tance, even hostility, toward bilingual education? Such antipathy seems to be rooted in nativistic and melting pot ideologies that tend to demonize the language and culture of the "other." Because bilingual education is much more than a pedagogical tool, it has become a societal irritant involving complex issues of cultural identity, social class status, and language politics. Is language diversity a problem? Is it a resource? Is it a right? On the surface these issues seem quite remote from the day-to-day realities of bilingual classrooms across the United States, yet they are the basis on which bilingual education is either loved or hated (Ovando 1990).

Along with issues of power, much of the opposition to bilingual education arises from the fact that its rationale seems to run counter to widely held popular beliefs about how humans acquire languages. Intuitively, one would think that a person learns another language by using it frequently and by avoiding use of the mother tongue. Using a new language is of course crucial to communicative and academic competence in that language. The quality of the instructional process, however, is equally important, and more time spent immersed in the new language is not necessarily associated with greater gains in that language if the student is not understanding the content of the lesson. Related to this, the climate for full cognitive development is absolutely crucial to the full development of the second language. One of the most common misconceptions is that children learn a second language with native-like pronunciation effortlessly and without pain – child's play, so to speak. Yet research suggests that young children may not reach full proficiency in their second language if cognitive development is discontinued in their primary language. Given the prerequisites for second language acquisition, older learners (approximately ages nine to twenty-five) who have built cognitive and academic proficiency in their first language are potentially the most efficient acquirers of most aspects of academic second language proficiency, except for pronunciation (Ovando, Collier, and Combs 2003).

Another problem in presenting a clear case for the effectiveness of bilingual education results from the confusion between program evaluation research and basic research. Much of the adverse publicity for bilingual education stems from a set of poor program evaluation results. Many researchers, however, feel that it is virtually impossible to control for all the background variables associated with bilingual education outcomes. A number of variables can have a negative effect on the outcome of a particular bilingual program: the number of qualified bilingual teachers, parental support, administrative support, material resources, time allocation for the child's first language and the second language, the sociocultural and educational background of the community, the general school curriculum and climate, and so on. Furthermore, it is not possible to have comparison groups of students – some receiving language assistance and others not – as the civil rights of the students not receiving any services would be violated. Because of these difficulties and the politicized nature of the field, researchers such as August and Hakuta (1997) tend to favour basic research in psycholinguistics, sociolinguistics, and developmental psychology rather than in program evaluation.

Researchers who are trying to get the word out about the empirical outcomes of bilingual instruction face a dilemma. They can be even-handed with the results and thus run the risk of providing fuel for the critics of bilingual education, or they can report findings that affirm mother tongue instruction results without providing enough empirical support for their claims (see, for example, Thomas and Collier 1996). In an ideal, nonpoliticized world researchers could concentrate on conducting empirical studies that illuminate pedagogical theories and practice. But because bilingual education has become an ideological lightning rod for groups with a variety of pedagogical agendas, language-minority educators *must* become better informed and engaged in the language policy debate. To hold their ground in the debate, they must have a clearly articulated strategy for addressing language issues within a political context to multiple publics. The beginning of such a strategy emerged at a 1999 session of the National Association for Bilingual Education. There, in a handout titled "¿Qué pasó en California? Lessons from Proposition 227," the presenters recommended that bilingual education be linked to the larger frameworks of quality education and access for language-minority and language-majority communities (Olsen 1999).

Higher English Standards for All

In the 1990s, the goal of promoting higher literacy expectations for all students resulted in a national drive for academic "standards" across the curriculum. Standards may have a number of positive effects as long as they are appropriate for all segments of the national population – that is, as long as they do not systematically advantage some students while disadvantaging others. Merely having standards is insufficient, however, if they are not fully implemented, scrutinized, and linked to the operative curriculum (Wiley with Hartung-Cole 2000).

In recent years, the International Reading Association (IRA) and the National Council of Teachers of English (NCTE) co-developed *Standards for the English Language Arts*, which has been among the more representative and influential standards documents. IRA-NCTE (1996, 3) presented twelve standards broadly applied across the curriculum, noting, "Although we present the standards as a list, we want to emphasize that they are not distinct, separable; they are in fact interrelated and should be considered as a whole." The document also makes an important qualification regarding the goal of educational equity: "It is clear, however, that we have frequently fallen short of this goal with children of the poor, students from certain linguistic and cultural groups, and those in need of special education" (8). The document's linking of "children of the poor" with students from "certain linguistic and cultural groups, and those in need of special education" is typical of many documents that allude to diversity without probing its dimensions, tending to frame it from a deficiency standpoint. But the document does offer the important qualification that "defining standards furnishes the occasion for examining the education" of those previously underserved (1).

The litmus test for such standards is that they be equitably applied to all students, which requires taking the needs of specific types of students into consideration. If particular ethnic, linguistic, or social groups of students consistently fail to meet the standards, the standards themselves and the instructional process designed to implement them must be scrutinized

(Wiley with Hartung-Cole 2000), with the recognition that "standards, by themselves, cannot erase the impact of poverty, ethnic and cultural discrimination, family illiteracy, and social and political disenfranchisement" (IRA-NCTE 1996, 9). If all students are to be assessed based on standards, they must have access to comparable resources, their schools must be similarly equipped, and their teachers must be comparably trained.

In the 2000 presidential elections, testing and high standards were touted as the reason for apparent educational gains in Texas and other states. Critics noted, however, that it is easy to maintain high standards in states with high dropout rates, because the standards are actually being applied to only an elite portion of the population – those who remain in school (see, for example, McNeil 2000; Ohanian 1999; Chapter 16). Thus, if high expectations are to be reasonably applied and equitably achieved, then all students must have an equal opportunity to reach them. In other words, schools must have comparatively equivalent resources to promote them, and students must have an equal opportunity to learn. These issues apply to IRA-NCTE Standard 8: "Students develop an understanding of technological and informational resources (e.g., libraries, databases, computer networks, video) to gather and synthesize information and to create and communicate knowledge" (IRA-NCTE 1996, 4).

IRA-NCTE also gave increasing recognition to linguistic and cultural diversity. For example, Standards 9 and 10 specifically address language and cultural diversity. The fact that national model standards were finally directed toward these issues represented substantial progress. However, even as that was happening, controversy erupted regarding Ebonics in Oakland, California, as the school district attempted to improve students' respect for their home languages. Note that IRA-NCTE Standard 9 called for such understanding: "Students develop an understanding of and respect for diversity in language use, patterns, and dialects across cultures, ethnic groups, geographic regions, and social roles" (IRA-NCTE 1996, 4). Nevertheless, such insight was lost on the media and the public at large (Baugh 2000; Perry and Delpit 1998; Ramírez et al. 2000).

During the 1990s, efforts came of age to develop content standards for English as a second language and to link those standards to academic content areas. Leaders in this area were Teachers of English to Speakers of Other Languages (TESOL), which published its own national standards, *ESL Standards for Pre-K-12 Students* (TESOL 1997; Snow 2000). TESOL's standards had three broad areas of application: English in social settings, English in academic content areas, and culturally appropriate English use.

The adoption of content standards, however, also implied the adoption and appropriate use of performance standards. The contemporary emphasis on performance standards recalls the stress on behavioural objectives during the 1960s and 1970s, when performance objectives were designed to make specific language behaviours explicit by describing the conditions of performance, stating the standard of acceptable performance. Despite the appeal of performance standards, they were criticized because they equated knowing a language "with the mastery of isolated, discrete items [that] would seem to have been disproved by the acknowledged failure of certain methods, such as audio-lingualism, which focused almost exclusively on the minutiae of language's building blocks" (Tumposky 1984, 303). The recent push for standards, however, appears to be less drastic in most US schools than the previous, more behaviouralist-oriented approaches (cf. Spolsky 1999).

For language-minority students, "near-native" or "native-like" English proficiency, as called for by model standards documents (TESOL 1997), is often presented as the ultimate goal of instruction. The importance of acquiring English is well understood by the overwhelming majority of language-minority learners and their parents. But overemphasizing native-like proficiency can eclipse the more important goal: for language-minority students to sustain progress in their academic subjects. *Lau* concluded that requiring students to attain full mastery of English as a prerequisite to their study of other academic content areas makes a "mockery of public education." Ideally, those for whom English is a second language should be able to pursue both the development of English *and* grade-level mastery of academic subjects. In states where anti-bilingual education laws have been passed, such as California and Arizona, so-called English immersion programs need to come under intense scrutiny to ensure that they are promoting both English and academic achievement (cf. Davis 1999; Singh 1998).

Conclusions and Prospects for Language Education

Language education in the United States remains a conflicted domain, as it has been through much of its history. Although some appreciate the value of many languages as a potential national resource, language diversity continues to be a surrogate marker for race and ethnicity. Thus the twenty-first century began, much as the previous one did, with a wave of English-only initiatives and persistent opposition to bilingual education (see Tatalovich 1995). Despite the perseverance of the attack on multilingualism, a minority American bilingual tradition, as well as social and regional varieties of English, remain as contested but enduring features of the American social landscape. Foreign language instruction prospers, but not at a level that poses any serious challenge to the "land of the monolingual" (Simon 1988), even as the spread of English around the globe confronts local linguistic traditions that both resist and co-opt English for their own purposes. In the United States, language educators and policy makers face an inevitable task in the new millennium: deal with the cognitive and academic issues involved, while making their way through a political, emotional, and ideological minefield.

Notes
From *World Yearbook of Education 2003*, ed. Jill Bourne and Euan Reid, 141-55. Copyright © 2003 Routledge. Reproduced by permission of Taylor & Francis Books UK.

References
Armas, G.C. 2001. New census survey offers glimpse into immigration, language spoken at home. Nando Media/AP Online. http://www.onenation.org/0108/080501a.htm.
August, D., and K. Hakuta, eds. 1997. *Improving schooling for language-minority children: A research agenda*. Washington, DC: National Research Council, Institute of Medicine.
Baugh, J. 2000. *Beyond Ebonics: Linguistic pride and racial prejudice*. Oxford: OUP.
Brod, R., and E. Welles. 2000. Foreign language enrolments in United States institutions of higher education. *ADFL Bulletin* (Association of Departments of Foreign Languages) 31(2): 22-29.
Cherokee Nation. n.d. A brief history of the Cherokee Nation. http://www.cherokee.org.
Crawford, J. 1997. *Best evidence: Research foundations of the Bilingual Education Act*. Washington, DC: National Clearinghouse for Bilingual Education.
–. 1999. *Bilingual education: History, politics, theory and practice*. 4th ed. Los Angeles: Bilingual Education Services.
Davis, A. 1999. Native speaker. In *Concise encyclopedia of educational linguistics*, ed. B. Spolsky, 532-39. Oxford: Elsevier.
Ehle, J. 1988. *Trail of tears: The rise and fall of the Cherokee nation*. New York: Anchor.
IRA-NCTE (International Reading Association and National Council for Teachers of English). 1996. *Standards for the English language arts*. Newark, DE, and Urbana, IL: IRA-NCTE.
Kirk Senesac, B.V. 2002. Two-way bilingual immersion: A portrait of quality schooling. *Bilingual Research Journal* 26(1): 85-101.
Kloss, H. 1971. Language rights of immigrant groups. *International Migration Review* 5: 250-68.
–. 1977/1998. *The American bilingual tradition*. Washington, DC: Center for Applied Linguistics.
Lau v. Nichols, 414 U.S. 563 (1974).
Leibowitz, A.H. 1971. *Educational policy and political acceptance: The imposition of English as the language of instruction in American Schools*. Washington, DC: Center for Applied Linguistics. ERIC No. ED047321.
Lepore, J. 2002. *A is for American: Letters and other characters in the newly United States*. New York: Alfred A. Knopf.
McCarty, T.L., and O. Zepeda, eds. 1995. Indigenous language education and literacy. Special issue, *Bilingual Research Journal* 19(1-4).
McNeil, L.M. 2000. *Contradictions of school reform: Educational costs of standardized testing*. New York: Routledge.
Macías, R.F. 1985. Language and ideology in the United States. *Social Education* (Feb.), 97-100.
Minami, M., and C.J. Ovando. 2004. Language issues in multicultural contexts. In *Handbook of research on multicultural education,* 2nd ed., ed. J.A. Banks and C.A.M. Banks, 567-88. San Francisco: Jossey-Bass.
Ohanian, S. 1999. *One size fits few: The folly of educational standards*. Portsmouth, NH: Heinemann.
Olsen, L. 1999. ¿Qué pasó en California? Lessons from Proposition 227. Handout distributed at the annual meeting of the National Association for Bilingual Education, 26-30 January, Denver, CO.
Ovando, C.J. 1990. Politics and pedagogy: The case of bilingual education. *Harvard Educational Review* 60: 341-56.
–. 1999. Bilingual education in the United States: Historical development and current issues. Paper presented at the annual meeting of the American Educational Research Association, 19-23 April, Montreal.
–. 2004. Language diversity and education. In *Multicultural education: Issues and perspectives*, 5th ed., ed. J.A. Banks and C.A.M. Banks, 289-313. New York: John Wiley and Sons.
Ovando, C.J., V.P. Collier, and M.C. Combs. 2003. *Bilingual and ESL classrooms: Teaching in multicultural contexts*. 3rd ed. Boston: McGraw-Hill.

Ovando, C.J., and P. McLaren, eds. 2000. *The politics of multiculturalism and bilingual education: Students and teachers caught in the crossfire*. Boston: McGraw-Hill.

PBS Video. 1999. *The News Hour with Jim Lehrer,* 1 February.

Perry, T., and L. Delpit. 1998. *The real Ebonics debate: Power, language, and the education of African-American children*. Boston: Beacon Press.

Ramírez, J.D., T.G. Wiley, G. DeKlerk, and E. Lee, eds. 2000. *Ebonics in the urban education debate*. Long Beach: Center for Language Minority Education and Research, California State University.

Rhodes, N.C., and L.E. Branaman. 1999. *Foreign language instruction in the United States: A national survey of elementary and secondary schools*. Washington, DC: Center for Applied Linguistics.

Schiffman, H.F. 1996. *Linguistic culture and language policy*. London: Routledge.

Simon, P. 1988. *The tongue-tied American: Confronting the foreign language crisis*. New York: Continuum.

Singh, R., ed. 1998. *The native speaker: Multilingual perspectives*. London: Sage Publications.

Snow, M.A. 2000. *Implementing the ESL standards for pre-K-12 students through teacher education*. Arlington, VA: Teachers of English to Speakers of Other Languages (TESOL).

Spicer, E.H. 1980. American Indians, federal policy towards. In *Harvard encyclopedia of American ethnic groups*, ed. O. Handlin, 114-22. Cambridge, MA: Harvard University Press.

Spolsky, B. 1999. Standards, scales, and guidelines. In *Concise encyclopedia of educational linguistics*, ed. B. Spolsky, 390-92. Oxford: Elsevier.

Spring, J. 1994. *Deculturation and the struggle for equality: A brief history of the education of dominated cultures in the United States*. New York: McGraw-Hill.

Tatalovich, R. 1995. *Nativism reborn? The official English language movement and the American states*. Lexington: University Press of Kentucky.

TESOL (Teachers of English to Speakers of Other Languages). 1997. *ESL standards for pre-K-12 students*. Alexandria, VA: TESOL.

Thomas, W., and V. Collier. 1996. *Language-minority student achievement and program effectiveness*. Fairfax, VA: Center for Bilingual/Multicultural/ESL Education, George Mason University.

Toth, C.R. 1990. *German-English bilingual schools in America: The Cincinnati tradition in historical context*. New York: Peter Lang.

Tumposky, N.R. 1984. Behavioral objectives, the cult of efficiency, and foreign language learning: Are they compatible? *TESOL Quarterly* 18(2): 295-307.

United States Census Bureau. 2000. Profile of selected demographic and social characteristics for the foreign-born population who entered the United States 1990-2000. http://www.census.gov/population/cen2000.

Unz, R., and Tuchman, G.M. 1997. *English language education for children in public schools*. California initiative statute (certified as Proposition 227 for the 2 June 1998 primary election). Available at English for the Children, http://www.onenation.org.

Weinberg, M. 1995. *A chance to learn: The history of race and education in the United States*. 2nd ed. Long Beach: California State University, Long Beach Press.

Wiley, T.G. 1998. The imposition of World War I era English-only policies and the fate of German in North America. In *Language and politics in the United States and Canada: Myths and realities*, ed. T. Ricento and B. Burnaby, 211-41. Mahwah, NJ: Lawrence Erlbaum.

–. 2000. Continuity and change in the function of language ideologies in the United States. In *Ideology, politics, and language policies: Focus on English*, ed. T. Ricento, 67-85. Mahwah, NJ: Lawrence Erlbaum.

–. 2002. Accessing language rights in education: A brief history of the U.S. context. In *Language policies in education: Critical issues*, ed. J.W. Tollefson, 39-64. Mahwah, NJ: Lawrence Erlbaum.

Wiley, T.G., with E. Hartung-Cole 2000. *ESL standards: Questions, answers and resources*. Long Beach: Center for Language Minority Education and Research, California State University.

Woodson, C.G. 1933/1990. *The mis-education of the Negro*. Reprint. Trenton, NJ: African World Press.

9

A Critical Examination of Language Policies and Practices in Canada and the United States

Karen M. Gourd

Language policies and practices in Canada and the United States have both provided and limited opportunities for language learners. They have been used as tools both to inspire unity and to control minority language groups. They have served to register dissent and to improve educational opportunities for language learners, as well as to present a traditional reading of history and current affairs. In both countries, language policies have been used to control specific populations in a range of ways: from explicit deculturalization to acculturation into the Westernized norms of the governing group, invisibility, assimilation, or symbolic recognition.

Two types of language policies will be critically examined in this chapter. One type explicitly addresses the education of language learners, including immigrants, indigenous communities, and historically forced residents such as enslaved Africans and peoples whose homes were annexed through wars and treaties. These policies include legislation and court decisions obligating districts to educate students who are not yet proficient in the national language.[1] The Bilingual Education Act of 1968 and the Supreme Court decision in *Lau* v. *Nichols* (1974) in the United States, and Canada's multiculturalism policy of 1971 and the Canadian Multiculturalism Act of 1988, for example, are national policies that explicitly address the education of language learners.

The second type of language policy is less explicitly connected with language learners' educational needs and opportunities, but no less relevant. Examples include legislation limiting immigration, privileging immigration from certain geographical regions, naming an official language or languages at the national or provincial/state level, and reducing or eliminating the rights of illegal immigrants (such as Proposition 187).[2] The naming of an official language or languages, in particular, not only sends powerful messages about the relative value and status of languages but limits the languages deemed acceptable for instruction. In these language policies, the importance of student learning can be trumped by other concerns, such as citizenship, economics, politics, race, and "coercive relations of power" (Cummins 1997, 106).

Language Policies as a Form of Control

Derwing and Munro note that at the time of the Confederation of Canada in 1867, Aboriginal languages were ignored. Subsequent language policies emphasized the "protection and promotion of our two official languages" (Speech from the Throne 2002, quoted in Chapter 7). Bilingual programs in languages other than English or French are not numerous, confined to specific geographic locations, and limited to particular "heritage languages." Indigenous languages are taught in parts of Canada, but generally within language revitalization programs, not bilingual programs that use the indigenous language as a language of content area instruction (T.M. Derwing, personal communication, 26 September 2003). The loss of indigenous languages underscores the serious invisibility issues of indigenous communities. Although some may symbolically recognize indigenous languages as part of the multilingual heritage of Canada, Aboriginal groups object to being lumped with immigrant groups under Canada's multicultural policies (Chapter 4).

Similarly, in the United States, except for separate policies specifically addressing indigenous populations (such as the 1990 Native American Languages Preservation Act), indigenous language issues have received much less attention than immigrant language issues (Wiley 2002). This lack of attention denies Native peoples' experiences of colonization and forced assimilation in the United States. Historically, control and oppression, not assimilation, motivated language and education policies aimed at indigenous peoples in the United States. Replacing indigenous languages with English, rather than developing bilingualism, was an explicit component of US language and education policies (see, for example, Lomawaima 1994; McCarty 2002; Prucha 1994). Yet the myth that survives is that Native Americans refused to learn English or to assimilate to US cultural norms; even when educated at government expense, they chose to "return to the blanket" (Spicer 1980). This myth implies that they were given a choice to become bilingual but chose to remain monolingual.

From 1619 to 1865, African Americans were restricted by "compulsory ignorance" laws. They were forced to learn English but forbidden to use their native languages and forbidden to learn to write in English. Enslaved Africans learned English, found ways to communicate across distinctly different linguistic backgrounds, and took great risks to learn and teach literacy skills in English (Douglass 1962). Yet the myth that survives in the minds of many, including educators, is that historically African Americans were not literate, that it remains difficult for them to learn standard English, and that they are best served educationally by remedial approaches. Punishment of individuals for using a language other than English, generally considered an obstacle to equitable educational opportunities by current standards, persisted after the Civil War. African Americans, Spanish speakers, and other language groups report being punished either physically or academically for using their home languages at school (see, for example, Nieto 1996; Chapter 4).

Language policies in educational settings are still used as a form of control. Students in Nieto's (1996) study clearly articulate links between their academic successes or failures and the teachers' attempts to control their linguistic choices. Students report being told only English was acceptable for use at school. The marginalization of their home cultures and languages was intended to accelerate their assimilation to monolingualism in English; instead, it caused them to resist the school curriculum. Their educational opportunities were compromised by their choice to use their home language and to identify with their home culture.

Immigration and language policies have also been used to give distinct advantages to some groups while restricting others. Both Canada and the United States have had immigration legislation that favoured groups that were most similar to the group in power while excluding groups that were perceived as more racially and linguistically distinct. As Derwing and Munro (Chapter 7) point out, language policies and programs often focused on controlling immigrant populations. Like domesticating policies in the United States (Chapter 8), language programs in Canada have been designed to quickly acculturate immigrants and to supply an obedient workforce for the Canadian economy.

While Canada has been officially bilingual since its founding, the United States has never had an official language. Recent attempts to name English as the official language, including a bill in the House of Representatives, were intended to limit the use of other languages and to reduce services to those who are not proficient in English by limiting the legal obligations of the government to provide them in other languages (Crawford 2000). Under this legislation, the legal obligation to provide equitable educational opportunities to *all* children would be replaced by a responsibility to equitably educate only those children who demonstrate proficiency in English.

Differences between the United States and Canada on the issue of official language were noted by M.E. Mujica, the head of US English, a group that advocates making English the official language of the United States. Mujica warns the United States against "creating an American Quebec" (US English 2005). In a discussion of the possibility of statehood for Puerto Rico, Mujica argues that admitting Puerto Rico into the Union would bring with it drastic cultural and linguistic problems for the United States, and equates this with the situation of Quebec in Canada. When I questioned Tracey Derwing about Mujica's reading of the Canadian issues, she responded: "For the most part, Canadians have come to grips with the fact that there are two official languages ... Having two languages has made people a bit more accepting of other languages. However, the situation is far more complex than this. A lot of the frictions between Quebec and the rest of Canada are related to historical factors other than language" (23 September 2003, personal communication).

Despite Canada's two official languages and the United States' lack of an official language, English remains the privileged language in both nations. While Mujica would have us believe that the difference between language policies in Canada and the United States lies in the naming of official languages, the motivations for naming official languages are quite different in the two countries. In Canada, the official language policy was intended to unify anglophones and francophones; specifically it was a bold move to *include* rather than *exclude* francophones and to increase the status of French in all of Canada.[3] Although the policy may not have achieved its goals, they remain very different from the goals of groups seeking to name English the official language in the United States, namely to ensure that minority language groups have no rights.

Language Policies Used to Register Dissent and Initiate Change

Language policies and education are complex, offering, as Joshee and Johnson (2005, 55) point out, multiple layers of a "discursive and dialectical space within which there are possibilities for change." Education is primarily the responsibility of the states in the United States and the provinces in Canada; however, federal policies related to the education of immigrants and multilingual residents also affect school-level programs and classroom practices. For example, 1968's Bilingual Education Act in the United States prompted the development of an increased number of language programs (Malakoff and Hakuta 1990). Initially, nearly all the programs were designed as transitional (Moran and Hakuta 1995). The use of the home language was viewed as a crutch that language learners were to leave behind as soon as possible.

Later revisions to the Bilingual Education Act were, in part, responses to the demands made by communities, researchers, and educators examining the experiences of language learners in the early programs. Although transitional bilingual education programs account for the largest number of bilingual programs, other programs such as two-way bilingual and maintenance bilingual programs have increased. Cultural sensitivity to students' home culture is recognized as a relevant component of language programs (Moran and Hakuta 1995).

State and provincial policies can either offset federal legislation or fill gaps perceived by local communities. Twenty-six US states have named English their official language, though this legislation has been found unconstitutional in at least three of these states. Despite the federal Bilingual Education Act, states such as Texas, Colorado, and California have introduced or passed legislation specifically intended to limit bilingual education programs. Alternatively, state-level policies can also extend support for language learners' needs and go beyond the federal policies. The Lau Remedies, designed to add teeth to the court decision in *Lau* v. *Nichols* (1974), were left unimplemented under Reagan. They were used, however, by some states to create guidelines to hold districts accountable for educating students acquiring English (Malakoff and Hakuta 1990).

Not only is the language policy context complex, it is also dynamic, and state/provincial-level policies are not without checks. Educators can mitigate these policies by relying on federal policies and their own experience to support bilingual programs. In conversations with bilingual teachers in California after the passage of Proposition 227 in 1998 (state legislation limiting the use of bilingual education as an instructional program in K-12 public schools), I heard many declare that "bilingual education continues in California. We just have to be creative in how we name and describe it." Even state-level policies that do not get implemented can have significant human effects. The documentary *Fear and Learning at Hoover Elementary* (Simón 1996) is testimony to the impact of 1994's Proposition 187 on individuals in California despite the fact its implementation was stopped by a federal district court decision.

Language Policies and Effective Education for Language Learners

Because policies and schools are complex, dynamic entities, superficial or simplistic fixes are unlikely to increase educational opportunities for language learners. Overnight changes in programs based on the highest quality research and theory can easily fall flat if the programs are implemented in contexts that are out of sync with them. This is not to say that language theory and research is irrelevant or detrimental to policies and programs. However, in both Canada and the United States, second language acquisition research appears to take a back seat to politics and social attitudes. Consequently, conventional wisdom cannot be overlooked as a component of policy making and implementation. For example, the decision in *Lau* v. *Nichols* (1974) was based on the common sense of the US Supreme Court members, who did not claim to be experts in second language acquisition research. Indeed, their decision plainly stated that it was up to educators to develop appropriate programs for the children who did not yet speak English. They knew, however, that giving children lessons in a language they did not understand was not an equitable educational opportunity. Conventional wisdom among the Supreme Court judges in 1974 was on the side of language learners. If the current US Supreme Court heard the *Lau* v. *Nichols* case, I am not convinced the outcome would be the same as the 1974 decision, despite the fact that subsequent research on second language acquisition clearly supports the Court's decision.

The justices on the US Supreme Court in 1974 determined "equitable education" to mean that different students' needs would require different services. Denying services obviously needed by language learners made a mockery of education. Cummins (2000, 6) explains that "to educate the whole child in a culturally and linguistically diverse context it is necessary to nurture intellect and identity equally in ways that, of necessity, challenge coercive relations of power." While effective policies and programs certainly can include instrumental focuses such as explicit instruction in the national culture and national or official language(s), programs must go further. Effective language policies and programs need to do more than prepare participants for the job market, cultural assimilation, or citizenship. They must "nurture the intellect" and provide opportunities for participants to challenge social and educational inequities.

Educators must be cognizant of three components of language learners' education. One has long been recognized: their need to learn the dominant language. Without skills in that language, immigrants have limited economic, social, and political opportunities. They can join the workforce only in low-paying jobs and can participate in the society only as second-class citizens even when they have full legal citizenship.

The second component of language learners' needs is their need for education in content areas even while they learn the dominant language. Immigrants in intensive programs that focus only on language skills miss content area knowledge necessary both to keep up with their peers and to maintain a sense of their own worth. Adult immigrants who must support their families and maintain their own usefulness need to be able to participate in social and work situations at more than a childlike level, even before they have achieved high levels of proficiency in the dominant language. Language policies and programs are beginning to acknowledge the skills and knowledge acquired through other languages, realizing that these skills and knowledge can be transferred to English.

The third component of language learners' needs is attention to their developing consciousness. Federal-level language policies have not yet explicitly acknowledged this need, but some national organizations and individual educators are attending to it. The US professional organization Teachers of English to Speakers of Other Languages has developed standards that explicitly support the development of home languages (TESOL 2002). The International Reading Association has position statements endorsing first language and second language literacy instruction (IRA 2001). The IRA's concern that intolerant social attitudes interfere with students' educational opportunities is made clear in its statement: "Children's proficiency in their country's dominant languages is a worthy and desirable goal. But efforts to deny students access to initial literacy instruction in their home language, often launched in the name of national unity, may reflect an underlying intolerance" (IRA 1998). Similarly, the National Council of Teachers of English (1986) warns that hostile attempts to "preserve," "purify," or "enhance"

English "will not only stunt the vitality of the language, but also ensure its erosion and in effect create hostility toward English, making it more difficult to teach and learn."

The NCTE has published several resolutions objecting to naming English the official language of the United States. Students learn much more quickly when they see themselves reflected in the lessons and are motivated to learn for reasons other than assimilation purposes. After an extensive review of the literature relating to immigration policy and the education of immigrants, Olneck (1995, 325) concludes, "Insistence on culturally discontinuous pedagogical regimes can often provoke disengagement and resistance, while culturally responsive pedagogy seems more often to prompt engagement and assent to learning. Maintenance of ethnic loyalty, not assimilation, appears associated with stronger school performance among immigrant children." Extending Olneck's conclusions to home language loyalty, we can expect that allowing choice in language learning for immigrants is more likely to secure their commitment to learning the national language. On the other hand, devaluing their home language and banning its use in public and official arenas, as intended by the proposed US official language legislation, is more likely to cause resistance and retard the acquisition of English. It seems obvious, then, that equitable learning opportunities for language learners should not be objectionable to those who want all immigrants to acquire English quickly. An effective educational program for language learners would include support for maintaining ties to the home language and culture, instruction in English, content instruction while acquiring English, development of social consciousness, and the development of social awareness for *all* educators and *all* students, not just those in bilingual or English as a second language programs.

The Way Forward

The histories of language policies and programs in the United States and in Canada are not dissimilar. As frustrated as bilingual education advocates may be, current language policies and programs in both countries have never been more supportive of bilingual programs. Despite its "conflicted" response to language learners and the role of other languages, the United States has more bilingual programs and more language learners in some sort of support program than ever before. Attention to the student's home language, although still not fully supported in all language programs, has become more common, even in states like California where legislation raised roadblocks to bilingual education programs (Crawford 2000). Programs give more attention to factors other than learning the structure of the English language. Although many teachers of language learners still claim they teach only the language, a growing number of educators pay attention to cultural information necessary for participation in society as well as developing an awareness of the injustices based on language use.

A critical examination of the Canadian and US contexts indicates that changes in language policies to ensure educational opportunities for language learners are likely to be limited as long as the policies are fuelled by conventional wisdom built on racist and exclusionary ideology rather than concern for the diverse needs of individuals. Until bilingualism is valued as a resource and strength of those who can operate in more than one language, language policies are likely to remain the site of political warfare between those who use policies to control and those who use them to resist control. Until issues of social justice are made foundational to all educational programs, language learners' educational opportunities will be restricted. Thus significant changes in the social, economic, and political contexts of schools and society are necessary but difficult steps to improved educational experiences for language learners. Citizenship education focused on preparing all citizens to create a fair and just world, rather than focused on teaching language learners to abide by cultural norms decided by those in power, could lead to the development and implementation of language policies that create open spaces for dialogue among diverse groups (Freire 1998).

Notes

1 In this chapter, I have adopted the distinction between a national language and an official language as explicated by Sonntag 1995. A *national* language is the language (or languages) most commonly used in a nation, whether or not it is has formally been labelled the official language. An *official* language is a language legislated at the federal or state/provincial level. Not all nations, states, or provinces have official languages. When there is an official language, it may be the only language in which instruction is permitted to take place.

2 Proposition 187 (1994) was designed to limit the rights of illegal immigrants in California. It made education, social services, and health care unavailable to illegal immigrants and their children. The proposition required teachers to report students they suspected to be illegally residing in the United States. The proposition passed by nearly 60 percent of the California voters. The US District 9th Circuit Appellate Court found the proposition to be unconstitutional, and Governor Davis chose not to appeal the court's decision.

3 T.M. Derwing contends that the status of French is not just a provincial question. Quebec's government recognizes that if French is to have real value inside and outside of Quebec, it must be recognized as an official language by *all* of Canada, not just by the province of Quebec (personal communication, 25 September 2003).

References

Crawford, J. 2000. *At war with diversity*. Buffalo, NY: Multilingual Matters.

Cummins, J. 1997. Cultural and linguistic diversity in education: A mainstream issue? *Educational Review* 49(2): 105-14.

–. 2000. *Language, power, and pedagogy: Bilingual children in the crossfire*. Toronto: Multilingual Matters.

Douglass, F. 1962. *Life and times of Frederick Douglass: His early life as a slave, his escape from bondage, and his complete history*. New York: Collier Books.

Freire, P. 1998. *Pedagogy of freedom: Ethics, democracy, and civic courage*. Lanham, MD: Rowman and Littlefield.

IRA (International Reading Association). 1998. *Summary of a policy resolution of the International Reading Association: First language literacy instruction.* http://www.reading.org/positions/first_language.html. No longer available.

–. 2001. *Second language literacy instruction: A position statement of the International Reading Association.* http://www.reading.org/resources/issues/positions.

Joshee, R., and L. Johnson. 2005. Multicultural education in the United States and Canada: The importance of national policies. In *International handbook of educational policy*, ed. N. Bascia, A. Cummings, K. Leithwood, and D. Livingstone, 53-74. Dordrecht, Netherlands: Kluwer Academic Publishing.

Lau v. Nichols, 414 U.S. 563 (1974).

Lomawaima, T. 1994. *They called it prairie light: The story of Chilocco Indian School.* Lincoln: University of Nebraska Press.

Malakoff, M., and K. Hakuta. 1990. History of language minority education in the United States. In *Bilingual education: Issues and strategies*, ed. A.M. Padilla, H.H. Fairchild, and C.M. Valadez, 27-43. Newbury Park, CA: Corwin Press.

McCarty, T.L. 2002. *A place to be Navajo: Rough Rock and the struggle for self-determination in indigenous schooling.* Mahwah, NJ: Lawrence Erlbaum.

Moran C., and K. Hakuta. 1995. Bilingual education: Broadening research perspectives. In *Handbook of research on multicultural education*, ed. J.A. Banks and C.A.M. Banks, 445-62. New York: Macmillan.

National Council of Teachers of English. 1986. *On English as the "official language."* NCTE Position Statement. http://www.ncte.org/about/over/positions.

Nieto, S. 1996. *Affirming diversity: The sociopolitical context of multicultural education.* 2nd ed. White Plains, NY: Longman Publishers USA.

Olneck, M.R. 1995. Immigrants and education. In *Handbook of research on multicultural education*, ed. J.A. Banks and C.A.M. Banks, 310-27. New York: Macmillan.

Proposition 187. 1994. Available at Glenn Spencer's American Patrol Report, http://www.americanpatrol.com/REFERENCE/prop187text.html.

Prucha, F. 1994. *American Indian treaties: The history of a political anomaly.* Berkeley: University of California Press.

Simón, L.A. 1996. *Fear and learning at Hoover Elementary.* Video. Los Angeles: Fear and Learning.

Sonntag, S.K. 1995. Elite competition and official language movements. In *Power and inequality in language education*, ed. J.W. Tollefson, 91-110. Cambridge: Cambridge University Press.

Spicer, E.H. 1980. American Indians, federal policy towards. In *Harvard encyclopedia of American ethnic groups*, ed. O. Handlin, 114-22. Cambridge, MA: Harvard University Press.

TESOL. 2002. TESOL/NCATE standards for the accreditation of initial programs in P-12 ESL teacher education. http://www.ncate.org.

US English, Inc. 2005. Publications page. http://www.us-english.org/foundation/publications.

Wiley, T.G. 2002. Accessing language rights in education: A brief history of the U.S. context. In *Language policies in education: Critical issues*, ed. J.W. Tollefson, 39-64. Mahwah, NJ: Lawrence Erlbaum.

Part 4:
Race-Based Policies

10
Race-Based Policies in Canada: Education and Social Context
Adrienne S. Chan

Policies that take up the concept of race as a category to regulate behaviour are race-based and provide a racialized consciousness because they legitimate ways of thinking about race. Different policies suggest practices that may be deleterious, contestatory, and, in some circumstances, supportive of racial equality. Race-based policies in Canada were established within a legacy of racialization, and this practice establishes a context for current policies that name race. Historically, a series of race-based policies outlined specific forms of discrimination and selected treatment. The Indian Act of 1876, the Chinese Exclusion Act of 1923, and the Act to Prevent the Employment of Female Labour in Certain Capacities of 1912 are some legislated examples.[1] Additionally, race-based policies have existed at the federal, provincial, and institutional levels, including school boards and postsecondary institutions.

In my discussion, I use racialization as a defining concept to think about policy and education. I examine how policy is used as a tool to meet particular racialized goals, such as separation and exclusion. Finally, I consider current examples of race relations policy, the emergence of an antiracism discourse in school boards, and the ongoing racialized debates fuelled by immigration, language, and wider social tensions.

Race-based policies are historical, but they continue and are a consideration in the social construction of education today. The terms *racialization* and *racialized relations* describe a process in which groups of people are objectified through the characteristics of race. Miles (1989) describes this as a process that takes an attribute (such as country of origin) and gives that particular category social significance, often as a negative feature. Groups of people are thus defined as different and as requiring some form of treatment to correct this differentiation. Policies and laws are created to address this differentiation (for example, segregation). Racialization can occur even without the use of the term *race* and may refer instead to, for example, "Black/White relations" (Satzewich 1998, 32). In these instances, racialization is invoked by the discussion of specifically identified racial groups and relations.

Racialization is embodied in ongoing discourses in education through institutional policies, practices, and norms. Structures and policies work within the demarcation of specific racial or ethnic groups; societal and institutional arrangements dictate polices or practices in legal, economic, housing, and education systems (Small 1998). Racializing policies are problematic insofar as they are linked to unexamined ideology, historical ideological processes, and structures that are part of the institution and the state (Small 1998).

This chapter discusses the period from the late nineteenth century to the present. This period began with race-based policies that were discriminatory, such as segregated "separate" schools, but later included inclusive policies oriented to social justice that articulate consideration of race, ethnicity, and culture. These include the multiculturalism policy (1971), the Canadian Multiculturalism Act (1988), and the Canadian Charter of Rights and Freedoms (1982). Through a discussion of separate schools, I will reveal the ways in which the public, parents, and school boards contributed to, or acceded to, policy to meet their own goals. I also review a range of more recent policies that identify race and ethnicity as important categories. This review reveals an emerging discourse regarding the construction of race and ethnicity within the notion of a pluralistic society. We see attempts to argue for the positive aspects of a racially and ethnically diverse society in Canada and the influence of these arguments on education.

Separate Schools and Educational Access

Segregated schools in Canada emerged both through policy and through practice as "separate" schools for Black children. These were most common in Nova Scotia and Ontario, where separate schools were a normative practice instituted by law (Walker 1980; Winks 1972). Segregation practices in schools were also present in other provinces, such as New Brunswick, Prince Edward Island, and British Columbia.

Separate schools in Nova Scotia were one of the results of Black migration from the United States to Canada in the late eighteenth century (Winks 1972) and were initially advanced as a source of opportunity for Black students. Early education for "Negroes" began with small schools organized by the church. Both "slave children"[2] and free children attended these schools, and Black teachers were placed in these schools. Nova Scotia passed an Education Act in 1836 that enshrined separate schools for Black children. Prejudice and a larger Black population fuelled the arguments for separate schools. If Black children were to have an education, it was argued, it should take place in separate schools from White children (Walker 1997, 1980). The act was amended in 1884 to specify that schools receiving "special aid" could not hire teachers with credentials "higher than a fourth class certificate." Since all Black schools received provincial aid, this amendment meant that less qualified teachers would be streamed into the separate schools (Walker 1997, 128).

In the case of New Brunswick, in 1820 the lieutenant governor requested that schools in Saint John have a "separate branch of the institution" for the instruction of "Negro" children (Winks 1972, 364). In Fredericton, where there were a large number of Blacks, a separate school was established because of community pressures. This was constructed as a choice between no schooling and separate schooling for Black students. Thus the practice of separate schools was embedded in New Brunswick without legislation. Separate schools often served all-Black communities, so that separation was, in part, constructed by the community (Walker 1997; Winks 1972).

Unofficial segregation was maintained in daily life in whole communities in Ontario, including Hamilton and Amherstburg. In education, segregation was legislated. The School Act of 1849 allowed for the "establishing of any number of schools for the children of colored people that they may judge expedient" (Backhouse 1999, 250). Intense prejudice and discrimination existed, and school trustees stated that they would not send their own children "to a School with niggers" in attendance (Winks 1972, 368).

As a result of ongoing tensions surrounding access to schooling, Ontario passed legislation in 1850 for a Separate School Act, which provided for separate schools with regard to religion and race (Walker 1980). The act allowed any group of five Black families to request the school trustees to establish a school for their families; a group of twelve or more White families could also request a separate school for Blacks (Walker 1997). This act provided a vehicle for White families and school officials to pressure Black families to apply for their own separate institutions. Such pressures were community-based because the act was framed to suggest to Black families that they would benefit from separate schools – particularly given the alternative of no school at all.

A section of the 1850 act outlined that where no separate schools existed, Black children had the right to attend a "common school." Common school was the name first given to public schools, as distinct from private schools and religious separate schools. Common schools were generally the local schools, and dominated by White students (Walker 1980). A court ruling made by Chief Justice Robinson in 1854 upheld this section of the act. A ruling in 1864 also provided that if a separate school was no longer in use, then Black children could access a common school (Walker 1997). These decisions opened the possibility for future challenges to separate schools and access to common schools.

Separate schools for Blacks were intended to "preserve the assumption of equality of opportunity while slowing cultural assimilation" (Winks 1972, 144). Many early separate schools lacked teachers who had competent training, pupil attendance was often irregular, and there were no library facilities. In some communities where it was not possible to establish separate schools, Black children were given separate benches, thus establishing internal segregation. In some districts, the taxes collected from Black taxpayers contributed to the White or common schools, the very schools that Blacks could not attend (Winks 1972).

Teachers protested the separate school system in Ontario, and in 1864 a teachers' association convention in Toronto adopted a resolution opposing segregation. In 1869, a segregated school in Amherstburg was integrated, but within six years the school was closed (Winks 1972). The following years saw unsuccessful court challenges to segregation. In *Hill* v. *Camden*, Dennis Hill challenged the school district to admit his two children, arguing that the nearest segregated "Negro" school was four miles away. The judge ruled that where a separate school was established for Blacks, then attendance "would be compulsory" (373). In a subsequent case, *Simmons* v. *Chatham*, a ruling was made that Blacks should attend "a separate school whether they lived near it or not" (374).

Separate schools were maintained in Nova Scotia through 1960, although a number of these schools resulted from community demographics rather than enforcement of the act. The last separate school closed in Ontario in 1965, although many had closed by the early 1950s (Winks 1972). In both Ontario and Nova Scotia, language identified White schools as "common" schools, while Black schools were "separate" schools. The definition of *common* then is a normative sense of which students have common access: White students. The discourse of "choice" also emerged as a vehicle for school boards and White parents to pressure Black parents to support separate schools in order to attain an education of any sort.

The experience of Chinese students in British Columbia was quite different from that of Black students. Chinese families were established in BC communities and schools in the late 1800s. School officials in Victoria attempted segregation of Chinese children from their schools as early as 1901. Chinese children had been attending public schools from the last decade of the nineteenth century, and many of these students were "overage" for the grade that they were assigned to.[3] Concern was expressed about the "social and moral effects" of the Chinese students on other students. The Department of Education took the view that such students "with language problems" were a "detriment to the progress of others" in the same grade, and this was one rationale for attempting segregation (Con et al. 1982, 128).

From 1908 through 1922, Victoria and Vancouver school boards put into effect partial segregation. In 1922, the situation came to a head in Victoria when the school board attempted to place 240 Chinese students, both Canadian-born and immigrants, into a separate building, called "the chicken coop" (Con et al. 1982, 129). The attempted segregation led Chinese parents to boycott the public school for a year until a compromise was reached to place only the students who were behind in their academic subjects in separate classrooms (Con et al. 1982; Wickberg 1980). The year-long boycott had deleterious consequences for some children, who did not return to school.

By the end of 1923, however, Chinese students were registered in mixed-race classrooms (Ashworth 1979).

While the situation with Chinese students was agitating in Victoria, general anti-Asian sentiments were widespread throughout the province. Attempts were made to segregate Japanese children in public schools throughout British Columbia as early as 1914 (Adachi 1976). Again, there were allegations that older Japanese children would "corrupt" White children and should be segregated. In one incident, a parent-teacher association in Vancouver claimed that Japanese students had infectious skin diseases and trachoma and were a health risk. After an investigation of thirty-three schools found that the majority of school principals considered their "Oriental" students to be "harmless," the Vancouver School Board did not carry out a policy of separation of Japanese children (Adachi 1976, 107).

With the bombing of Pearl Harbor in December 1941, the Canadian government debated whether Japanese Canadians were a threat to national security. Several authors have documented the political, economic, and security arguments given by the state for the internment of Japanese Canadians (see Adachi 1976; Kitano 1969; Li 1990). Government policies outlined separation initially by partial evacuation and, ultimately, by full evacuation of "Japanese nationals" from the coast of British Columbia (Adachi 1976, 208).

The impact of evacuation and internment on Japanese children is an example of the culmination of a racialized federal policy on education. In the spring of 1942, evacuation began and Japanese children who resided in communities near Vancouver left their regular classrooms for temporary buildings used as schools at Hastings Park. Volunteers with no training staffed these classrooms. In September 1942, a thousand students were turned away from schools in Vancouver, since these children were expected to be sent to camps in interior British Columbia before winter. Strathcona Public School had an enrolment of six hundred Nisei (second-generation Japanese Canadians, born in Canada) students in 1941, but would not admit any Japanese students in 1942. No provision had been made for the interim period prior to the move to interior camps. The provincial minister of education, H.G.T. Perry, in fact proposed that the School Act be amended to prohibit Japanese students from the provincial school system entirely (Adachi 1976). Thus, at the same time that some branches of the federal government were preparing the way for later multiculturalism (see Chapter 1), others were enacting racist policies.

The BC government's unwillingness to address the lack of education for interned Japanese students forced the Canadian government to reluctantly step in to deal with the situation. However, no schools were built to accommodate Japanese students. Rather, the responsibility for the schools fell to the Japanese families themselves. They set up makeshift schools in a range of buildings, including bunkhouses and barns. Many students missed a year of formal education before they were established in any type of classroom again. High school students were left to take correspondence courses at their own expense until several local churches took responsibility for staffing and financing high school and kindergarten classes (Adachi 1976, 264). Japanese children in the internment camps also suffered from the lack of adequate books, teaching materials and qualified teachers. In one camp with over two thousand children, there were only two Nisei with teaching credentials. In 1943, a four-week teacher training course for 125 Nisei was delivered in the New Denver camp as a measure to address the education of the children. Japanese children remained in internment camp schools, with substandard resources and staffing, until the war ended.

In the case of Chinese and Japanese children, race-based objectification constructed Asian students as morally threatening to White students or as a security risk to Canada more generally. Because of anti-Asian sentiments, Canadian-born and immigrant children were racialized under one gaze as "Chinese" and "Japanese." The internment of Japanese students is a stark example of how education may be affected by wider national policy that is fuelled by fear and racism.

Access to education and to public life was also affected by race-based provincial policy in British Columbia. British Columbia was the primary Canadian destination for Chinese, Japanese and South Asian immigrants at the end of the nineteenth century. Chinese people were recruited as indentured labourers to support the building of the Canadian Pacific Railway. Japanese people worked on the railway as well as in fishing, lumber, and mining industries, while South Asian people (then called Hindus) worked on the railway and on plantations. Against a backdrop of a racialized economy, Chinese, Japanese, and South Asians were all disenfranchised in British Columbia, commencing in 1875 when the Chinese lost the right to vote (Bolaria and Li 1985).

The loss of the right to vote in the province had additional negative consequences, including the loss of the right to vote federally. Moreover, the voters' list was a requisite for serving in such public offices as school trustee (Bolaria and Li 1985). The absence from the voter's list and lack of franchise also meant denial of admission to professional schools, such as law and pharmacy (Angus 1937; Krauter and Davis 1978; Ward 1978; Raj 1980). All three groups were thus denied these opportunities until they regained the right to vote in 1947.

The separation of Black, Chinese, and Japanese Canadian children in the schools reveals how school boards and provincial and federal governments contributed to the racialization of education through policy and practice. Parents, teachers, and public figures all participated in the discourse of separation through the debates and actions regarding children who had been racialized for publicly expressed reasons of morality or safety. These children and their education were constructed through race, and thus, subject to discrimination and social practices of power. The effects of these events extended far beyond the children and the schools to become part of a family, community, and social discourse on race.

Canadian and Provincial Legislation

When Canada established a national policy on multiculturalism in 1971 it became the first country in the world to do so. The policy set the stage for goals that emphasized equality in economic, social, cultural, and political spheres in Canadian life and citizenship. The naming of race, ethnicity, language, and religion in the policy was significant in a country that had largely made culture, beyond British and French, invisible. The policy suggested that an inclusive, respectful society for all Canadians could be achieved by creating an environment that acknowledged, valued, and promoted cultural diversity. A contested policy at the time, the text was considered a hallmark move toward a social justice and egalitarian philosophy that characterized the Liberal government (Fleras and Elliott 1996).

I will not review the successes and failures of the multiculturalism policy nor the 1988 Canadian Multiculturalism Act (for reviews and critiques, see, for example, Fleras and Elliott 1992; James 1995; Rezai-Rashti 1995; Tator and Henry 1991). Instead, I will review the resulting emergence of policy, the consideration of race within multiculturalism, and the linkages between policy, education, and the schools.

As evident from the discussion of separate schools, Canada was culturally diverse at the turn of the twentieth century. Changes in the Immigration Act of 1966 also affected the cultural composition of the country. The development of the multiculturalism policy was foreshadowed by efforts to gather ethnic support for the Second World War, the Royal Commission on Bilingualism and Biculturalism in 1963, and the Official Languages Act of 1969 (Chapter 1; Joshee 1995b; Moodley 1995). Education had been identified during the 1940s as a means to implement policy on cultural diversity (Joshee 1995a).

The multiculturalism policy officially recognized cultural, ethnic, and racial diversity as categories of consideration, rather than categories of separation and exclusion. The policy opened up debates that questioned the deficit model of difference and valorized a pluralist model of community participation. Yet the complexity of race, ethnicity, and culture was not necessarily taken into account in the use of multiculturalism as an overarching term. Race is referred to in the policy, which emphasizes cultural and racial diversity. The racial element of the multiculturalism policy, however, was not clearly defined and was subject to a range of interpretations. Because race and racialization extend beyond race or colour, and occur within ethnicity and other ethnic markers (Moodley 1995), I suggest that race is implied in the consideration of cultural, ethnic, and racial diversity. Nevertheless, an effect of the policy was the engagement of people in discussion on the subject of

race and racial equality. The federal government supported the multiculturalism policy by establishing a minister of multiculturalism in 1973 and a race
relations unit in 1981. The latter initiative conferred a specific focus on race
relations and increased the extent to which multiculturalism would include
the goals of equality of access and elimination of racial discrimination.

Education was implicated in at least three of the multiculturalism policy's
objectives, as outlined by the prime minister:

· The government will assist members of all cultural groups to overcome
  cultural barriers to full participation in Canadian society.
· The government will promote creative encounters and interchange among
  all Canadian cultural groups in the interest of national unity.
· The government will continue to assist immigrants to acquire at least
  one of Canada's official languages in order to become full participants in
  Canadian society. (Canada, House of Commons 1971)

Awareness of cultural barriers, cultural group interchange, and language
acquisition became more prevalent with the changing cultural make-up of
educational institutions, particularly in British Columbia (Nelson 1992) and
Ontario. Ultimately, the Canadian multiculturalism policy implicated the
education system as a site where "multicultural ideas, views, and principles
could be diffused among young Canadians" (Rezai-Rashti 1995, 3). The influence of multiculturalism policy on education and schooling was articulated
in a number of discussions: "[We] must recognize the key, vital and essential
role which teachers, our schools and our educational institutions can and
must play if we are ultimately to make significant progress toward the goals
of multiculturalism in Canada" (Canada, House of Commons 1986, 6:15).

Legislation following the multiculturalism policy heightened the profile of
race and ethnicity. The Canadian Human Rights Act, passed in 1977, protected
Canadians from discrimination on numerous grounds; those implicated in
racial categories included race, ethnicity, colour, and religion. In 1982, the
Charter of Rights and Freedoms came into force under the new Constitution.
Section 15 of the Charter addresses the protection from discrimination on
the basis of race, national or ethnic origin, colour, and religion, as well as sex,
age, and mental or physical ability. In 1988, the multiculturalism policy was
revised and embedded in the Canadian Multiculturalism Act.

Although federal policy has no explicit jurisdiction over education, it may
suggest directions in provincial policy. Since the creation of the multiculturalism policy in 1971, provincial and school board policies have emerged
that emphasize cultural awareness. It is important to note that the existence
of policy does not guarantee any action or particular practice (Anderson and
Fullan 1984; Ball 1990; Chan 1998). Policies may exist as goals in and of
themselves without any expectation of affecting change in practice, while

other policies will stimulate practices that are already supported by existing attitudes and motivation – as was demonstrated by the policies for separate schools. However, I suggest that the federal policy, contemporary immigration trends, and changes in the ethnocultural composition of Canada brought the subjects of multiculturalism and policy together into sharper focus, with the consequent potential for impact on practice.

In 1974, Saskatchewan became the first province in Canada to approve a provincial Multiculturalism Act. In the same year, the School Act in Saskatchewan was amended to permit languages other than English or French to be used for instruction for a limited time in the school day. Other provincial initiatives included the establishment of a K-12 Indian and Métis policy, a Native Curriculum Review Committee, the expansion of heritage-language education, and the articulation of the role of the education system in a multicultural society (Saskatchewan Learning 1994).

In 1977, Ontario established a provincial multicultural policy. The policy recognized the racially and ethnically diverse population of Ontario, and the citizenship entitlement of all people regardless of race or religion (Fleras and Elliott 1992). Following the development of a policy on race relations in 1983, the Ontario government established an Advisory Committee on Race Relations in 1985 through its Ministry of Education. The provincial policy was also followed by a series of activities related to education, including revision of the objectives of schooling at the elementary level to reflect multiculturalism and a course in cross-cultural education offered by a faculty of education (McLeod 1992). In 1987, the Ontario government renewed its commitment by articulating a number of principles to support multiculturalism.

Other provinces in Canada, such as Alberta in 1984, Manitoba in 1992, and British Columbia in 1993, have followed suit with Multiculturalism Acts or combined acts and policies that include human rights and citizenship. Since 1995, some of these acts have been revised, repealed, or reduced in composition and stature. The legislation on multiculturalism has also been subject to change and debate concerning the role of race within the policy. Race relations policy and activities in the schools have emerged concurrently with the development of federal and provincial policies. These policies have also been the result of racial tensions, incidents, and awareness of demographic changes in schools and communities. As such, their political context is subject to change as local and provincial governments and school boards change.

Contemporary Schooling and Race Relations

I return now to the three regions discussed in the early history of segregation in schools: Nova Scotia, Ontario, and British Columbia. These three examples illuminate the ways in which race relations have been shaped in the current context of schooling. The tension between policy and practice is a key factor when considering the impact of race-based initiatives.

Cole Harbour School District High School is part of the Halifax Regional School Board in Nova Scotia. In 1997, an external review of the high school was conducted following a series of racial incidents in the school. The review was preceded by a race relations policy in 1990 and a report on race and racism in Nova Scotia education by the Black Learners Association (BLAC 1994). Race and racism were at the forefront of the Cole Harbour inquiry, although it raised a more complex web of issues that included class, poverty, sexism, and the changing structure of the school and school district (Frank 1997b). The high school was a microcosm of its community, and the racial and other tensions in the community had embedded themselves in the school.

Cole Harbour was a racialized school district and a number of issues related to race emerged in the review. Among these issues were cultural competence. Black students viewed White teachers as lacking sufficient (Black) cultural knowledge and lacking experience with diverse students. Accordingly, Black students and parents alike expressed the opinion that there should be more Black teachers and staff and curriculum that reflected the rich cultural history of Black people in Canada (Frank 1997b). Interviews with teachers, staff, students, parents/guardians, and community members exposed a charged sense of frustration and struggle: "The issue here for me is to try to understand HOW with a Race Relations Policy, a Race Relations Department, a Monitoring Committee, a student support worker – all the mechanisms are in place – but they can't be attached. Unless these things connect, and get connected to other policies and practices as well, there is little use in having them" (senior employee of the board, quoted in Frank 1997a, 14). As a teacher concluded, "Overall we have a poor plan of implementation" (quoted in Frank 1997a, 14). Ultimately the external review made seventy-five recommendations, with a key recommendation for "school improvement." In 2001, another review was conducted to evaluate progress since the 1997 report. While the Nova Scotia Education Act had been amended in 2000 to guarantee African Canadians a seat on anglophone school boards, little else had been accomplished. In 2002, the Halifax Regional School Board revised its Race Relations, Cross Cultural Understanding and Human Rights Policy.

In Ontario, where a multicultural policy was established in 1977, the Toronto school board became the first school board in Canada to develop an official policy on race relations, in 1979. This example was followed elsewhere in the greater Toronto area. The pressure for policy has tended to be the result of advocacy from parents and community groups, although the actual policy implementation was often an administrative task given to a staff consultant or an advisor in race relations or antiracism (Rezai-Rashti 1995). The Ontario Ministry of Education's Advisory Committee on Race Relations was established in 1985 with objectives that included the development of a race and ethnocultural equity policy for provincial school boards. One of the articulated factors contributing to the focus on race and ethnicity was a high level of migration to Ontario, particularly Toronto, although there has been a significant Black population in the province since the late 1800s.

The work of the Advisory Committee on Race Relations contributed to guidelines for policy development and implementation for antiracism and ethnocultural equity (Ontario Ministry of Education and Training 1993). The guidelines identified the linkages among policies, guidelines, and practices, including the necessity of articulated objectives, action plans, outcomes, resources, timelines, and people with responsibility and accountability. The guidelines also specified the need for flexibility: "Policies and implementation plans should respond to community needs and local conditions, while also recognizing the need to reflect the wider society" (6).

The Ontario government mandated in 1993 that all school districts develop and implement antiracism policies in accordance with the guidelines. By 1995, over forty school boards had some form of race and ethnic relations policy, and twenty-five boards were in the process of formalizing policies (Rezai-Rashti 1995). However, these boards represented less than half the school boards of Ontario. As well, implementation of the existing policies remains problematic due to lack of resources, priorities within schools, and the need for staff development and awareness of racial and ethnic issues (Rezai-Rashti 1995). Teachers and administrators play a significant role in transforming race relations policy into practice, and in whether any form of multiculturalism education takes place in the schools (McLeod 1992), and it is difficult for schools to have policy embodied in everyday practice.

In British Columbia, the Vancouver School Board established a race relations policy with nineteen policy statements in 1982. The policy was designed "to improve race relations and to increase cultural understanding in Vancouver Schools." To facilitate its implementation, schools were asked to develop action plans, and the school board produced an accompanying document, "Guidelines for Implementation of VSB Race Relations Policy," in 1983. The school board had established a Race Relations Advisory Committee in 1980. This committee supported and guided the implementation of the policy and guidelines, focusing on "better race relations, fairness and equity through multiculturalism" (Fisher and Echols 1989, 6).

A review of the Vancouver policy was initiated in 1987 with an evaluation report produced two years later (Fisher and Echols 1989). The review was not precipitated by specific racial or cultural tensions, as in Cole Harbour. Nevertheless, the report identified racism, and comments by participants in the study suggested that racism often appeared in subtle and systemic ways as well as overtly. Racial incidents were reported, but they were often not distinguished from students acting out more generally. The evaluation report recommended the allocation of greater resources to promote and implement the policy.

Two school board staff positions were instrumental in facilitating awareness and implementation of the policy: the race relations and multicultural education (later called antiracism) consultant[4] and the manager of multiculturalism and antiracism. The role of the consultant emphasized the provision of program and pedagogical services. The manager worked on policy implementation, and, later, established related policies such as equity and harassment prevention (Eric Wong, personal communication, 12 September 2003). In 1996 a policy entitled "Multiculturalism and Anti-racism" was approved by the school board. It was shorter than the 1982 policy and lacked statements about action, focusing instead on descriptive and values statements. Phrases such as "that the Board direct the Superintendent" were eliminated from the policy. The position of antiracism consultant was eliminated in 1997, after over ten years, despite considerable objection from teachers, parents, and the community.

In 1997, twenty-seven school districts in British Columbia had a multicultural policy, a race relations policy, or a multiculturalism and antiracism policy. These policies generally expressed a goal of valuing cultural diversity, along with other objectives relating to citizenship, social justice, and the elimination of racism (Joshee and Parhar 1997). Since then some school districts have amalgamated for administrative purposes. A similar reorganization of Ontario school districts has taken place in order to reduce the number of districts and administrative costs. The impact of merging districts and thus incorporating policies has not been documented.

Conclusion

This chapter has charted the course from race-based policies that were directed at racial segregation and the exclusion of particular groups, to race relations and multiculturalism policies that include an appreciation of ethnic and cultural differences. The relationship between policy and practice was contrasted in these two contexts. In the historical examples of racial segregation, policies were implemented with the support of racism and cultural prejudices in the community. These policies were developed in a context of racialization and had a profoundly negative impact on particular racial groups. In the contemporary examples, such as Cole Harbour District High School, the race relations policy was insufficient as a tool to address racism, in part due to lack of implementation strategies. There are still school boards that have not developed race relations policy as a means of addressing racial, ethnic, and cultural diversity.

Race relations are not always an explicit goal of multicultural education or multicultural policies, yet they are implicated through the goal of promoting better intergroup relations (Fleras and Elliott 1992). Antiracist education more precisely articulates the ideals of addressing race and racial discrimination, particularly within institutional systems and structures. Policies that suggest that Canada operates within principles of cultural pluralism and cultural democracy are consistent with multiculturalism. James (1995, 35) argues that "insofar as these policies [i.e., multiculturalism policy] set out how the governments will respond to, and *accommodate* the diverse population, then they provide a framework which will inform the practices and policies of institutions such as schools."

Policies that identify race as a category for race relations and multiculturalism are still found in many school district policy manuals. However, greater attention is required to facilitate implementation and action. The Vancouver School Board example suggests the need for greater resources to promote and implement policy. Race relations and multiculturalism are always politicized when resources are involved. Many provinces are currently funding schools with operating deficits, which has had serious consequences for engagement with multicultural policy implementation. Administrators in school districts without a policy may argue that policy is not necessary because of the (partial) evidence that policies have failed to address racism, cultural bias, and problems of access, and have no effect on these issues. Without a policy, however, there are no fundamental principles to guide behaviour or strategically plan for change.

Education of racially, culturally, and ethnically diverse populations requires an engagement with the issues of race-based policy and implementation. Included in this engagement should be a consideration of the differences and similarities of the goals of race relations and multiculturalism. These issues should be articulated in the context of historical racialization and the political and social elements of education. This articulation of both issues and context is necessary before policy goals can be realized and normalized in educational institutions.

Notes

1 This Saskatchewan act prohibited business owners who were Asian or "Oriental" from employing White women or taking them in as residents or lodgers (Backhouse 1999, 136). Japanese and Chinese people were specifically identified in the act, which used the derogatory term "Chinaman."

2 Slavery was referred to in Canada as early as 1752 and continued into the early nineteenth century (Winks 1972).

3 The term *overage* was commonly used to denote students who were older than the other students in their grade school class. Immigrant families arriving from China came with children in their early teens and younger. These children and adolescents had little, if any, English-language training before arriving in Canada and therefore tended to be assigned to classes with younger children (Con et al. 1982).

4 The Vancouver School Board uses the term *consultant* to denote a seconded teacher. Secondment is a practice by which staff are transferred to a position for a finite period without losing their original job position, seniority, status, or rank. On completion of a secondment, individuals often return to their original positions.

References

Adachi, K. 1976. *The enemy that never was: The history of Japanese Canadians*. Toronto: McClelland and Stewart.

Anderson, S.E., and M. Fullan. 1984. *Policy implementation issues for multicultural education at the school board level*. Toronto: Ontario Institute for Studies in Education.

Angus, H.R. 1937. *The problem of peaceful change in the Pacific area*. London: Oxford University Press.

Ashworth, M. 1979. *The forces which shaped them*. Vancouver: New Star Books.

Backhouse, C. 1999. *Colour-coded: A legal history of racism in Canada, 1900-1950*. Toronto: Osgoode Society for Canadian Legal History and University of Toronto Press.

Ball, S. 1990. *Politics and policy making in education*. London: Routledge.

BLAC (Black Learners Association of Canada). 1994. *Report on education: Redressing inequity – Empowering Black learners*. Halifax: BLAC.

Bolaria, S., and P. Li. 1985. *Racial oppression in Canada*. Toronto: Garamond Press.

Canada. House of Commons. 1971. *Debates* (8 October, Pierre Trudeau), p. 8545.

–. 1986. *Proceedings of the Standing Committee on Multiculturalism*. Sixth session of the 33rd Parliament.

Chan, A. 1998. Impact of race relations policy on practice. Unpublished paper. Vancouver: David Lam Chair in Multicultural Education, University of British Columbia.

Con, H., R.J. Con, G. Johnson, E. Wickberg, and W.E. Willmott. 1982. *From China to Canada*. Toronto: McClelland and Stewart in association with the Multiculturalism Directorate, Department of the Secretary of State, and the Canadian Government Publishing Centre, Supply and Services Canada.

Fisher, D., and F. Echols. 1989. *Evaluation report on the Vancouver School Board's race relations policy*. Vancouver: Vancouver School Board.

Fleras, A., and J.L. Elliott. 1992. *The challenge of diversity: Multiculturalism in Canada*. Scarborough, ON: Nelson Canada.

–. 1996. *Unequal relations: An introduction to race, ethnic and Aboriginal dynamics in Canada*. Scarborough, ON: Prentice Hall Canada.

Frank, B. 1997a. *An external review of Cole Harbour District High School*. Halifax: Halifax Regional School Board.

–. 1997b. *(Re)search, (re)searching and (re)searcher: Reflections on the process of the external review of Cole Harbour District High School*. Paper presented at the conference "Multiculturalism, Nationalism and Anti-Racism Education: Research and Debates in Canada," 12-13 November, Vancouver.

James, C. 1995. Multicultural and anti-racism education in Canada. *Race, Gender and Class* 2(3): 31-48.

Joshee, R. 1995a. Federal policies on cultural diversity and education, 1940-1971. PhD diss., University of British Columbia.

–. 1995b. An historical approach to understanding Canadian multicultural policy. In *Multicultural education in a changing global economy: Canada and the Netherlands*, ed. T. Wotherspoon and P. Jungbluth, 23-41. New York: Waxmann Munster.

Joshee, R., and A. Parhar. 1997. Analysis of school district policies in British Columbia addressing multicultural education. Unpublished paper. Vancouver: David Lam Chair in Multicultural Education, University of British Columbia.

Kitano, H. 1969. *Japanese Americans: The evolution of a subculture*. Englewood Cliffs, NJ: Prentice Hall.

Krauter, J.F., and M. Davis. 1978. *Minority Canadians: Ethnic groups*. Toronto: Methuen.

Li, P. 1990. *Race and ethnic relations in Canada*. Toronto: Oxford University Press.

McLeod, K. 1992. Multiculturalism and multicultural education in Canada: Human rights and human rights education. In *Beyond multicultural education: International perspectives*, ed. K.A. Moodley, 215-42. Calgary: Detselig.

Miles, R. 1989. *Racism*. London: Tavistock.

Moodley, K.A. 1995. Multicultural education in Canada: Historical development and current status. In *Handbook of research on multicultural education*, ed. J.A. Banks and C.A.M. Banks, 801-20. New York: Macmillan.

Nelson, P. 1992. *Lower mainland multicultural education project*. Vancouver: Social Planning and Research Council of British Columbia.

Ontario. Ministry of Education and Training. 1993. *Antiracism and ethnocultural equity in school boards: Guidelines for policy development and implementation*. Toronto: Ministry of Education and Training.

Raj, S. 1980. Some aspects of East Indian struggle in Canada, 1905-1947. In *Visible minorities and multiculturalism: Asians in Canada*, ed. K.V. Ujimoto and G. Hirabayashi, 63-80. Toronto: Butterworth.

Rezai-Rashti, G. 1995. Multicultural education, anti-racist education, and critical pedagogy: Reflections on everyday practice. In *Anti-racism, feminism and critical approaches to education*, ed. R. Ng, P. Staton, and J. Scane, 3-20. Westport, CT: Greenwood Publishers.

Saskatchewan Learning. 1994. *Multicultural education and heritage language education policies*. http://www.sasked.gov.sk.ca/docs/policy/multi/index.html.

Satzewich, V. 1998. Race, racism and racialization: Contested concepts. In *Racism and social inequality in Canada*, ed. V. Satzewich, 25-45. Toronto: Thompson Educational Publishing.

Small, S. 1998. The contours of racialization: Structures, representation and resistance in the United States. In *Racism and social inequality in Canada*, ed. V. Satzewich, 69-86. Toronto: Thompson Educational Publishing.

Tator, C., and F. Henry. 1991. *Multicultural education: Translating policy into practice*. Ottawa: Department of Multiculturalism and Citizenship.

Vancouver School Board. 1983. *Guidelines for implementation of VSB race relations policy*. Vancouver: Vancouver School Board.

Walker, J.W. St. G. 1980. *A history of Blacks in Canada*. Hull: Minister of Supply and Services Canada.

–. 1997. *"Race," rights, and the law in the Supreme Court of Canada*. Waterloo, ON: Osgoode Society for Canadian Legal History and Wilfrid Laurier University Press.

Ward, W. 1978. *White Canada forever*. Montreal: McGill-Queen's University Press.

Wickberg, E. 1980. Chinese and Canadian influence on Chinese politics in Vancouver, 1900-1947. *BC Studies* 45: 37-55.

Winks, R. 1972. *The Blacks in Canada*. New Haven, CT: Yale University Press.

11

Education, American Style: Race-Based School Policies and Practices in the United States

Christopher M. Span, Rashid V. Robinson, and Trinidad Molina Villegas

In 2004, numerous locales across the United States commemorated the fiftieth anniversary of the *Brown* v. *Board of Education* decision. This landmark ruling declared that schools legally segregated by race were inherently unconstitutional. In a unanimous decree, the Supreme Court mandated that states that purposefully segregated children on the basis of race or ethnicity revamp their educational systems. *Brown* radically challenged the race-based policies and practices that had shaped schooling in the United States since the colonial era. Few Americans today are aware of the legacy of race-based schooling that *Brown* v. *Board of Education* confronted and eventually upended. *Brown* not only challenged the legal exclusion of students of colour – in particular southern African American schoolchildren – from a quality education, it ended the policies and practices that reserved a quality education almost exclusively for White children.

The history of public schooling in the United States is premised upon race and ethnicity. From its beginnings to the near present, the schooling opportunities American children received have depended more on their racial or ethnic background than on their educational aptitude, residence, or parental income. The well-documented educational histories of African Americans and Whites in the nineteenth and twentieth centuries chronicle this argument excellently, but race-based policies and practices were not exclusive to these two groups. America was, as it still is today, a multiracial, multiethnic, and multilingual society; accordingly, race, ethnicity, and language directly shaped the educational experiences of other groups, including Native Americans, Asian Americans, and Latinos (see also Chapters 2, 3, 8, and 9). How these groups fared alongside African Americans and Whites in the grand narrative of American schooling depended as much on their ascribed racial or ethnic characteristics as it did on the ideology, political economy, and schooling opportunities of the time.

These race-based schooling practices did not go unchallenged. African American, Native American, Asian American, and Latino parents vehemently opposed their children receiving an inferior education because they were perceived as inferior or regarded as members of the wrong racial or ethnic group. These challenges – grassroots, legal, and otherwise – insisted that the United States live up to its democratic ideals and offer their children the same access to a quality education being offered to Whites (Chapter 2). These groups started their own schools, made the most of the segregated schooling provided by local officials, or sought remedy in the courts. What is unknown to most Americans today is that the determination of these concerned parents unintentionally served as precedent for *Brown*. This chapter chronicles their history and offers a very brief overview of the role race and ethnicity conventionally played in the attitudes, policies, and practices that shaped the schooling experiences of African American, Asian American, and Latino schoolchildren in the nineteenth and twentieth centuries. As importantly, this chapter also illustrates how members of these varying groups fought, and, in some cases, successfully challenged a school system that segregated or denied their children an education because of their race or ethnicity.

African Americans

Arguably no group has been more researched with regard to race-based schooling than African Americans. Without question, race has always been a factor in the educational policy and practices pertaining to African Americans. From the introduction of Africans as slaves to colonial Virginia in 1619 to at least fifteen years after the *Brown* decision, race has determined not only the schooling opportunities of African Americans, but their overall livelihood as well. Simply take a look at some of the laws regarding literacy and African Americans prior to the Civil War (1861). Southern colonies made it a crime to teach slaves. In 1740, colonial South Carolina was the first to enact legislation to forbid the teaching of reading and writing to enslaved African Americans (Raffel 1998, xiii). In 1770, colonial Georgia enacted similar legislation (Cornelius 1991, 18). By 1830, Georgia – now a state – as well as North Carolina, Virginia, and Louisiana imposed fines, public whippings, or imprisonment on anyone caught teaching enslaved or free African Americans these prohibited skills. In the years leading up to the Civil War, Arkansas, Alabama, Tennessee, Maryland, Missouri, and Mississippi, among others, passed a series of similar antiliteracy laws or customarily denied African Americans – enslaved or free – the means of acquiring the rudimentary skills of reading and writing (Span 2003).

North of slavery, where approximately 250,000 out of 4.5 million African Americans lived on the eve of the Civil War, schooling opportunities for African Americans were also restricted by race-based considerations. In the northeastern and midwestern states, segregation, by law or cultural practice, overwhelmingly determined the educational opportunities of children. Practically every northern state with state-funded schools established a segregated or dual school system for its White and "coloured" residents. "Prejudice and discrimination," historian Christopher M. Span (2003, 6) notes, "served as the guidepost for free Blacks' blatant educational exclusion or segregation." At the beginning of the nineteenth century, for instance, local school committees in Connecticut, New Hampshire, New York, Massachusetts, and Rhode Island frequently assigned children "to separate institutions, regardless of the district in which they resided" (Litwack 1961, 114). In the Midwest, similarly, local school boards in Ohio, Indiana, Michigan, Illinois, and Kansas separated African American children from White children as late as 1900 (McCaul 1987; Mohraz 1979). Black children attended dilapidated schools, received an inferior education, and were not allocated their just proportion of local school funds.

When we think of segregated race-based schooling, we often think of the American South between the years 1896 and 1954, from the *Plessy* v. *Ferguson* decision to the *Brown* decision. This segregated schooling took place in an era commonly referred to as Jim Crow. But Jim Crow schooling was not a late nineteenth and early twentieth century phenomenon. The dual system of race-based schooling that epitomized African American and White education in the American South originated in the North before the Civil War. This invidious segregated school system was a northern concept.

Throughout the nineteenth century, African American parents challenged the laws and societal practices that restrained or denied altogether the educational opportunities of their children. Some started their own private schools, others attempted to enhance the quality of the segregated schools their children attended, and a handful used the courts in an effort to gain access to a quality education for their children (Franklin 2000; Litwack 1961; Span 2003; Woodson 1998). Arguably, the most noteworthy pre-Civil War example of African American use of the courts to address the educational needs of their children occurred in Boston, Massachusetts. *Roberts* v. *City of Boston* (1849) was the first desegregation case in the United States.

In 1849, Benjamin F. Roberts, on behalf of his five-year-old daughter Sarah, sued the city of Boston for perpetuating a system of unequal segregated schools. Sarah Roberts had to walk past five White elementary schools to attend Smith School, a dilapidated facility for the area's Black children. Roberts argued the Smith School was vastly inferior to those five White schools and requested his daughter be allowed to attend one of them. His request coincided with a new city ordinance mandating that all Boston children attend the school nearest to their residence. Roberts's lawyers, abolitionist Charles Sumner and Boston's first Black attorney, Robert Morris, argued that all persons were equal before Massachusetts law and that race-based distinctions were therefore not permissible in the state. They further argued that racial segregation characterized all African Americans as inferior and that a segregated Black school could not equal a segregated White school because of the stigma associated with segregation.

The Massachusetts Supreme Court, however, was not persuaded by the argument. Chief Justice Lemuel Shaw ruled against Roberts and argued that schooling segregated by race was not a violation of Massachusetts law as long as schools were equally provided for. The criterion was quantity, not quality, of schooling. It did not matter that the Smith School was dilapidated, overcrowded, poorly funded, and understaffed; what mattered was that Boston had provided a school for the city's Black residents. But Benjamin Roberts was not dismayed. He continued to agitate on behalf of his daughter and, in 1855, as the nation debated the future of American slavery, Massachusetts passed a law prohibiting race-based schooling. Despite the legal defeat, *Roberts*, as desegregation scholar Jeffrey A. Raffel notes, was a monumental case. For instance, the case introduced the phrase "separate but equal," which became synonymous with African American life and education in the years to come. Moreover, *Roberts* was cited in the 1896 *Plessy* decision as support for the segregation ruling, "for if even in Massachusetts, where the rights of Blacks had been enforced, segregation was considered legal, surely it would be legal in the South" (Raffel 1998, 221).

Asian Americans

Although the impact of race-based schooling on the African American experience has been thoughtfully investigated, the same cannot be said about Asian Americans, particularly the Chinese. At the time of the *Roberts* decision, Chinese immigrants were arriving in California, and they too were demanding that their children receive access to a quality education. San Francisco was a chief point of arrival and departure for Chinese immigrants working in California's mining industries, and the city soon became home to a thriving Chinese community. California's first public school for Chinese immigrants opened there in the fall of 1859. It immediately faced harsh criticism, despite the fact it was segregated by race.

As well documented by Charles Wollenberg (1978), school superintendent James Denman was among the first public school officials in the city to express his discontent with the use of public resources to educate people of Asian decent. When he visited the school reserved for the Chinese in the spring of 1860, Denman deemed it a waste of public resources, noting both the low attendance (three children and seven adults) and the difficult task of educating the Chinese into American culture. By autumn of that year, Denman reorganized the school, establishing it as a night institution to allow Chinese workers to learn English alongside their children. This reorganization did boost enrolment, but Denman was still unsatisfied. Low enrolment was always a factor, as Liza Ketchum (2000, 102) notes, because the school was outside of Chinatown, and "Chinese children were afraid of being stoned" if they attended the school during evening hours. After Denman was re-elected in 1869, he resumed his campaign to close the Chinese school, this time citing an 1870 change in state legislation that had deleted the word "Mongolian" from school law. To Denman, this deletion signified that the city was no longer obligated to fund the education of its Chinese residents; accordingly, the school board suspended funding and closed the school in 1871 (Wollenberg 1978). Denman's actions ignored both the spirit and letter of the recent Burlingame Treaty, which had established the rights and privileges of Chinese immigrants in the United States.[1] From 1871 to 1884, there were no public schools of any kind for the Chinese. While succeeding school superintendents proved to be more favourable to the Chinese sending their children to school, staunch racial prejudice meant that most were unable to convince the San Francisco board of education or state taxpayers to improve or extend the schooling opportunities of Chinese children.

In response to this situation, Chinese parents petitioned state representatives, established their own schools, and used the courts to ensure that their children attended school. For instance, in 1877, approximately 1,300 Chinese residents petitioned California legislature to open schools for their children; their request went unanswered (Wollenberg 1978). Between 1871 and 1890, and with the assistance of religious organizations such as the American Missionary Association, the Chinese in San Francisco and elsewhere in the state opened nearly fifteen schools (Woodbury 1885, 368). In addition, several Chinese language schools were established in San Francisco, including one founded by the Chinese Consolidated Benevolent Association. This organization had been established in 1854 to address the overall concerns of Chinese immigrants (McClain 1994). In 1885, the persistence of Chinese parents was rewarded (so to speak) when the California Supreme Court in *Tape* v. *Hurley* upheld a lower court ruling that declared, "All children, regardless of race, had the right to attend public school" in the state (Yung 1995, 49). Mary and Joseph Tape were Chinese immigrants who in 1884 attempted to enrol their eight-year-old American-born daughter Mamie into Spring Valley School. Spring Valley was the closest school to the Tapes' home, it was all White, and it absolutely refused to accept Mamie. In fact, on the first day of school, the principal, Jennie Hurley, stood at the door and barred Mamie Tape from entering.

The San Francisco school board circumvented the *Tape* ruling by reestablishing a separate school for Chinese children; the California legislature went even further and promptly legalized separate educational facilities for "Mongolian" and White children. Both responses proved to be legal, for when the California Supreme Court validated the right of Chinese-descent students to attend public schools, it left unchallenged the doctrine of "separate but equal" that would be established in *Plessy* a few years later.

By the time Mamie Tape completed her requirements for enrolment in Spring Valley, which included a medical exam and proof of vaccination, the new "Chinese only" school had opened, and, by law, she was forced to attend it. These actions enraged Mary Tape, who firmly believed in the value of education and her child's rights as an American citizen. In April 1885, five months after she and her husband began their crusade to enrol Mamie into Spring Valley, she wrote an open letter to the school board. It candidly expressed her discontent at the ill-treatment of her daughter. "Dear sirs," she wrote,

> I see that you are going to make all sorts of excuses to keep my child out off the Public schools ... Didn't God make us all!!! What right have you to bar my children out of the school because she is a chinese Decend. They is no other worldly reason that you could keep her out, except that. I suppose, you all goes to churches on Sundays! Do you call that a Christian act to compell my little children to go so far to a school that is made in purpose for them ... You have expended a lot of the Public money foolishly, all because of a one poor little Child. Her playmates is all Caucasians ever since she could toddle around. If she is good enough to play with them! Then is she not good enough to be in the same room and studie with them? May you never be persecuted like the way you have persecuted little Mamie Tape. Mamie Tape will never attend any of the Chinese schools of your making! Never!!! I will let the world see Sir What justice there is When it is govern by the Race prejudice men! (in Yung 1995, 49)

Despite her objections, Mrs. Tape did enrol Mamie in the Chinese school. Eventually, as historian Judy Yung has illustrated, the San Francisco school board allowed Chinese children to attend integrated high schools. This process of integration, however, did not occur until the 1920s, much too late for Mamie and Mrs. Tape's other children. Still, it is important to note that the struggles for school desegregation in San Francisco occurred significantly earlier than *Brown* and among a people other than African Americans.

Chinese children were also placed in segregated schools in the American South. Most Americans are unaware of the migration of the Chinese to the American South, but a significant minority made states such as Louisiana and Mississippi their home. Most Chinese arrived in these Deep South states following the Civil War, contracted by White landowners as agricultural labourers to challenge the economic aspirations of newly freed African Americans. By the beginning of the twentieth century, most southern Chinese owned their own lands and businesses. The South was vastly different from California. Whereas White Californians labelled the Chinese as "Mongolian" and attempted to restrict or deny their educational opportunities because of their ascribed racial characteristics, the Chinese in Mississippi were deemed "coloured." As such, when Chinese children came of age in the delta of the Mississippi they were required by law to attend the segregated schools reserved for African Americans and other "coloured" children. These segregated schools were vastly inferior to the schools reserved for White children. They were dilapidated structures with shorter school terms, far fewer resources, and less qualified teachers. They typically educated children for only three years, and most prepared their pupils for a life of industrial labour or domestic servitude.

Chinese parents understood the ramifications of sending their children to these neglected and inferior schools: an inferior education meant an inferior life after schooling. Accordingly, in 1924, Gong Lum of Bolivar County, Mississippi, tried to enrol his American-born child Martha in an all-White school (Lim de Sanchez 2003). As Richard Kluger (1977, 120) puts it, "The superintendent of schools was momentarily perplexed when Martha Lum, aged nine, presented herself bright and early one morning for enrolment in the white school." In this state of confusion, he enrolled Martha, but at noon he summoned her to his office and informed her that she was not allowed to attend school with White children because she was "yellow." Martha was required to attend a coloured school. Gong Lum, "a merchant and taxpayer," as Kluger aptly points out, sued the state education superintendent on behalf of his daughter, claiming that his daughter was not coloured. His lawsuit ultimately reached the US Supreme Court. In *Gong Lum* v. *Rice* (1927), Mr. Lum's lawyers argued that the Chinese were not "colored" but Chinese, because "colored described only one race, and that is the Negro." They further argued that "Whites maintained separate schools to protect their children from Blacks" and concluded that "the white race may not legally expose the yellow race to a danger that the dominant race recognizes and guards itself against" (Irons 2002, 53-54).

Since Mr. Lum did not challenge the legality of segregated schools, the Supreme Court ruled against him and in favour of Mississippi. It affirmed the state court's verdict that Mississippi was "not compelled to provide separate schools for each of the colored races" and that all persons deemed coloured, regardless of their "non-white" racial background, did have the benefit of attending "colored public schools." With these words, the US Supreme Court upheld *de jure* segregation in Mississippi schools and a school system that efficiently divided its educable youth into two categories: "those of the pure white or Caucasian race" and those of "the brown, yellow, and black races" (*Gong Lum* v. *Rice* 1927).

Latinos

Like African and Chinese Americans, Latinos, particularly Mexican Americans, were also discriminated against in race-based segregated schools. Throughout the first half of the twentieth century, Mexican Americans in California experienced segregationist practices. Jim Crow had reached the west coast by 1900, and it was strictly enforced in all areas of public life, from housing to transportation, restaurants, churches, businesses, shops, bars, swimming pools, and public schools (Cooke 1948; García 1981; Ruiz 2001; Wollenberg

1974). Mexican Americans resisted these discriminatory policies and practices, especially in the realm of public education.

Under the guise of Americanization, schools throughout the Southwest created a separate school system for immigrant children (Alvarez 1987; Weinberg 1995). Children of Mexican descent were segregated into separate schools from their White counterparts, irrespective of their citizenship status or knowledge of the English language (Alvarez 1987; Cooke 1948; Gonzalez 1990; Ruiz 2001). As an educational ideal, Americanization – the belief that all immigrant people should learn how to be "American" in school – galvanized the xenophobic sentiments Whites maintained against Mexican Americans, justifying their segregation and exclusion from participating in mainstream society. Demographics had a lot to do with the racist sentiment of Whites in the Southwest, in particular California. Alvarez (1987, 4) contends that by 1924, "most large American cities had Mexican enclaves," with the majority in Arizona, Colorado, New Mexico, and California. Wollenberg (1974), relying on data from the 1930 US census, reported that Mexican residents in California increased to 368,000 from 121,000 in 1920. The number of people of Mexican descent had tripled in only a decade to constitute "California's largest 'minority group'"[2] (319). This demographic growth was also apparent in California public schools, particularly in and around the "citrus belt" area of Los Angeles and Orange County, where more than half of all Mexican Americans lived (Alvarez 1987; Wollenberg 1974).

Whites in California had a disdain for children of Mexican descent, especially regarding issues of school integration. Throughout the state, Whites attempted to deny, restrict, or segregate the schooling opportunities of Mexican American children. Like the Chinese Americans in San Francisco and the Mississippi delta, and African Americans in Boston and elsewhere, Mexican American parents refused to let their children be discriminated against or receive an inferior education. Two significant legal cases within the Mexican American community illustrate how Latino parents challenged these overt discriminatory practices: *Roberto Alvarez v. The Board of Trustees of the Lemon Grove School District* (1931) and *Mendez v. Westminster School District of Orange County* (1947). These cases were fundamental in dismantling educational segregation in California. Furthermore, *Alvarez* and *Mendez* served as testament to the unity and determination of Mexican Americans during a racially hostile era to stand up for the rights of themselves and the future livelihoods of their children.

In the summer of 1930, the all-White Lemon Grove school board unanimously and arbitrarily decided that children of Mexican descent should attend separate schools. On 5 January 1931, Jerome T. Green, principal at Lemon Grove Grammar School, prohibited 75 of its 169 students (approximately 44 percent) from enrolling in school. The 75 Mexican American children were sent to a nearby *caballeriza* (barn) to attend class. This barn was designated as their school (Alvarez 1986). In response to this discriminatory action against their children, a group of outraged parents formed *El Comité de Vecinos de Lemon Grove* (the Neighbours' Committee of Lemon Grove; Balderrama 1982): "Comadres and compadres (godparents) had banded together for grassroots political action" (Ruiz 2001). The parents decided to boycott the school, and with the exception of one family, the rest of the community supported the action. Parents simply refused to have their children educated in a place reserved for animals; schooling their children in a barn was both humiliating and degrading. The idea symbolized the degree of racism Whites practised against Mexican Americans and their children (Alvarez 1986). With the assistance of Mexican consul Enrique Ferreira and San Diego attorneys Fred C. Noon and A.C. Brinkely, Lemon Grove parents sued the school board (Balderrama 1982).

In February 1931, the parents submitted a writ of mandate to the school board, arguing that the exclusion of Mexican American students "was clearly an attempt at racial segregation ... by separating and segregating all the children of Mexican parentage ... from the children of American, European and Japanese parentage." They further argued that the board had no legal right or power to exclude their children "from receiving instruction upon an equal basis" (Alvarez 1986, 8). The board denied the accusations and argued that the separate school and the White school were equally equipped. They further argued that the new school was closer to the homes of Mexican American children and that its Americanization curriculum would better serve the needs of these students. They concluded that "the deficiencies of the children of Mexican descent could be corrected" under these schooling arrangements without affecting the educational experiences of White children (9).

When the case went to trial, however, the judge did not accept the rationale or practices of the school board. On 13 March 1931, Judge Claude Chambers ruled in favour of the Mexican students, arguing that segregating children "would probably hurt them academically in terms of learning the English language and customs" (cited in Griswold del Castillo, Ortiz, and Gonzalez 2003, 3). Chambers further pointed out that the school board could not segregate children of Mexican descent from White children because, according to California law, both belonged to the same race; such acts of discrimination violated the Fourteenth Amendment, which guarantees equal protection of the law to all US citizens (Balderrama 1982). This ruling demonstrated that people of Mexican descent were not affected by sections 8003 and 8004 of the California Educational Code, which established separate schools for Indians and for Asians, because Mexican Americans in California were deemed "White" by law (Wollenberg 1974; Balderrama 1982). Notwithstanding, *Alvarez* was the first desegregation case in the twentieth century.

The decision gave Mexican Americans in southern California the opportunity to challenge the societal forces attempting to deny them a place in society, a place that ignored their needs and silenced their voices. According to the historian Charles Wollenberg (1974), ordinary people from working-class backgrounds were able to restore a sense of ethnic pride and dignity within the community at large. In retrospect, Roberto Alvarez, one of the chief plaintiffs from the *Alvarez* case, agreed. Looking back, he stated, "They [Mexican parents] were not just wetbacks ... they had schooling. They had the guts in a strange country to get together and say 'this is wrong.' They fought and won. I think that's important" (in Espinosa and Christopher 1985).

The struggle for equitable schooling was not over for children of Mexican descent, however. In 1945, Mexican American children were still being seg-regated in California schools. In his 1948 study, Cooke pointed out that "one fifth of all non-metropolitan schools still segregated Mexican-Americans in one form or another" (419). After *Alvarez*, the labels that segregated Latino children in schools changed from ethnicity and language to mental apti-tude. In 1934 in Orange County, for example, approximately 70 percent of Mexican American pupils were labelled "retarded" because "they were older than the normal student at their grade level" (Wollenberg 1974, 322). The reality was that the majority of these students had limited English proficiency and attended vastly inferior schools to Whites. Research by social scientists and educators alike nonetheless validated the actions of local school officials; this research reinforced the suggestion that segregation was necessary and that it served the interest and advancement of both Mexican American and White children.

These segregationist practices once again prompted parents, community organizers and other concerned citizens, regardless of their racial affiliation, to continue the battle against segregated schools. *Mendez* exemplified this collaboration across ethnic and racial lines. The Mexican American com-munity received support from the American Jewish Congress, the American Civil Liberties Union, the National Lawyers Guild, the National Association for the Advancement of Colored People, the Japanese-American Citizens League, and Attorney General Robert W. Kenney of California. In fact, Thurgood Marshall and Robert L. Carter, later lead counsel for the *Brown* decision, also assisted in *Mendez*. Marshall and Carter filed an *amicus curiae* brief in support of the desegregation of children of Mexican descent.

The *Mendez* case was spurred on by the League of United Latin American Citizens and Mexican American parents who filed a lawsuit against four school districts (Westminster, Garden Grove, El Modeno, and Santa Ana) in California. Parents argued that their children's Fourteenth Amendment rights were being violated and that school officials used language – namely, limited English proficiency – as a proxy for race to segregate children of Mexican descent. *Mendez* charged that children of Mexican descent were "excluded from 'attending, using, enjoying, and receiving the benefits of the education, health, and recreation facilities of certain schools' within their respective districts and systems, 'while other schools are maintained, attended, and used exclusively and for persons of children purportedly known as White or Anglo-Saxon children'" (in Cooke 1948, 419).

The presiding judge, Paul J. McCormick, reiterated Chambers' ruling in *Alvarez*: segregating children of Mexican descent on any basis violated the Fourteenth Amendment and the laws of California. "We think such practices [educational segregation]," McCormick continued, "clearly and unmistakably disregard rights secured by the supreme law of the land" (quoted in Cooke 1948, 420). In spite of the favourable ruling, the "separate but equal" legacy of *Plessy* was not overturned by *Mendez*. Judge McCormick concluded only that the state laws "did not provide for the establishment of 'Mexican' schools."

Nonetheless, *de jure* segregation in California generally diminished significantly after the ruling. The collective efforts of the Mexican American community helped pave the way for cases dealing with the segregation of children of Mexican descent throughout the Southwest and elsewhere. *Alvarez* and *Mendez* have an important place in American educational history as the first legal challenges to the "separate but equal" clause of *Plessy*. Many scholars suggest they were the first cases to "sound the death knell of Jim Crow in education" (McWilliams cited in Ruiz 2001).

Conclusion

This chapter argues that the history of American education with regard to people of colour has been predicated on race-based considerations. African Americans, Asian Americans, and Latinos were systematically segregated or denied an education on the basis of their race, ethnicity, or language. But these groups challenged the systems of segregation that denied their children a quality education, they attempted to use the American justice system to challenge historical wrongs, and they insisted that the nation respect them as citizens in a democracy and educate their children with the same vigour as White children. The actions and agency of these concerned parents unquestionably served as precedent for *Brown*.

Today, the struggle for equitable schooling and the struggle to dismantle the role of race, ethnicity, and language in American education continue. For example, Gary Orfield (2001) offers compelling data to illustrate that African Americans and Latinos, in particular, continue to live in segregated neighbourhoods and attend segregated and dilapidated schools. Thus, as we examine race relations, specifically in the area of education, we must not forget the implications of past events for present-day society. Educators, policy makers, and the community at large should strive to improve the educational experiences of historically underserved and overlooked students, especially with an increasing demand for high-tech skills in a globalized society. Moreover, parents and community activists of all backgrounds should look to the educational pasts of African Americans, Asian Americans, and

Latinos for both the guidance and the motivation necessary to eliminate vestiges of the race-based schooling that defined our American education system for more than two centuries.

Notes

1 Under the terms of the Burlingame Treaty (1868), both the United States and China recognized "the inherent and inalienable right of man to change his home and allegiance, and also the mutual advantage of the free migration and emigration of their citizens and subjects, respectively for purposes of curiosity, of trade, or as permanent residents." The treaty stipulated that "Chinese subjects visiting or residing in the United States, shall enjoy the same privileges, immunities, and exemptions in respect to travel or residence, as may there be enjoyed by the citizens or subjects of the most favored nation." The privileges and immunities provision was aimed at protecting Chinese immigrants in the United States against discrimination, exploitation, and violence. For additional information on the Burlingame Treaty, see McClain 1994.

2 According to the 1930 US census, California's total White population (native and foreign born) was 3,710,595.

References

Alvarez, R. Jr. 1986. The Lemon Grove incident: The nation's first successful desegregation court case. *Journal of San Diego History* 32(2). http://www.sandiegohistory.org/journal.

–. 1987. *La familia: Migration and adaptation in Baja and Alta California, 1800-1975*. Berkeley: University of California Press.

Arriola, C. 1995. Knocking on the schoolhouse door: *Mendez v. Westminster*, equal protection, public education, and Mexican Americans in the 1940s. *La Raza Law Journal* 8(2): 166-207.

Balderrama, F.E. 1982. *In defense of la raza, the Los Angeles Mexican consulate, and the Mexican community, 1929 to 1936*. Tucson: University of Arizona Press.

Carroll, A. 1999. *Letters of a nation*. New York: Broadway.

Cooke, H.W. 1948. The segregation of Mexican-American school children in Southern California. *School and Society* 67: 417-21.

Cornelius, J. 1991. *When I can read my title clear: Literacy, slavery, and religion in the antebellum South*. Columbia: University of South Carolina Press.

Espinosa, P., and F. Christopher. 1985. *The Lemon Grove incident*. Video. New York: Cinema Guild.

Franklin, J.H. 2000. *From slavery to freedom*. 8th ed. New York: McGraw Hill.

García, M.T. 1981. *Desert immigrants: The Mexicans of El Paso, 1880-1920*. New Haven, CT: Yale University Press.

Gong Lum v. *Rice*, 275 U.S. 78 (1927).

Gonzalez, G. 1990. *Chicano education in the era of segregation*. Philadelphia: Balch Institute Press.

Griswold del Castillo, R., I. Ortiz, and R. Gonzalez. 2003. What was the Lemon Grove School desegregation case all about? Chapter 7, section 2 of *San Diego's Mexican and Chicano history*. http://www.rohan.sdsu.edu/dept/mas/chicanohistory.

Irons, P. 2002. *Jim Crow's children*. New York: Viking.

Ketchum, L. 2000. *Into a new country: Eight remarkable women in the West*. New York: Little, Brown, and Company.

Kluger, R. 1977. *Simple justice*. New York: Vintage.

Lim de Sanchez, S. 2003. Crafting a delta Chinese community: Education and acculturation in twentieth-century Southern Baptist mission schools. *History of Education Quarterly* 43(1): 74-90.

Litwack, L. 1961. *North of slavery*. Chicago: University of Chicago Press.

McCaul, R.L. 1987. *The Black struggle for public schooling in nineteenth-century Illinois*. Carbondale: Southern Illinois University Press.

McClain, C.J. 1994. *In search of equality: The Chinese struggle against discrimination in nineteenth century America.* Berkeley: University of California Press.

Mendez v. *Westminster School District of Orange County.* 161 F.2d 774 (9th Cir. 1947) (No. 11310).

Mohraz, J. 1979. *The separate problem: Case studies of Black education in the North, 1900-1930.* Westport, CT: Greenwood Press.

Orfield, G. 2001. *Schools more separate: Consequences of a decade of resegregation.* Cambridge, MA: Civil Rights Project, Harvard University. http://www.civilrightsproject.harvard.edu.

Plessy v. *Ferguson,* 163 U.S. 537 (1896).

Raffel, J. 1998. *Historical dictionary of school segregation and desegregation: The American experience.* New Haven, CT: Greenwood Press.

Roberto Alvarez v. *Lemon Grove School District.* 1931. Superior Court of California, County of San Diego, Petition for writ of mandate no. 66625.

Ruiz, V.L. 2001. South by southwest: Mexican Americans and segregated schooling, 1900-1950. *OAH Magazine of History* (Organization of American Historians) 15(2). http://www.oah.org/pubs/magazine.

Span, C.M. 2003. "Knowledge is light, knowledge is power": African American education in antebellum America. In *Surmounting all odds: Education, opportunity, and society in the new millennium,* ed. C.C. Yeakey and R. Henderson, 3-30. Greenwich, CT: Information Age Press.

US Census. 1930. Available at University of Virginia Library Historical Census Browser, http://fisher.lib.virginia.edu/collections/stats/histcensus.

Weinberg, M. 1995. *A chance to learn: The history of race and education in the United States.* 2nd ed. New York: Cambridge University Press.

Wollenberg, C. 1974. *Mendez* v. *Westminster:* Race, nationality and segregation in California schools. *California Historical Quarterly* 53(4): 317-32.

–. 1978. *All deliberate speed.* Berkeley: University of California Press.

Woodbury, F.P. 1885. Address on Chinese work. *American Missionary* 39(12): 368-71.

Woodson, C.G. 1998. *Education of the Negro prior to 1861.* New York: A+B Publisher Group.

Yung, J. 1995. *Unbound feet: A social history of Chinese women in San Francisco.* Berkeley: University of California Press.

12
Canadian and American Race-Based Education Policies
Njoki Nathani Wane

Race is one of many lenses through which we understand and see the world, and it colours everything before us. In affirming this racialized lens of seeing and making meaning, itself a challenge to the prevailing racial blindness, there are perils: the lens of race simultaneously clarifies and distorts social reality. It both illuminates and obscures, creating false dichotomies and distinctions between people where none really exist (Marable 1995). Beyond recognizing and naming racial blindness, there is a call to act. This dialogue attempts to provide an overview of the similarities and differences in Canadian and American race-based education policies as they have been articulated by the previous two chapters. Although both chapters address race-based policies in Canada and United States, each takes a different approach. Chan reviews Canada's race-based policies and cites the Indian Act of 1876, the Chinese Exclusion Act of 1923, and The Act to Prevent the Employment of Female Labour in Certain Capacities of 1912 as examples of legislated policies. Span, Robinson, and Villegas, on the other hand, cite US court cases that challenged race-based policies as examples of unfair treatment and discrimination of African Americans, Chinese Americans, and Mexican Americans. In highlighting the selected laws and court cases, this response hopes to create a dialogue on how we read and understand discriminatory practices in the two countries.

From the outset, the two chapters clearly state the historical challenges that people of non-European ancestry have faced in order to attain an education. Race-based policies outlined specific forms of discrimination and differential treatment for peoples of non-European descent. These policies met with different forms of resistance, both individual and collective. Such policies have been employed as tools to meet racialized goals of creating segregated communities. Chan states, regarding Canada: "Race-based policies are historical, but they continue and are a consideration in the social construction of education today ... Policies and laws are created to address ... segregation. Racialization can occur even without the use of the term *race* ... Structures and policies work within the demarcation of specific racial or ethnic groups; societal and institutional arrangements dictate policies or practices in legal, economic, housing, and education systems" (pp. 131-32). Span, Robinson, and Villegas express the same sentiments eloquently in reference to American policies: "The history of public schooling in the United States is premised upon race and ethnicity. From its beginnings to the near present, the schooling opportunities American children received have depended more on their racial or ethnic background than on their educational aptitude, residence, or parental income" (p. 146).

Segregated schools were the norm in Canada and the United States until the early twentieth century, and a close examination of educational legislation in both countries indicates that education for non-Europeans was regulated and governed by race-based policies. For example, before the US Civil War in 1861, it was a crime to teach enslaved African American children how to read and write. At one point, anyone caught teaching enslaved Black children was whipped and imprisoned. In places where there were schools for Black children, they were segregated from children of European ancestry. In Canada, however, separate schools were encouraged as a source of opportunities for Black children to learn how to read and write. Prejudice fuelled the creation of separate schools throughout Canada. In both countries, the early separate schools lacked qualified teachers or enough resources to create facilities conducive to learning. These segregated school systems for Black children did not go uncontested. Both chapters describe court challenges to segregation whereby Black parents challenged the laws and societal race-based educational practices.

The experience of Chinese students in both countries was slightly different from that of Black students. Span, Robinson, and Villegas discuss the segregated schools for Chinese students in San Francisco, California, while Chan gives examples from Victoria and Vancouver, British Columbia. In both countries, Chinese families tried to set up schools for their children and faced numerous challenges. In Canada, the Chinese families boycotted the public school system, while in San Francisco, the Chinese schools were closed, thus eliminating the educational opportunities for Chinese students. Chinese schools were later established through the assistance of the American Missionary Association. From this time on, there were struggles between Chinese parents, school authorities, and law courts.

Students of other non-European backgrounds, such as Japanese, South Asian, East Asian, and Latino, also were denied equal educational opportunities in both Canada and the United States. For example, the education of Japanese Americans and Japanese Canadians was greatly jeopardized after the bombing of Pearl Harbor in December 1941. Mexican Americans experienced segregationist practices similar to those experienced by African Americans in the South. And, like African Americans, Latinos challenged these discriminatory policies and practices. Span, Robinson, and Villegas provide numerous examples of how parents challenged in court the race-based policies that were designed to keep Mexican American children out of White schools.

Realities and Rhetoric in the Education of Racial Minority Students

Are all the children in these two nations provided with equal educational opportunities? The official end of slavery in 1833 did not see an end to racial segregation in Canada. In many parts of Canada, access to schools and universities was governed by race. Although compulsory education was introduced for Aboriginal students through the Indian Act of 1880, it left a lot to be desired as the government forced these children to attend residential schools. The segregation and experiences of Aboriginal students in residential schools had an impact on Aboriginal children's education. On the US side, Span, Robinson, and Villegas have clearly demonstrated that the history of American education with regard to people of colour has been predicated on race-based considerations.

Responding to the 1948 UN Declaration of Human Rights endorsement of equality for all people, regardless of race, creed, gender, and other grounds enumerated under human rights law, many Canadian provinces authorized racial desegregation in the mid-1960s. Subsequent policies and directives affirmed ethnoracial difference: the Royal Commission on Bilingualism and Biculturalism (1963), Canadian Bill of Rights (1960), the federal Multiculturalism Policy (1971), the Indian control of Indian education policy (1972; see Chapter 4 for a fuller discussion), and section 15 of the Charter of Rights and Freedoms (1982), which recognized every individual to be equal before and under the law and to have the right to equal protection and equal benefit of the law, without discrimination. Despite the implementation of the official policy on multiculturalism, systemic and differential treatment continues to be accorded to racialized communities in such areas as educational attainment, socioeconomics, and the criminal justice system.

The rhetoric of additive multiculturalism refuses to challenge the social advantages accorded to the dominant group or the denial and stigmatization of racialized groups. The challenge becomes naming those groups for whom multiculturalism offers safe ethnic pluralism without the necessity of challenging relations of power and domination. In Canada, despite the official political rhetoric of diversity and inclusion, most clearly articulated in the Multiculturalism Act (1988), a profound dichotomy exists between the purported egalitarianism and the actual racial divides in the country. The boundaries of racial identity are maintained to ensure stability in a neocolonial era. Social structures maintain and reproduce systemic inequalities wherein race functions as the grounds of exclusion. Unlike the contemporary scientific preoccupation with a common humanity and shared genetic basis, previous scientific experiments sought to bring forward minute racial differences as evidence of profound human differences. Being raced was the basis for exclusion and discrimination. Particularly in the pursuit of imperial policies, a great deal of institutional effort determined and maintained racial affiliation and boundaries in schools.

In the year 2007, have exclusionary race-based education policies and practices been phased out? Race-based policies remain, among other issues, a taboo in mainstream conversation. In multiracial spaces in both Canada and the United States, talking about race is always a difficult, emotional engagement; its entangled and inconspicuous nature entails discomfort and unresolved issues. In other words, how a person participates in dialogues that address race-based policies often depends on the ways in which he or she understands his or her own racial identity in society. The two previous chapters have shown that major changes have taken place when there was some kind of meaningful dialogue that challenged race-based policies and practices. Clearly, the continuation of such dialogues is crucial for change in education. Chan has shown that race issues continue in the Canadian landscape. She cites the Cole Harbour story, a story intensely charged with frustration as the parents and students struggled to show that the system of education was discriminatory and did not provide adequate provisions for educational growth. The Cole Harbour situation shows, according to Chan, that "policies ... developed in a context of racialization ... [are] insufficient as a tool to address racism, in part due to lack of implementation strategies. There are still school boards [in Canada] that have not developed race relations policy as a means of addressing racial, ethnic, and cultural diversity."

Both chapters conclude by reminding us of the necessity to understand and articulate the past when examining the current state of race and education. Span, Robinson, and Villegas remind the readers, "As we examine race relations, specifically in the area of education, we must not forget the implications of past events for present-day society." And, Chan notes, "Education of racially, culturally, and ethnically diverse populations requires an engagement with the issues of race-based policy and implementation ... These issues should be articulated in the context of historical racialization and the political and social elements of education. This articulation ... is necessary before policy goals can be realized and normalized in educational institutions."

Conclusion

The two chapters highlight the point that although overt racial segregation has ended in both countries, racial differences and their intersections with class, gender, and ethnicity influence the degree and quality of access to the basic right of education. In addition, the authors show that the collective efforts of marginalized communities have brought about great changes toward the provision of equal education opportunities for all children. There is a clear need for critical awareness of racial constructions and the social factors influencing racial engagement for oppression and liberation, showing why it is necessary to raise and answer significant questions about power, influence, mobilization, and resistance. Critical awareness and self-determination are needed in order to develop more feasible, inclusive approaches to accessible education for both Canadian and American children of all races, creeds, sexual orientations, abilities, and classes.

References
Marable, M. 1995. *Beyond Black and White: Transforming African-American politics*. New York: Verso.

Part 5:
Employment Equity and Affirmative Action

13

Canada's Employment Equity Act: Perspectives on Policy and Implementation

Carol Agocs

Canada is distinguished by the significant and growing diversity of its population, and consequently of its workforce. However, this diversity is accompanied by persisting patterns of inequality in access to good jobs, career advancement, and compensation. Recognizing the impact of systemic or institutionalized employment discrimination on women, racialized ("visible") minorities, persons of Aboriginal ancestry, and persons with disabilities, the Government of Canada enacted the Employment Equity Act and the Federal Contractors Program in 1986. Section 2 of the act describes its goal: "to achieve equality in the workplace so that no person shall be denied employment opportunities or benefits for reasons unrelated to ability and, in the fulfillment of that goal, to correct the conditions of disadvantage in employment experienced by women, Aboriginal peoples, persons with disabilities and members of visible minorities by giving effect to the principle that employment equity means more than treating persons in the same way but also requires special measures and the accommodation of differences."

Although it covers only a small proportion of the Canadian workforce, the policy framework created by the act has many strengths as a proactive and mandatory response to systemic discrimination in employment. It has therefore been considered a model by other jurisdictions including the Netherlands, Australia, Northern Ireland, South Africa, and Belgium. Scholarly research on the results of employment equity and affirmative action in several countries suggests that when such policies are implemented by employers and enforced by government, they can be effective in reducing systemic disadvantage (Agocs 2002b).

Over the twenty years since the report of the Royal Commission on Equality in Employment (Abella 1984) first proposed a framework called "employment equity" as a policy remedy for systemic discrimination, the act has been reviewed and revised twice, most recently in 2002. A body of evidence has accumulated regarding the impacts of this policy framework as well as its deficiencies in addressing intractable issues of systemic discrimination.

Clearly its results are mixed: White able-bodied women and "visible minority" men and women have made some gains, but Aboriginal people and persons with disabilities have seen few benefits (Agocs 2002a). Furthermore, the potential impact of employment equity has been limited by a failure of employers to implement it, and a failure of government to commit to vigorous monitoring and enforcement (Agocs 2002a). These issues reflect the critical role of political power relations and political will.

The legislative reviews of the act and the responses of the Government of Canada to those reviews yield a unitary set of conclusions and recommendations that are intended to guide the government's policy direction on employment equity. Taking inspiration from standpoint theory and postmodern critiques of empiricism, this chapter provides an overview of the Employment Equity Act and its results, with attention to the differing perspectives of key stakeholders. These perspectives are revealed in an analysis of testimony before the Parliamentary Standing Committee on Human Resources Development and the Status of Persons with Disabilities, which reviewed the act in 2002. The analysis of stakeholders' perspectives reinforces the observation that having a well-crafted policy is not enough: effectiveness depends upon the context of power relations and how they are enacted both in the workplace and in the federal political arena. Additionally, this analysis demonstrates how the existing review process effectively undermines the stated intent of the policy.

Diversity and Inequality: The Context of Employment Equity

The 2001 census of Canada showed that demographic and immigration trends are making Canada's population and workforce increasingly diverse. People of Aboriginal ancestry represent 4.4 percent of the population, and people who identify themselves as Aboriginal account for 3.3 percent (in comparison, 1.5 percent of the population of the United States is Native American). Because the median age of the Aboriginal population is thirteen years younger than that of the non-Aboriginal population, Aboriginal people will constitute a larger proportion of the Canadian labour force in years to come. About half of Aboriginal people live in cities, and there is a long-term trend toward migration to the larger cities. Aboriginal people currently represent 8 percent of the population of Winnipeg and 9 percent of Saskatoon's residents (Statistics Canada 2003a).

The 2001 census also revealed that over 18 percent of the Canadian population are immigrants, that is, people born in other countries and settled as permanent residents in Canada. This is the highest proportion of any country in the world except for Australia – in comparison, only 11 percent of the US population is foreign-born (Statistics Canada 2003b). Over the past decade, 40 percent of immigrants to Canada came from China, India, the Philippines, Hong Kong, Sri Lanka, Pakistan, and Taiwan. A majority of immigrants are younger adults, thus enriching the diversity of Canada's workforce, especially in the larger cities. Three-quarters of immigrants arriving during the 1990s settled in Canada's three largest metropolitan areas: Toronto, Vancouver, and Montreal. Forty-four percent of Toronto's population, and 40 percent of Vancouver's, now consists of immigrants (in comparison, New York's population is 24 percent foreign-born). Only about 10 percent of immigrants who arrived during the 1990s reported no knowledge of either of Canada's official languages, and their average educational level is higher than that of the Canadian-born population (Statistics Canada 2003b).

Visible minorities, defined in the Employment Equity Act as "persons, other than Aboriginal peoples, who are non-Caucasian in race or non-white in colour" (s. 3) constituted over 13 percent of Canada's 2001 population, and 73 percent of immigrants arriving in the 1990s (this figure approached 80 percent for those settling in Toronto). Approximately 37 percent of the populations of the Toronto and Vancouver metropolitan areas are visible minorities. Visible minorities are projected to account for a fifth of Canada's population by 2016. While a majority of the populations of Asian and South Asian[1] origin were born abroad, about 80 percent of Blacks (or African Canadians) and 90 percent of people of Japanese origin were born in Canada. Both historical influences and recent immigrant settlement patterns account for notable variations in the diversity of populations of cities across the country. For example, Canadian-born Blacks are a majority of the visible minority population in Halifax and Montreal, while people of Asian and South Asian origin are most numerous among Toronto's and Vancouver's visible minorities (Statistics Canada 2003b).

These demographic facts have significant implications for employment equity policy and implementation. First, Canada's workforce is clearly highly diverse at present, and will become even more diverse in the future on the basis of race, ethnic origin, religion, and culture – particularly in urban areas. Second, across Canada there is significant variability in the composition of the population, suggesting that employment equity policy must be both flexible and broad in order to effectively address local demographic characteristics, and that employment equity goals should vary significantly from one locality to another to reflect these differences. Third, because of the significant increase in the representation of visible minorities and Aboriginal people in the population from the census of 1996 to the census of 2001, current employment equity goals that are based on 1996 census data (and on a 1991 survey in the case of persons with disabilities) are inaccurate and insufficient.

The diversity of Canada's workforce is accompanied by marked patterns of inequality on the basis of gender, immigrant status, race, disability, and Aboriginal ancestry. Data on earnings indicate the extent of this inequality, since pay represents the distribution of material rewards for the work people do. According to the 2001 census, women working full time for a full year earn just over 70 cents for every dollar earned by their male counterparts. Even women aged twenty-five to twenty-nine with university degrees made only 81 cents for every dollar earned by their male peers for full-time, full-year work. Moreover, an 11 cent pay gap remained for women and men of the same age and educational groups working in the ten most common occupations chosen by men. Nearly 47 percent of women now work on a full-year, full-time basis, and a higher proportion of women earners than of men have university degrees (Statistics Canada 2003c; also see Hadley 2001).

Pay disadvantage is also evident for visible minority women and men when they are compared with White women and men of similar characteristics. Pendakur and Pendakur (2002) conducted a multivariate regression analysis of census data for Canadian-born residents aged twenty-five to sixty-four whose earnings came from wages and salaries. They compared earnings of visible minority, Aboriginal, and White women and men for Canada as a whole and for eight census metropolitan areas for several census years, the most recent being 1996. Their analysis controlled for the effects of age, education, marital status, household size, official language, and city of residence. The analysis for 1996 showed that Aboriginal women earned 14 to 41 percent less than White women of similar characteristics. The pay gap between visible minority and White women was 19 percent in Montreal, 15 percent in Halifax, and 12 percent in Toronto. In Canada as a whole and in some cities, Aboriginal men earned only about half the pay received by White men. The pay gap for visible minority men was 15 percent. In general, Pendakur and Pendakur found that the pay disadvantage of Aboriginal and visible minority women and men in comparison with White women and men worsened from 1991 to 1996, regardless of city of residence. They concluded, "A decade after the implementation of employment equity programming, inequity is seen to be on the rise at the same time as larger and larger numbers of Canadian-born minorities can be seen entering the labour market. It appears that the labour market may be neither colour blind nor moving toward employment equity" (510).

Considering the earnings disadvantage suffered by visible minorities, it is not surprising that a recent study of urban poverty based on 1996 census data found "extreme poverty rates ... in most communities" among Aboriginal people, recent immigrants, visible minorities, persons with disabilities and lone-parent families (Lee 2000, xvi). An analysis of census data for 1980, 1990, and 2000 found a rise in low income rates among immigrants, including those with postsecondary degrees, as the primary sources of immigration shifted to Asia and Africa (Picot and Hou 2003).

Canada's Employment Equity Act: Overview and Results

Canada's first Employment Equity Act, passed in 1986 by a Progressive Conservative government, was inspired by the report of the Royal Commission on Equality in Employment (Abella 1984), which presented an analysis of systemic discrimination suffered by women, visible minorities, Aboriginal people, and people with disabilities. The purpose clause of the act, quoted earlier, reflects its origin as a policy response to systemic discrimination, which may be defined as "patterns of behaviour that are part of the social and administrative structures of the workplace, and that create or perpetuate a position of relative disadvantage for some groups, and privilege for other groups, or for individuals on account of their group identity" (Agocs 2002b, 2).

Also in 1986, the Government of Canada initiated the Federal Contractors Program (FCP), which applies to organizations with one hundred or more employees that sell goods or services to the government valued at $200,000 or more. This discussion addresses experience with the act but not the FCP, which does not require public reporting of workforce data or of the results of audits of FCP employers; therefore very little is known about its results. The FCP's lack of sanctions for noncompliance and lack of meaningful enforcement of compliance, however, have long been criticized by equality seekers.

The Employment Equity Act imposed twelve requirements on federally regulated employers of one hundred employees or more, including federal Crown corporations and some private sector employers such as banks and firms in the interprovincial communication and transportation businesses. From the outset there were concerns that employment equity in Canada not be seen as the same as affirmative action in the United States. One of the major concerns voiced to the Abella commission was that affirmative action was an interventionist government policy imposed on employers (Abella 1984). As a result, part of the philosophy of employment equity was to concentrate on the public sector. Because the legislation is federal, it covers only those in the federal public sector. In 1987, when the act took effect, only about 4 percent of the Canadian labour force was covered, and that proportion has since declined. The FCP covered about 7 percent of Canada's workforce in 1988, but only about 6 percent by 1998 (Agocs 2002a). Quebec is currently the only province with mandatory employment equity legislation that covers the provincial government and the broader public sector. Thus employment equity policy covers only a small proportion of the Canadian workforce.

The Employment Equity Act requires employers to conduct a workforce census based upon voluntary self-identification by members of the four designated groups. The results must be reported annually to Human Resources Development Canada, which publishes a compilation of the reports and also provides information and consultation to employers. Employers can be fined for failure to report, but the 1986 act did not provide sanctions for failure to implement employment equity. Employers are also required to compare the representation of designated group members in their firms with relevant labour force data, most of which comes from the census. Based on this comparison, employers must establish numerical goals and timetables for hiring, training, and promotion of designated groups, and must prepare a work plan for attaining these goals. An important part of implementation is the requirement to conduct an employment systems review to identify and remove discriminatory barriers that limit the access and career development of designated group members. The work plan is supposed to include a program for barrier removal as well as special measures and actions to accommodate differences between designated group employees and White, able-bodied, male employees. The employer is required to inform employees about employment equity, and to monitor the results attained and revise the work plan to ensure its effectiveness.

Under the provisions of the Employment Equity Act, there have been two legislative reviews of the legislation, in 1994-95 and 2002. The first of these reviews resulted in the passage of a new Employment Equity Act in 1995. The 1995 act requires employers to "consult" and "collaborate" with "employees' representatives," but notes that these "are not forms of co-management" (s. 15). The most significant new features were that the federal public service was covered by the act, and that employers were subject to compliance audits by the Canadian Human Rights Commission (CHRC). An Employment Equity Review Tribunal was also empowered to enforce compliance using the existing tribunal structure under the Canadian Human Rights Act. This power has never been used, however, because the CHRC is directed to use persuasion and negotiation to encourage employers to work toward compliance, and to apply sanctions only as a "last resort."

While the 1995 act gave the CHRC a new enforcement role, it also weakened the possibilities for holding employers accountable. It forbids the CHRC or a tribunal to impose a "quota" on an employer, where "quota" is defined as "a requirement to hire or promote a fixed and arbitrary number of persons during a given period." The Canadian Human Rights Act was also changed to disallow the use of data collected under the Employment Equity Act as the basis for a complaint – thus the CHRC could no longer use this data as a basis for negotiating voluntary agreements with employers to step up their equity activities. Furthermore, a tribunal could no longer order an employer to implement "positive policies and practices" or "goals and timetables" as a remedy for discrimination (Agocs 2002a, 68). Both the use of employment equity data as evidence in complaints, and orders to implement employment equity as a remedy for discrimination, had previously been features of landmark human rights cases.

Table 13.1 summarizes some indicators of results under the act drawn from the earliest and the most recent annual reports of federally regulated private sector firms. The 2001 report uses 1996 census data as the standard in assessing the representation of visible minorities, Aboriginal people, and women in the Canadian labour force, and 1991 data for people with disabilities. The 2001 census data published so far, which are used in Table 13.1, clearly indicate that using 1996 and 1991 data as indicators of availability would lead employers and the compliance audit to set employment equity goals that are far too low. The table also provides some useful information about what has and has not been accomplished under employment equity policy. All the equity groups are poorly represented among senior managers. Women in general, and women who are visible minorities, Aboriginal, or persons with disabilities, are all much more likely than men to earn less than $30,000 for full-time work.

Visible minority representation in the employment equity firms has increased roughly to the same degree as visible minority representation in the population has increased. Visible minorities are somewhat overrepresented among part-time workers. As well, they are somewhat more likely than the total workforce to be paid less than $30,000, and less likely to be paid $70,000 or more. In 2001, hires and promotions of visible minorities exceeded their representation in the firms under the act – an encouraging finding. The representation of persons with disabilities remains strikingly low in the firms covered by the act even after fourteen years of employment equity. Terminations continued to exceed hires in 2001, as was true every year for the past decade (HRDC 2003). The representation of Aboriginal people in firms covered by the act also continues to be far below their representation in the population. They are equally represented among those hired and those terminated, and overrepresented among part-time workers. Aboriginal men are poorly represented among men earning $70,000 or more.

Women's representation in the employment equity firms still falls below their representation in the Canadian workforce, though they were more likely than men to be promoted in 2001. Nearly two-thirds of part-time employees are women. The pay gap for women in the employment equity firms – 21 percent for full-time, full-year employment – is about 9 percent less than it is for the Canadian workforce as a whole (HRDC 2003, 5).

The data derived from employers' mandatory reports for 2001 give little reason for enthusiasm about the results of employment equity policy. While there are some signs of progress for women and visible minorities, results for 2001 did not show the gains one might expect given that the number of employees hired "increased dramatically in 2001, and this was the highest level since 1990" (HRDC 2003, 2). Gains for Aboriginal people were negligible, and no benefits of employment equity can be detected for persons with disabilities.

Elsewhere (Agocs 2002a) I have argued that the logic of the Employment Equity Act is essentially sound in terms of its purpose and its requirements of employers, including the workforce census, employment systems review, goal setting, consultation with employees, reporting to the government, and compliance audits by the Canadian Human Rights Commission. Furthermore, academic research in Canada, Northern Ireland, and the United States has shown that affirmative action or employment equity improves the representation,

Table 13.1

Representation of employees who are members of designated groups in firms covered by the Employment Equity Act, Canada, 1987 and 2001

Designated group as percentage of:	Designated groups							
	Visible minorities[2]		Persons with disabilities		Aboriginal people[2]		Women	
	1987	2001	1987	2001	1987	2001	1987	2001
Canadian workforce/population[1]	6.3	13.4	5.4	6.5[3]	2.1	3.3	44.0	46.7
Workforce in firms under the Act:								
Total	5.0	11.7	1.6	2.3	0.7	1.6	40.9	44.9
Banks	9.5	17.1	1.8	2.0	0.6	1.1	76.1	71.0
Communications	4.0	10.8	1.4	2.3	0.6	1.4	39.6	41.3
Transportation	2.6	7.6	1.4	2.5	0.7	2.0	16.9	24.7
Other sectors[4]	2.6	7.7	2.3	2.7	0.9	2.7	21.2	28.0
Hires	5.3	12.7	0.7	1.2	0.6	1.7	37.4	41.6
Promotions	7.4	14.6	1.4	1.9	0.6	1.6	51.1	53.2
Terminations	3.3	10.8	1.2	1.9	0.6	1.7	36.4	40.2
Upper level/senior managers	2.1	3.7	1.6	1.9	0.2	1.5	4.7	19.6
Salary ≥ $70,000[5]								
Total	1.5		1.2		0.2		3.1	
Men	n/a	18.0	n/a	16.7	n/a	11.2	n/a	n/a
Women	n/a	7.3	n/a	6.1	n/a	3.4	n/a	8.7
Salary < $30,000[5]								
Total	7	12.7	1.7	7.5	0.8	13.5	56.0	n/a
Men	n/a	19.8	n/a	18.4	n/a	26.4	n/a	n/a
Women	n/a	12.7	n/a	1.7	0	1.7	n/a	17.7
Part-time employees (permanent)	6.4	12.7	1.2	1.7	0	1.7	74.6	66.0

Notes on sources:

1 Census of Canada 1986 (workforce), 2001 (total population), reported in Employment and Immigration 1988 (1987 data), and Human Resources Development Canada 2003 (2001 data).

2 Employment and Immigration 1988 (1987 data), and Human Resources Development Canada 2003 (2001 data). Includes women and men. The 1987 data are for full-time employees; 2001 data are for total employees, except salary data. Salary data for 2001 are for full-time employees only and are shown by gender.

3 Health and Activity Limitation Survey 1991, reported in Human Resources Development Canada 2003.

4 Includes metal mines, grain elevators, electric power systems, business financing, business services.

5 Percentage of all permanent full-time employees in the specified designated group/gender category. Of all men, 8.6 percent earn less than $30,000 and 20.8 percent earn $70,000 or more.

career progression, and relative pay levels of women and racialized minorities when it is implemented by employers, when employers set goals, and when equity requirements are enforced (see, for example, Agocs 2002b; Holzer and Neumark 2000; Leck and Saunders 1992; Leonard 1989, 1990, 1996; Rogers and Spriggs 1996; Rogers 2002).

My argument has been that Canada's employment equity policy has not been effective because it has not been implemented by employers, primarily because enforcement has not been rigorous or adequately resourced, and because employers do not face sanctions for failure to comply. A policy that is not enforced is unlikely to be implemented. A policy that is not implemented cannot be fairly evaluated, and it cannot be expected to get results (Agocs 2002a).

What Changes Are Needed in the Act? Stakeholder Perspectives

We turn now to a consideration of the Employment Equity Act through the eyes of spokespersons for employers, unions, and organizations representing women, persons with disabilities, racialized minorities, Aboriginal people, and immigrants. Their views were presented to the Parliamentary Standing Committee for Human Resources Development and the Status of Persons with Disabilities as part of the legislative review of the 1995 Employment Equity Act during the Thirty-seventh Parliament, first session. The committee meetings at which they testified occurred between December 2001 and April 2002, and transcripts of these meetings, except for in-camera sessions, are posted on the committee's website as "Evidence" (Standing Committee on Human Resources Development 2002). The transcripts contain brief opening statements by each witness, followed by their responses to extensive questioning by the committee.

The hearings included political dramaturgy that drifted away from the purpose at hand, such as MPs' comments on the accomplishments or attractions of their home communities or provinces for the benefit of any constituents who might be listening, and their particular interest in witnesses from the same riding or place in the political spectrum. For example, the transcripts record that Alexa McDonough, leader of the social democratic political party, the New Democratic Party, attended and addressed friendly questions to witnesses at the meeting where union representatives made their presentations. On the other hand, another MP delighted in questioning union representatives on whether they were implementing employment equity in their organizations and on their own representation of the designated groups.

The transcripts were reviewed to identify stakeholders' concerns about the Employment Equity Act in its present form, and recommendations for change. My analysis encompasses the testimony of representatives of forty different employers, unions, and designated group organizations in eleven meetings of the committee, but did not include expert witnesses, individuals, or technical briefings or presentations made by the agencies charged with implementing the legislation. The testimony displays themes common across stakeholder groups as well as significant differences in perception among them. These can be summarized briefly as follows; the number of witnesses mentioning each point is shown in parentheses. Only ideas mentioned by more than one witness are included in this summary.

Employers
Ten representatives testified; nine had substantive comments about the act:

· The act does not need to be changed. (8)
·· There should be more government resources to support employer (and nongovernmental organization) activities and for public education. (5)
· Enforcement should not be strengthened, or should be helpful to the employer. (4)
· Reporting requirements are too complex. (4)
· Definitions and requirements need to be clarified. (3)
· There should be no additional requirement for union involvement. (2)

Unions
Eight organizations testified:

· The act needs strengthening and/or amendment. (6)
· The act should require the involvement of unions in all aspects of employment equity (mandatory joint committees). (8)
· The Federal Contractors Program needs the same requirements as the act, as well as compliance audits. (4)
· The act and issues faced by designated groups need to be viewed in a larger context and a more comprehensive policy approach is needed. (3)
· Resources are needed for education. (3)
· The quality of availability data is inadequate. (3)
· Goals and timetables should be mandatory. (2)
· Employment equity has failed people with disabilities. (2)
· Results are inadequate for Aboriginal people. (2)
· Disadvantaged cultural communities should be covered as designated groups. (2)
· A complaints provision is needed. (2)
· A process of accreditation of foreign credentials is needed. (2)
· An Employment Equity Commission is needed. (2)

Organizations Representing Designated Groups

Visible Minority and Immigrant Women and Men
Four organizations testified:

- Lack of recognition of foreign credentials is a serious problem. (2)
- The act should cover federal government employers not currently covered. (2)
- Better enforcement is needed. (2)

Aboriginal Women and Men
Five organizations testified, and four offered specific ideas:

- The act has not helped Aboriginal people. (2)
- The organization supports the act. (2)
- Better enforcement is needed. (3)
- Poor quality jobs are created for Aboriginal people under the act. (2)
- Poor quality availability data and poor procedure for their use result in inadequate goal setting for Aboriginal people. (2)
- Self-identification is problematic. (2)
- Issues affecting Aboriginal people require a broader approach. (2)
- Non-Aboriginal employers and employees need cross-cultural training. (2)
- There is a lack of useful data on multiple disadvantage. (2)
- Special measures and accommodation are needed for Aboriginal employees. (2)

Women and Men with Disabilities
Ten organizations appeared before the committee:

- The act has not benefited people with disabilities. (2)
- The organization supports the act. (3)
- Better enforcement is needed. (4)
- A broader coordinated strategy, involving federal and provincial governments, is needed. (4)
- Employers need training about disability issues. (3)
- Disability organizations should be funded and involved in employment equity implementation. (3)
- An improved accommodation process is needed. (3)
- Human Resources Development Canada and the Canadian Human Rights Commission need more resources. (2)

Women
Three organizations testified:

- Stronger enforcement and monitoring are needed. (3)
- The act should recognize multiple disadvantage. (2)
- Measures are needed to address work-life balance. (2)
- Better workforce data are needed. (2)

These summaries show that employers have a different perception of the act than unions and designated group organizations. Employers are generally satisfied with the act as it is, and oppose any changes that would add enforcement or requirements of any kind, such as expanded union involvement. They would support an expanded role for government in education and providing incentives to employers and perhaps designated group organizations. Unions, in contrast, are quite critical of the act's limited effectiveness and inadequate enforcement. They unanimously recommend a role for unions in employment equity implementation, most often through a joint committee process. Unions and designated group organizations raise many of the same issues regarding specific impediments to making employment equity effective for people with disabilities, Aboriginal people, and visible minorities.

Aside from suggestions as to how to make employment equity more effective for the groups they represent, designated group organizations are inclined to see employment equity as part of a much broader set of policy instruments needed in order to address the complex issues of disadvantage affecting people with disabilities, Aboriginal people, and people with overlapping identities. Reading the transcripts of the committee meetings left me impressed by the analysis and the specificity of the suggestions offered by many of the witnesses from unions and designated group organizations. While many suggestions appear predictable and self-interested, such as when groups recommend an expanded role for themselves, there is also ample evidence of concern for the positions of people outside the speaker's sector.

The Report of the 2002 Legislative Review

The parliamentary committee's task was to arrive at an analysis and set of recommendations to present to the Liberal government regarding what changes, if any, should be made to the 1995 Employment Equity Act. The committee was chaired by a Liberal, and its vice-chairs were a Liberal parliamentary secretary for Human Resources and Development Canada and the senior critic of HRDC for the Canadian Alliance, the official opposition party. The fifteen committee members included eight Liberals (three of whom were parliamentary secretaries), three members of the Canadian Alliance (the caucus chair, the HRDC critic, and the member assigned to persons with disabilities issues), two members of the Bloc Québécois, one Progressive Conservative, and one New Democratic Party member. Members of the Liberal Party were clearly the majority. But the Canadian Alliance had four powerful members on the committee and was thus in a position to threaten the act, given its well-known opposition to employment equity and the absence on the committee of a countervailing weight of influence from the left.

The committee's report proposed twenty-nine recommendations, none of which involved substantial amendments to the Employment Equity Act. In the committee's words, "The recommendations in our report are best characterized as directions for fine-tuning administrative processes, clarifying legislative ambiguity, enhancing awareness and supporting the labour market needs of disadvantaged workers. We recognize that there is a need to focus more resources in specific areas, particularly in terms of facilitating greater access to employment for persons with disabilities and Aboriginal people" (Canada, House of Commons Standing Committee on Human Resources 2002, 2). The committee explicitly rejected the suggestion of many witnesses representing unions and designated groups that enforcement and penalties should be stronger. It also rejected the suggestions that additional designated groups be considered, that the act's coverage be expanded to cover smaller employers, and that employment equity be negotiated with unions. Many of its recommendations, on such issues as the recognition of foreign credentials, the strengthening of the Federal Contractors Program, and the development of data on multiple disadvantage, suggested further discussion, study, or consideration rather than action.

By its own admission, the committee reframed the issue from a matter of principled political commitment to the transformative potential of employment equity, to a technical and administrative matter. In the end, the committee's report endorsed the position put forward by employer representatives: that the act not be changed, that better enforcement not be recommended, and that the insights of unions and designated group representatives be adopted only if they do not cost much and do not require much of government or employers. The issue of reforming the act to make it more effective in attaining its purpose was never raised, although the report acknowledged that employment equity has not helped Aboriginal peoples or persons with disabilities. Tellingly, while the Canadian Alliance members submitted a minority report, they did not recommend the repeal of the Employment Equity Act, or even the rejection of the committee's report. Both the witnesses for employers and the Canadian Alliance members evidently regarded the act as so benign they had no need to oppose it.

The response by the Government of Canada to the committee's report was noncommittal, and promised discussion or study, but no action or resources, in response to most of the recommendations for administrative changes, minimal as they were. The government reaffirmed that existing enforcement arrangements are adequate (HRDC 2002, 8).

The 2002 legislative review of the Employment Equity Act, then, was an exercise that consumed the time and energy of hundreds, but produced little change. Neither the committee's report nor the government's response referred to the need to ensure that the act's purpose is realized.

Reframing Employment Equity: Comparing Policy Lenses

The 2002 legislative review of the Employment Equity Act is a case study of the process of policy change within a political and administrative context.

The case raises two obvious questions:

- Why did the committee not use this opportunity to improve the effectiveness of employment equity policy by amending the act to make it more capable of achieving its purpose?
- Evidence available to the committee made clear what kinds of changes are needed to make the act more effective, such as a stronger enforcement regime. Why were they not adopted?

The case and the questions it raises present an opportunity to seek explanation and understanding through reframing – considering the case from the perspectives of several of the most influential frames of reference in policy studies. This exercise may facilitate an understanding of the case and at the same time offer insights into the strengths and limitations of these policy lenses.

In *Whose Science? Whose Knowledge?* Sandra Harding (1991) compares three epistemological programs in feminist thought: empiricism, standpoint theory, and postmodernism. Feminist empiricism seeks truth and social justice by attempting to reform and rigorously apply the norms of conventional science. Standpoint approaches seek understanding and policy change by using life experience, particularly the experience of women's struggles against oppression, as the starting point for analysis. Postmodernism (or postpositivism) challenges conventional assumptions of rationality and truth, pointing to the social construction of knowledge claims within contexts of power relations. Each of these three fundamental frames of reference can provide an epistemological foundation for influential and competing interpretations in policy studies. I will consider the case through the lenses of the rational decision-making model, policy as emergent strategy, stakeholder analysis, and postmodern or postpositivist approaches, in the spirit of Sandra Burt's (1995) suggestion that there is value in feminist approaches to policy that involve frame shifting.[2]

The Rational Model
Empiricist assumptions and the rational model of decision making have long served as the ideal toward which policy analysis is enjoined to strive. The model is that the stated objective of a policy drives the search for information, the consideration of options, and decisions about policy content.

Like many others, I have used the rational model and the empiricist frame to guide a search for the content of policy most likely to be effective in achieving the stated purpose of the legislation. According to this analysis of the evidence, the content of an equality policy most likely to reduce systemic discrimination in employment against women, racialized minorities, persons with disabilities, and Aboriginal people is essentially contained in the logic of the Employment Equity Act as it is written. The act can be effective if it is implemented, but this will happen only if enforcement, monitoring, sanctions and a complaints process are established and made effective.

The rational model guides thinking about what the content of a policy should be if it is to achieve its purpose. But it does not explain why policy decision makers do not choose to create and maintain effective policy – in this case, why the committee did not recommend changes to the Employment Equity Act that would make it effective. Indeed, the committee's report provides no indication that it even explicitly considered the objective of Employment Equity Act, stated at the beginning of this chapter. The unreal world of the rational model assumes that policy decision makers are motivated to create effective policy – an assumption that is evidently unfounded in this case.

The rational model builds in a separation of policy from implementation, as well as a dichotomy of politics and administration. In previous work (see, for example, Agocs 2002a; Agocs, Burr, and Somerset 1992) I have positioned the problem of the limited results of employment equity policy as a policy-implementation gap: the policy is sound, but it is not being implemented. This interpretation is not wrong, but it begs the question of why this is the case, and it perpetuates an artificial conceptual boundary between policy and implementation. In fact employment equity *is* being implemented – in ways that reflect and maintain the interests of employers, and that enable bureaucrats and politicians to claim that employment equity is government policy.

Policy as Emergent Strategy

Mintzberg and Jorgensen (1987) have challenged the rational model from a basis in organization theory and analysis, arguing that policy is not formulated consciously and explicitly and implemented formally. Nor is it the product of incrementalism in the form of "groping," "muddling," or random collisions in a policy "garbage can," as some influential theorists have proposed (see, for example, Lindblom 1959; Cohen, March, and Olsen 1972); such analyses do not explain why one policy idea is taken up while others are rejected. Instead, policy emerges through a process of implementation enacted in the behaviour of organizational actors: policy is what people in organizations actually do, not what they claim to do or what a formal policy prescribes. Focusing on emergent strategy – an evolving mix of ideas and actions – thus breaks down the policy/implementation dichotomy by reframing policy as what actually happens on the ground. Policy makers in organizations set out broad outlines of a policy – an "umbrella" in Mintzberg and Jorgensen's word – while leaving the details to emerge as actors respond to situations. The content of policy, then, emerges through action, learning, and experience, and is as likely to come from the bottom of an organization as from the top.

Mintzberg and Jorgensen's formulation of policy as process offers insight into how actors without official policy-making roles create and transform policy. It provides the beginning of an account of the ways in which employers, unions, and designated group representatives each develop distinctive and conflicting conceptualizations and working approaches to employment equity at the workplace level. The theory opens a window on the agency of organizational actors, including those who work for change inside organizations on behalf of the designated groups. But Mintzberg and Jorgensen (1987) remind us that in the end, there must be "central control" at the workplace, and that the formalization of intended policy in statutes and regulations is institutionalized in government. The implication is that emergent policy, by and large, is in the hands of those with power in the policy process – actors whose priority may not be progress toward equality.

Stakeholder Perspectives

Frustration with the limitations of the rational model stimulates a search for responses to the questions it leaves unanswered, and prompts a move from the ideal world of policy modelling to the real world of struggle over policy-related decisions and outcomes. Working from a standpoint frame of reference, I have examined the review of the act from the perspectives of the principal stakeholders in employment equity: employers, unions, and organizations representing women, persons with disabilities, racialized minorities, and Aboriginal peoples. To this list of stakeholders we must add government agencies, particularly HRDC and the CHRC, the committee, the political parties, and the Government of Canada. Each stakeholder's position on the case reflects a specific configuration of experiences, interests, aspirations, and values.

The contributions of designated group representatives, in particular, challenge the paradigm of equity as a process of forcing women, minorities, Aboriginal people, and persons with disabilities to conform to an organizational structure and culture created by and for White able-bodied men. They make reference to the act's promise that difference will be acknowledged and accommodated, and that the workplace, and its decision makers, must change. In testimony before the parliamentary committee, the suggestions of unions and representatives of designated group organizations were more nuanced, specific, and convincing regarding changes in employment equity policy than those of employer representatives. Yet the report of the committee adopted few of these ideas.

Pluralist theory suggests that the system of democracy is characterized by the opportunity for "interest groups" to be heard and to influence policy making. The committee hearings provided opportunities for union and designated group representatives to speak, but not to be heard, in the sense that their ideas were not taken up by the committee as the basis for substantive recommendations. In the words of Sandra Burt (1995, 357), "Public policy consists of actions that governments choose to take, as well as actions that they choose not to take."

A pluralist perspective and a stakeholder analysis brings into focus the realities of decision making on policy content, but does not explain the result that some stakeholders' ideas matter a great deal, while the ideas of those who know first-hand about discrimination and disadvantage count for little. Standpoint analysis makes this clear, but does not provide an explanation.

Postpositivist Lenses

The final meetings of the parliamentary committee, during which it decided on the recommendations to be offered in the report, were held in camera and not open to scrutiny. What is known is that the outcome of the legislative review of the Employment Equity Act explicitly validated the positions of employers within a competitive marketplace. The majority of the committee's recommendations dealt with assistance to employers by government, such as "clarifying" definitions, providing information and technical support, and fine-tuning supply-side labour market programs. Even the recommendations to involve unions and designated group organizations in partnerships were designed to use the knowledge of these stakeholders in developing strategies to assist employers with hiring, accommodation, and training – not to ensure that those who understand discrimination first-hand would have a voice and role in making employment equity work effectively for themselves.

In putting forward the employers' agenda, the committee's recommendations clearly reflected the assumption that the lack of progress toward equity in the workplace for Aboriginal people and persons with disabilities was attributable to deficiencies in their skills, education, or work experience, not to systemic discrimination. The committee's discourse constructed and labelled these groups as "disadvantaged" and in need of remedial programs. The issue of employers' lack of action in proactive implementation of the special measures and reasonable accommodations required by the legislation was not raised. Thus the committee's report strayed far from the purpose and intent of the Employment Equity Act. Once again, the designated groups, not the organization, are framed as in need of change.

Feminists and postpositivist theorists have developed a critique of institutional structures within which policy issues are identified and policy choices are made, and analyses of the ways in which elites exclude some problems from consideration while embracing others. This critique clearly resonates in the case under discussion. For example, despite the consensus among designated group and union witnesses that employment equity policy must recognize the specific conditions and barriers that affect women of colour, women with disabilities, Aboriginal women, and women who are triply disadvantaged, the committee chose not to recommend action to acknowledge this. Unions and designated groups proved unable to problematize the issue of multiple disadvantage, while employers' interest in being free of constraints was taken up by the committee as a central concern. An analysis of the struggle over what was constructed as an issue and what problems were left untouched can illuminate the case (Bacchi 1999).

Policy making is inherently political. Hence the question of rationality in policy decision making arises not only in relation to the content of policy choices but also in relation to how actors develop political strategies. Many of those testifying before the committee, understanding the workings of parliamentary politics and party discipline, and fearing the potentially destructive influence of the Canadian Alliance on the committee, would be wary of presenting a fundamental critique of the Employment Equity Act. Rather than tempting a damaging attack or even repeal by advocating fundamental change in the legislation, recommending administrative fine-tuning represented a safer strategy. Thus the political context may have influenced advocates of employment equity to compromise and moderate their positions on the need for change in the legislation. Equity advocates, then, may have censored themselves, disciplining and denying their own experience under employment equity so as not to lose everything in a potentially risky and high-stakes game.

This possibility engages Foucault's analysis of governmentality, or the institutionalization of power relations under the auspices of the state. Foucault (2000, 342) suggests that "power is exercised only over free subjects," who can choose among various possibilities for action. Confronting the complex systems of modern government influences individuals to monitor and control their own behaviour while believing themselves to be free (Bacchi 1999, 47). In this manner, "individuals can be governed through their freedom to choose" (Rose and Miller 1992, 201). Governments employ a variety of technologies and expert administrative processes, such as legislative reviews, structured public consultations, and program evaluations, to enact and legitimate the outcomes desired by such powerful actors as business, federal agencies, and leading political parties. Clearly, a rational/positivist frame of reference does not explain what amounts to an official endorsement of a gap between the stated purpose of state policy and what is being implemented in the name of that policy. In the words of Rose and Miller (1992, 190), "Government is a congenitally failing operation: the sublime image of a perfect regulatory machine is internal to the mind of the programmers. The world of programmes is heterogeneous, and rivalrous. Programmes complexify the real, so solutions for one programme tend to be the problems for another."

Postpositivist analysis offers a frame of reference that may fruitfully examine the power relations and institutionalized practices that shape policy making on issues such as employment equity. An understanding of why and how policy inaction and resistance to change are perpetuated is part of the unfinished business of policy research.

Conclusion

Reframing the case of the legislative review of the Employment Equity Act through the lenses of several theoretical perspectives can move us, step by step, toward an understanding of why the potential for change offered by this moment in policy development was not taken up. Clearly, policy studies must move beyond traditional assumptions and frames of reference to gain insight into the choices that create and constrain the transformative potential of public policy.

Notes

1 The term *Asian* (as in Asian Canadian) is typically used to designate people of East Asian origin, while *South Asian* refers to people whose origins are from the subcontinent.
2 The four approaches are different approaches to policy analysis. The three epistemological programs are positions that allow us to look critically at the different forms of policy analysis. There is no one-to-one link between the epistemic positions and the approaches.

References

Abella, R.S. 1984. *Equality in employment: A Royal Commission report*. Ottawa: Supply and Services Canada.
Agocs, C. 2002a. Canada's employment equity legislation and policy, 1986-2000: Unfulfilled promises. In *Workplace equality: International perspectives on legislation, policy and practice*, ed. C. Agocs, 65-89. The Hague: Kluwer Law International.
–. 2002b. Systemic discrimination in employment: Mapping the issue and the policy responses. In *Workplace equality: International perspectives on legislation, policy and practice*, ed. C. Agocs, 1-33. The Hague: Kluwer Law International.
Agocs, C., C. Burr, and F. Somerset. 1992. *Employment equity: Cooperative strategies for organizational change*. Scarborough, ON: Prentice Hall Canada.
Bacchi, C. 1999. *Women, policy, and politics*. London: Sage.
Burt, S. 1995. The several worlds of policy analysis: Traditional approaches and feminist critiques. In *Changing methods: Feminists transforming practice*, ed. S. Burt and L. Code, 357-78. Peterborough, ON: Broadview Press.
Canada. House of Commons. Standing Committee on Human Resources Development and the Status of Persons with Disabilities. 2002. *Promoting equality in the federal jurisdiction: Review of the Employment Equity Act*. June. Ottawa.
Cohen, M.D., J.G. March, and J. Olsen. 1972. A garbage can model of organizational choice. *Administrative Science Quarterly* 17(1): 1-25.
Employment and Immigration. 1988. *Employment Equity Act, Annual Report to Parliament 1988*.
Employment Equity Act. S.C. 1995, c. 44.
Foucault, M. 2000. *Power*. Essential works of Foucault, 1954-1984, vol. 3. Edited by James D. Faubion, translated by Robert Hurley. New York: New Press.
Hadley, K. 2001. *And we still ain't satisfied: Gender inequality in Canada, a status report for 2001*. Toronto: National Action Committee on the Status of Women and Centre for Social Justice.
Harding, S. 1991. *Whose science? Whose knowledge? Thinking from women's lives*. Ithaca, NY: Cornell University Press.
Holzer, H., and D. Neumark. 2000. Assessing affirmative action. *Journal of Economic Literature* 38(3): 483-568.

HRDC (Human Resources Development Canada). 2002. *Government of Canada response to the 9th Report of the Standing Committee on Human Resources Development and the Status of Persons with Disabilities.* Ottawa: Publications Social Development Canada.

–. 2003. *Annual report: Employment Equity Act, 2002.* Ottawa: Human Resources Development Canada.

Leck, J., and D. Saunders. 1992. Hiring women: The effects of Canada's Employment Equity Act. *Canadian Public Policy* 18(2): 203-20.

Lee, K. 2000. *Urban poverty in Canada: A statistical profile.* Ottawa: Canadian Council on Social Development.

Leonard, J.S. 1989. Women and affirmative action. *Journal of Economic Perspectives* 3(1): 61-75.

–. 1990. The impact of affirmative action regulation and equal employment law on Black employment. *Journal of Economic Perspectives* 4(4): 47-63.

–. 1996. Wage disparities and affirmative action in the 1980s. *American Economic Association Papers and Proceedings* 86(2): 285-93.

Lindblom, C. 1959. The science of "muddling through." *Public Administration Review* 19(2): 79-88.

Mintzberg, H., and J. Jorgensen. 1987. Emergent strategy for public policy. *Canadian Public Administration* 30(2): 214-29.

Pendakur, K., and R. Pendakur. 2002. Colour my world: Have earnings gaps for Canadian-born ethnic minorities changed over time? *Canadian Public Policy* 28(4): 489-512.

Picot, G., and F. Hou. 2003. *The rise in low-income rates among immigrants in Canada.* Research paper. Ottawa: Statistics Canada, Analytical Studies Branch.

Rogers, S. 2002. Northern Ireland – Gender, race and the new equality agenda. In *Workplace equality: International perspectives on legislation, policy and practice,* ed. C. Agocs, 201-24. The Hague: Kluwer Law International.

Rogers, W.M. III, and W.E. Spriggs. 1996. The effect of federal contractor status on racial differences in establishment-level employment shares: 1979-1992. *American Economic Association Papers and Proceedings* 86(2): 290-93.

Rose, N., and P. Miller. 1992. Political power beyond the state: Problematics of government. *British Journal of Sociology* 43(2): 173-205.

Standing Committee on Human Resources Development. 2002. Edited Committee evidence. http://www.parl.gc.ca/infocomdoc/37/1/huma/meetings/evidence.

Statistics Canada. 2003a. *Aboriginal peoples of Canada: A demographic profile.* 2001 Census: Analysis series, cat. no. 96F0030XIE2001007. Ottawa: Statistics Canada.

–. 2003b. *Canada's changing ethnocultural portrait: The changing mosaic.* 2001 Census: Analysis series, cat. no. 96F0030XIE2001008. Ottawa: Statistics Canada.

–. 2003c. *Earnings of Canadians: Making a living in the new economy.* 2001 Census: Analysis series, cat. no. 96F0030XIE2001013. Ottawa: Statistics Canada.

14

Critical Race Theory and Interest Convergence in the Backlash against Affirmative Action: Washington State and Initiative 200

Edward Taylor

In November 1998, Washington State became yet another lost battleground in the national debate on affirmative action with its passage of Initiative 200, which promised to "end discrimination" by eliminating most forms of affirmative action. Washington thus followed in the footsteps of California and Texas, where the passage of Initiative 209 and the Hopwood decision, respectively, have resulted in lower numbers of African American and Hispanic students in undergraduate and graduate programs and reversed decades of affirmative action policy in state hiring. How did fairly small, relatively homogenous Washington come to share national billing with such populous and ethnically diverse states as California and Texas as the next test case for the elimination of affirmative action? This question leads to an even more central one: how is it that affirmative action, once the bulwark of liberalism and racial progress, is looking so frail?

This chapter is the result of my quest not only to understand the story of Initiative 200, but to look at it as a useful metaphor for the failure of liberalism's promises. Critical examination of I-200 challenges both traditional liberalism and conservative calls for colour blindness. It is also an opportunity to look at the backlash against affirmative action through the lens of a newer form of oppositional scholarship called critical race theory. CRT uses a paradigm of racial realism to critique the incrementalism of liberalism and traditional civil rights programs. My purpose is to introduce some of the tenets of CRT into the national debate about affirmative action, in search of both a cogent explanation for current trends and some roadmap toward resistance and hope, rather than fatalism and despair.

Liberalism and Multiculturalism

As a political philosophy, liberalism has been the dominant force in civil rights legislation and multiculturalism (Sleeter 1996). With its commitment to equality, concern for the less well-off, and belief in government and the law as tools against oppression, liberalism's values are more aligned with antidiscrimination movements than are conservative philosophies. Because of its reliance on political and legal strategies, progress is stepwise, sometimes requiring healthy doses of patience. But its promise is optimistic: as time goes on, truth will be revealed and things will change for the better. Liberalism, however, has been weakened by critiques from both the left and right. And its creed of certain, gradual improvement has been sorely tested as its gains are reversed by the pressure of successful legal challenges – pressure that is likely to be persistent.

In a parallel way, multiculturalism, although grounded in an era of change and a vision of equality, has seen its goals diluted. Its original activist agenda has been diminished as the political climate shifts toward "colour-blindness" and attempts at an inclusive curriculum are reduced to cultural tourism. Some adherents believe that for multiculturalism to reassert its relevance, it must openly identify and more explicitly struggle against oppression by keeping *race* at the centre of its agenda (Ladson-Billings 1994; Sleeter 1996).

Critical Race Theory

Like multiculturalism, critical race theory grew out of the civil rights movement of the 1950s and 1960s (Gay 1983). Both originated as intellectual, academic forms of resistance to oppressive social relationships. Although they share a common ancestor, they have evolved in different arenas; multicultural education is focused on the reform of educational institutions (J.A. Banks 1984), while CRT challenges legal doctrine and methodology.

Critical race theory is an eclectic and dynamic type of legal scholarship that matured during the 1980s as a result of the perceived failure of traditional civil rights litigation to produce meaningful racial reform (Taylor 1999). What started as informal exchanges between law professors and students gradually grew into a movement. Watching the gains of the civil rights era being slowly eroded sparked interest in new strategies to achieve racial justice, strategies informed by critical theory, feminism, postmodernism, and other intellectual traditions. This scholarship gradually grew into a group identity that has not only made a significant impact in the legal field, but is now being extended into areas such as education (Ladson-Billings and Tate 1995), women's studies (Crenshaw 1995; Wing 1996), and economics (Rubin 1996).

As an oppositional intellectual movement, CRT is not an abstract set of ideas or rules. Critical race scholars have identified some defining theoretical elements (Lawrence et al. 1993). The first is that racism is a normal, not aberrant or rare, fact of daily life in society, and the assumptions of White superiority are so ingrained in our political and legal structures as to be almost unrecognizable (Delgado 1995). Racial separation has complex historical and socially constructed purposes that ensure political and legal power vests in groups considered superior to people of colour (Calmore 1995a). CRT opposes the common tendency to disregard the historical context in which racial conflict was spawned. Bond (1991, 222) contends that this widespread historical illiteracy reveals "an astounding ignorance of our racist past." CRT also posits that because racism is permanent, periods of seeming progress are often followed by periods of resistance and backlash as societal forces reassert White dominance (Bell 1992). In reaction, CRT challenges the experience of Whites as the normative standard (Calmore 1995b) and grounds its conceptual framework in the distinctive experiences of people of colour (Williams 1991). This "call to context" insists that the social and experiential context of racial oppression is crucial for understanding racial dynamics, an understanding thus based on what Bell (1990) calls "racial realism."

CRT is grounded in the realities of the lived experience of racism, which has singled out, with wide consensus among Whites, African Americans and others as worthy of suppression (Crenshaw 1988). CRT thus embraces this subjectivity of perspective and openly acknowledges that perceptions of truth, fairness, and justice reflect the mindset, status, and experience of the knower. In contrast, traditional legal definitions claim neutrality and colour-blindness as the basis for the ideology of equal opportunity and meritocracy (Brown 1992; Litowitz 1997). CRT challenges those claims, noting how purportedly objective facts are used to promote the interests of the majority. Delgado (1989) points out an important distinction between the viewpoints of Blacks and Whites: Whites don't see it as their perspective, but as the truth.

One powerful way to challenge the dominant mindset of society – shared stereotypes, beliefs, and understandings – is the telling of stories. Stories can not only challenge the status quo, but help build consensus and create a shared, communal understanding. They can, at once, describe what is and what ought to be. As a result, CRT scholars often use storytelling, narrative, autobiography, and personal history as a way to engage and contest negative stereotyping. This strategy makes use of the experience of people negatively affected by racism as a primary means to confront the beliefs held *about* them by Whites. Crenshaw (1988, 1387) calls this confrontation a condition "for the development of a distinct political strategy informed by the actual conditions of black people."

CRT is deeply dissatisfied with traditional civil rights litigation and liberal reforms. Having watched the backlash against the gains of the 1960s by an increasingly conservative judiciary, CRT scholars have lost faith in traditional legal remedies. They have seen restrictive definitions of merit, fault, and causation render much current antidiscrimination law impotent. Progress in employment and contracting laws designed to end discrimination has been stalled as courts promote popular preferences at the expense of minority interests. Two commonly held ideologies have contributed to the backlash against civil rights litigation: the myths of meritocracy and colour-blindness. By relying on merit criteria, or standards, the dominant group can justify its exclusion of Blacks from positions of power, believing in its own neutrality

(Harris 1993). CRT asserts that such standards are *chosen*, not inevitable, and should be openly debated and reformed so as to no longer benefit privileged Whites alone. The neoconservative colour-blind view calls for the repeal of affirmative action and other race-based remedial programs, arguing that Whites are the true victims. CRT notes that colour-blindness makes no sense in a society in which people, on the basis of group membership alone, are treated differently. Colour-blindness allows us to ignore the racial construction of Whiteness and reinforces its privileged and oppressive position. Thus, Whiteness remains the normative standard and Blackness remains different, other, and marginal. Even worse, a rhetoric that disallows reference to race means Blacks cannot name their reality or point out racism (Taylor 1998).

A central tenet of CRT's criticism of liberalism is Bell's theory of "interest convergence": Whites will promote advances for Blacks only when those advances also promote White interests (Bell 1980). The concept of interest convergence stems from the Marxist theory that the bourgeoisie will tolerate advances for the proletariat only if these advances benefit the bourgeoisie even more. Class conflict is therefore intractable and progress is possible only through revolution.

Washington State

Washington, unlike California or Texas, is neither particularly populous nor diverse. Of its 5.5 million residents, 82.2 percent are White (Washington HECB 1997). Although there have been changes in demographic trends, none amount to seismic shifts. For the last decade, the Native American population has been steady at 2 percent and the African American population at just over 3 percent. Asian/Pacific Islander and Hispanic groups have grown, from 4 percent or so to just over 6 percent each. In a parallel way, Washington's colleges and universities are fairly homogenous. At four-year institutions, Whites make up 82 percent of students. The more rural state universities (such as Washington State University and Western Washington University) are 87 percent White (Washington HECB 1996). Undergraduate enrolments at community colleges are 19.3 percent ethnic minority and 80.7 percent White.

Washington has a racial history, which, while far from ideal, is less virulent than in many other states. The first African Americans came to Seattle around the time of the Civil War (Taylor 1994). Excluded from the main industries of logging and shipbuilding by the labour unions, most of their job opportunities were menial. Locally, there was more racial antipathy directed toward Asian immigrants and American Indians than toward African Americans, in part because of their low numbers. African Americans thus escaped the savage, organized violence prevalent in other parts of the United States and built a small but vigorous community. The progression of the twentieth century, however, saw increasing residential and educational segregation and continued severe economic hardships due to exclusionary employment practices. Nonetheless, Washington was relatively racially tolerant; for example, it was one of a handful of states that did not have antimiscegenation laws (Taylor 1994).

The civil rights movement mobilized Washington's African American population, especially in Seattle, to seek equitable economic and educational opportunities by the use of marches, sit-ins, and boycotts. Outcomes of this activism included the reduction of racial barriers in labour unions and employment practices, and a busing program that took African American students from the central district to White, suburban schools (Taylor 1994). Although busing programs have ended, in part because of objections by African American parents, a variety of affirmative action programs continue to operate.

Affirmative action programs in Washington include outreach programs in middle and high schools to encourage girls and ethnic minorities to participate in math and science, college mentorship programs targeting high schools with majority African American, Hispanic, and Asian enrolment, and training programs for those traditionally excluded from skilled trades. Affirmative action programs also help shape state hiring goals and provide opportunities for women and minority-owned businesses to receive city, county, and state contracts. For example, of nearly sixteen thousand hirings by the state over the past five years, 7 percent have been under affirmative action (Brune 1998). Notably, nearly half of those hired were White.

Responsibility for issues regarding diversity in higher education rests with the Higher Education Coordinating Board (HECB). Beginning in 1987, the board included in its master plan for higher education the goal of "establishing and implementing policies and practices that ensure the full participation of minorities in higher education programs as students, faculty, staff, and administrators" (Washington HECB 1987, 36). As part of this plan, alternative standards for admissions were established. These standards allow access for students whose combined indices of grades and standardized test scores do not meet regular admissions criteria, and take into account issues of race, income, educational attainment of family members, and college-preparatory high school courses. According to the Washington State Commission on African American Affairs (1995), White students are by far the greatest beneficiaries of the alternative standards. In 1994, for example, 978 first-time freshmen (1.4 percent of a total of 70,883 undergraduates) were admitted under the alternative standards; 80 percent were White.

Nor have policies aimed at increasing the diversity of college staff and faculty created much change. People of colour constitute 14.7 percent of staff at community colleges (as of 1996) and 9.8 percent at four-year institutions, numbers that have not changed significantly since 1990. Whites comprise 90.8 percent of faculty at four-year institutions and 88.9 percent at community colleges, also consistent proportions over this decade. Against this backdrop of modest policies and practices, the Washington State Civil Rights

Initiative emerged (Washington State Commission on African American Affairs 1995).

Initiative 200

Initiative 200 originated from the Center for Equal Opportunity, a conservative think-tank based in Washington, DC. Modelled closely on California's Proposition 209, I-200 uses the language of civil rights. In full, the text reads: "The state shall not discriminate against or grant preferential treatment to any individual or group on the basis of race, sex, colour, ethnicity, or national origin in the operation of public employment, public education, or public contracting."[1]

With the financial support of Steve Forbes, former Republican presidential candidate, and buoyed by appearances by William Bennett, drug czar under President George H.W. Bush, I-200 began collecting signatures to qualify for the ballot in 1997. Because supporters of I-200 could not collect the requisite number of signatures (8 percent of the number of votes cast in the previous election for governor) by the deadline (four months before election day), the initiative did not make it directly on to the ballot. The next option was to submit it to the legislature ten days before the start of a regular session. The state Republican party contributed statewide mailings. Forbes gave $35,000 to the campaign, much of it in the three weeks before the deadline for signatures, and over $10,000 for radio ads primarily heard on KVI-AM. I-200 came to public consciousness through the efforts of John Carlson, a conservative talk-show host at KVI-AM and chair of the I-200 campaign. Affirmative action became the daily subject for his radio call-in show. Management concerns about this "one-beat" programming (as well as low ratings) led to his ouster from KVI in February 1998 (Serrano 1998).

I-200 came to national awareness with a *New York Times* story in December 1997 that chronicled the unusual experience of signature gatherers recruited by a firm hired by the I-200 campaign. African Americans from California and the Midwest had been offered bus fare, meals, motel expenses, and $600 a week to work on a "civil rights drive." Pro Mayes, from Rancho Tehama, California, said the recruiter came to his house and "brought my family a turkey for Thanksgiving" (in Egan 1997). For many, it seemed like a good opportunity to earn Christmas money. Five African Americans, including one disabled woman and a homeless man, were bused to Seattle.

Problems arose as soon as they began work. "I was getting cursed at by people and having a lot of trouble getting signatures," said Arthur Tillis, of Chicago. "Then I finally read the thing real carefully and I said: 'Wait a minute. This is against affirmative action. It's not a civil rights thing like it says.'" Beverly Mosely of Milwaukee had a similar experience. "I got all the way to Seattle and they still wouldn't tell me what the initiative was all about. I'm out there with a clipboard and a couple of people came up to me and said, 'Do you know what you're doing?' I said yes. Getting signatures to keep affirmative action from being abolished. After reading it real carefully, then, let me tell you: I decided I would never sign something like this myself." All left the state, broke and discouraged. "They wanted some black faces," said Tyrone Wells of Toledo, Ohio. "We were used." Mayes summed up his feelings: "You want to know what this whole thing really cost me? My pride. I was duped. And now I got nothing to bring home to my two kids" (in Egan 1997).

According to Sherry Bockwinkel, the owner of the recruiting firm: "The only way they could be misled is if they can't read. Petitioners are motivated by money. They tend to be lazy. If they say they were misled, they are lying" (in Egan 1997). Dee Jones, who hired the workers, said they were fired for failing to meet their quotas: "All they wanted to do was sleep and treat this like a vacation" (in Brune and Serrano 1998, A1).

Carlson, the campaign manager, defended the use of African Americans. He said, "You want people who are known as 'horses,' people who can get the signatures, and get them fast. You don't want people with little or no experience of any race." He denied race was a factor in the petition drive and said that, although the ballot measure "deliberately borrows" language from the 1964 Civil Rights Act, it is not misleading. In his view, "This initiative will restore the moral principal of protecting all Americans from discrimination" (in Egan 1997).

This borrowed language has been controversial. When Proposition 209 passed in California, exit polling showed that 28 percent of those who had voted in favour did not realize that 209 banned affirmative action (Foster 1997). A similar measure banning affirmative action in the city of Houston failed after Mayor Bob Lanier insisted that Proposition A be described as ending affirmative action. This choice of wording was believed to be a key factor in voters' rejection of Proposition A. The American Civil Liberties Union went to the Thurston County Superior Court in Washington to have the words "affirmative action" added to the language of Initiative 200, but the judge ruled against changing the language. The state attorney general's office, which wrote the title and text of the initiative, had decided to basically reflect the language that was in the initial proposed ballot, "trusting that voters would make an informed choice if and when the time comes" and deliberately avoiding "loaded" terms, said James Pharris, senior assistant state attorney general (in King 1997).

I-200 obtained the 180,000 signatures required to be submitted to the Washington State Legislature. Without enough support to pass (35 of 98 House members and 17 of 49 senators), the initiative was referred to the November election ballot as a referendum (Initiative process 1997). It was approved by 58 percent of the voters. Buoyed by this success, national opponents of affirmative action discussed pursuing similar ballot measures in Florida, Nebraska, and Michigan (Holmes 1998).

Public Opinion

Like voters in California and Houston, Washington residents' opinion appeared to depend on language. Early polls (conducted by the *Seattle Times*) found 64 percent of respondents in favour of I-200. Knowing that I-200 would eliminate affirmative action in state employment, contracting, and education, support dropped to 49 percent (Postman and Brune 1998). Although 93 percent believed that racial discrimination still exists and 80 percent felt that bias against women is still a problem, 48 percent thought that affirmative action programs, while good in principle, need to be reformed. There was a significant racial gap – 55 percent of Whites and 37 percent of minorities – among those in favour of the initiative.

When views on specific affirmative action programs were polled, the response ranged widely. Eighty-five percent supported programs encouraging girls and minorities in math and science, 62 percent favoured the alternative admissions standards in higher education admissions, and 56 percent wanted to continue apprenticeship programs for those previously excluded from skilled trades. Only 44 percent defended set-asides for women and minorities in government contracting, and 36 percent endorsed specific hiring goals for women and minorities (Postman and Brune 1998). In sum, outreach (especially for White women) met with general approval; numeric goals were disliked.

How did the loss of affirmative action affect minority enrolment in colleges? At the University of Washington, for example, the number of minorities is already quite low, at 7.5 percent of entering freshmen. In the year following the passage of I-200 about 40 percent fewer African Americans, 30 percent fewer Hispanics, and 20 percent fewer Native Americans were admitted (Verhovek 1999).

I-200 through the Lens of Critical Race Theory

To examine whether the case of I-200 supports the central tenets of CRT, several issues must be addressed.

Racism as Normal

Charging racism is a volatile exercise, but much depends on how it is defined. The insistence "I'm not a racist" has become the defence *du jour* of even the most blatant of hate criminals. Indeed, when racism is defined as specific, individual acts against persons of colour, most Whites can rightly deny this charge. They see themselves as good and fair people, not as members of a group that enjoys special, undeserved privileges. Such a perspective is distressing, and many Whites react with defensiveness and withdrawal if confronted.

If, on the other hand, racism is defined as a political and social force that has benefited a certain group, through no single action on the part of individuals, the terms change. If those benefits include nonsegregated housing, employment opportunities reserved for persons of European ancestry, access to better schools, absence of organized racial violence, and protection from negative racial stereotyping, the net casts wide. Almost no White can reasonably claim to have avoided some of the privileges that are part and parcel of Whiteness. Then the equation inverts. As Sleeter (1996, 30) asserts, "I am a racist ... because I benefit from racism."

Rather than attempting to prove widespread acts of racial discrimination against ethnic minorities in Washington State, we must examine the centrality, and invisibility of, White privilege. The problem in Washington is the multitude of benefits extended to the majority population by virtue of group membership – benefits enjoyed at the expense, and exclusion, of others. Affirmative action programs attempt to widen some of this privilege base with women and people of colour. But many perceive such programs as victimizing deserving and honest people who are not personally guilty of racist acts.

Ultimately, I-200 enshrines the view that the protection of "innocent" Whites from displacement is more important than the protection of ethnic minorities from long-standing, "normal," race-based exclusion, although nearly all agree that racial and gender discrimination still exist. Crenshaw (1988, 1342) describes this dilemma: "Even when injustice is found, efforts to redress it must be balanced against, and limited by, competing interests of white workers – even when those interests were actually created by the subordination of Blacks. The innocence of whites weighs more heavily than do the past wrongs committed upon Blacks and the benefits that whites derived from these wrongs."

The Role of Social/Historical Context

Perhaps because of its relatively benign history, at least as compared to the South, Washington voters may be relying on a "things haven't been that bad here" theory. Thus, the groundwork is laid for assumptions about equality in opportunities for jobs, contracts, and college preparation. The systemic ways in which the majority has favoured its own in housing, employment, schooling, and contracting, to name a few, are not seen as aberrant or unjust.

The reasoning goes something like this: although there is a history of racial and gender discrimination in Washington (that still exists), it is now time to end programs designed to reverse its effects. Affirmative action has been a useful tool to give women and minorities equal opportunity but is no longer needed. Such policies force employers to hire unqualified women and minorities over qualified White men (Postman and Brune 1998).

I-200 guides the state into what Tushnet (1996) calls the "we've done enough" phase. He says that a common pattern in antidiscrimination law is that, after Whites have one of their periodic outbursts of support for minorities, particularly African Americans, they eventually and inevitably decide to reverse themselves.

Narrative

Narrative plays two roles in the story of Initiative 200. First is the priority of myths of affirmative action over the notably absent voices of minorities or women and their experiences seeking college admissions, public employment, promotions, or public contracting. Second is the curious story of the African Americans recruited to gather signatures.

Stories wield influence, perhaps more than they should. Think scientifically, as the saying goes, act anecdotally. In the case against affirmative action, a story of almost mythic proportions is told of the child of a neighbour who did not get accepted into his college of choice because of minority set-asides. There are the reports of the friend not hired by the school district because of "diversity needs," or the long-deserved promotion lost to someone less qualified. This collective account, now deeply and widely held, fuels a feeling of despair at the senselessness of it all. I-200 taps into these stories, and data-based evidence that affirmative action has largely benefited Whites seems to hold little sway.

What I-200 avoids are the stories of those who have lived lives continuously shaped, and limited, by racism and sexism in schooling and employment. It is unclear if Whites possess a collective consciousness of these stories: the grandmothers who spent lives scrubbing floors, the fathers denied all but the most menial of jobs, the school counsellors who insisted on shop classes or home economics rather than algebra. These experiences have forged a collective consciousness for African Americans and feminists that have informed a political agenda. I-200 ignores, by necessity, this collective identity. The terms of the debate are defined by a rhetoric that does not permit the telling of these stories, much less access to a reservoir of public support.

The unusual story of the I-200 signature gatherers illustrates this point. The decision of I-200 to recruit African Americans was disingenuous at best, cynical at worst. Some Whites, who felt they were misled, asked to have their names removed from the initiative. As one sociology professor remarked, "I guess I thought that African Americans, being a minority, would not engage in any activity that would make their life chances less." In a similar paradox, the initiative used race-neutral language to advance a race-based cause. John Carlson's confusing justification of the signature gatherers underscored this quandary: race was not a factor in the petition drive, he insisted, yet, "You don't want people with little or no experience of any race" (in Egan 1997, A12). The explanation offered by Sherry Bockwinkel was more direct, charging that the African Americans couldn't read, were lazy, and were lying. These accusations resonate deeply with commonly held stereotypes about African Americans. Claims of race-neutrality, however, make defence difficult.

Interest Convergence

Assessing the degree of interest convergence in affirmative action programs requires some tally of advantages. But such interests are difficult to measure. In a state with a relatively small minority population, race-specific policies and goals have a correspondingly small impact. And, when over 70 percent of the state workforce qualifies for consideration under affirmative action (women plus minorities), interest divergence and convergence are hard to distinguish. Although the case can be made that Whites, especially White women, have benefited considerably, it does not change public perception that affirmative action is about favouritism for unqualified Blacks (Sniderman and Carmines 1997).

Does the popularity of I-200 then contradict the principle of interest convergence? Would not programs that benefit Whites enjoy the support of other Whites? That turns out to be true for those programs that target Whites, such as those promoting math and science to girls or assisting displaced homemakers. Those that specify race, for hiring goals or contract set-asides, are distinctly unpopular. What appears to be objectionable about affirmative action in Washington State is not its Whiteness, but its Blackness.

Sniderman and Carmines (1997) have conducted extensive national public opinion polls about affirmative action using computer-assisted interviewing. They found White opposition to affirmative action is "intense, unvarying, and pervasive" and that its primary beneficiaries are believed to be Black (30). In fact, the mere mention of affirmative action causes Whites to significantly increase their expressed dislike for Blacks and makes them more likely to describe Blacks as lazy, irresponsible, and arrogant (39). This is true for men and women of all classes, and true for self-described liberals (57 percent), Democrats (65 percent), and Republicans (64 percent). Whites also overwhelmingly believe that most Blacks are poor and violent.

Although national studies of public opinion have shown an overall reduction in overt racial prejudice, Sniderman and Carmines found no shortage of Whites who are willing to admit their racist stereotypes: 52 percent describe Blacks as violent, 45 percent as boastful, 42 percent as complaining, and 34 percent as lazy. The authors comment: "Given that it is virtually cost-free to say something nice about Black Americans in the course of a public opinion interview, what is striking is how few white Americans actually do. Apart from a general willingness of 3 out of 4 whites to describe Blacks as 'friendly' – surely as innocuous a positive quality as one can imagine – only a modest majority of whites are willing to attribute specific positive characteristics to most Blacks" (Sniderman and Carmines 1997, 61).

Because of these widespread anti-Black sentiments, Sniderman and Carmines recommend that future attempts to garner support for affirmative action policies refrain from any mention of race. They also note that arguments based on underrepresentation or a history of discrimination are fairly ineffective. Even if a company has a proven policy of racist hiring policies, support for affirmative action goes only to 42 percent from 21 percent. Rather, they suggest changing the terms of the argument to the grounds of moral principles centred on broader views of social justice. This colour-blind strategy, they believe, can increase the support of both prejudiced and self-interested Whites. For example, affirmative action policies aimed at helping the poor or disabled, if they specifically avoid any mention of race, can garner support from up to two-thirds of Whites (Sniderman and Carmines 1997, 25). Such a strategy, they maintain, does not rely on interest convergence but on common, shared principles of fairness and justice.

This is a distinction without much difference. Others have argued that replacing race- and gender-based affirmative action with a need-based approach is not an adequate substitute but will, because of absolute numbers, redirect resources back to White males (Feinberg 1997). Nonetheless, Sniderman and Carmines' point was not lost on the "No I-200" campaign. Its ineffective strategy was to avoid mention of race and appeal to White men who might worry that their daughters or wives could be denied equal pay or benefits, or lose funding to participate in sports. Appeals to economic prosperity (again, avoiding any mention of race) were the thrust of a series of full-page ads in the *Seattle Times* endorsed by Microsoft, Boeing, and others that urged votes against I-200 "Because it's bad for business" (No. I-200 Campaign 1998).

Conclusion

The case of I-200 not only illustrates and confirms some of the tenets of critical race theory, but suggests CRT as a model with explanatory power. The counterargument, however, is that the I-200 supporters believe they are endorsing fundamental principles of fairness. It is unfair to discriminate by race or gender in public hiring, contracting, or college admissions. Affirmative action discriminates against people who, by no fault of their own, lose out to women and minorities. And, despite their commitment to ideals of justice, they are being criticized as racist.

What has gone wrong? CRT believes that the problem lies in the methods and process of our legal system, where insistence on race-neutral language has negated the social and historical context of racial exclusion and White privilege. Worse still, the benefits of this context go unrecognized and unchallenged. Brown (1992), in her analysis of the legal principles of race-neutrality, points out the fallacious assumption that Blacks and Whites occupy equal positions in society. By disengaging cases from their historical context, in a process known as "disaggregation," the legal process removes the voices of people harmed by racism and refuses to acknowledge the deeply held beliefs of Black inferiority and White superiority.

In the case of I-200, although White women, veterans, and persons with disabilities have also had their opportunities widened by affirmative action, the greater concern is the protection of those Whites displaced by such policies. In short, protecting Whites trumps protecting Blacks.

For advocates of affirmative action, the options come down to trust in traditional liberalism or racial realism. This distinction is more than an academic exercise. The choice between the two makes all the difference, not only in how we conceptualize and formulate public policy, but in how we vote. Liberalism, to its discredit, has underestimated the depth of resentment among Whites for race-based policies and has avoided facing the contradiction between its stated goal of racial equality and its reluctance to confront White privilege. Liberalism may be too weakened to mount a serious defence of affirmative action.

Not all critical race theorists agree with this dismissal of liberalism. Crenshaw (1988) has argued that liberal ideology, although far from being perfect, has visionary ideals that should be developed. She also notes that, given the limited range of options for Blacks to challenge racism, liberalism should not be too quickly discarded. As such, she follows in the tradition of the activists discussed by Johnson (Chapter 2).

Racial realism, on the other hand, directly confronts racism and White privilege. This approach offends many, who accuse it of excessive cynicism and nihilism. Yet Cornel West (1995, xi) says that CRT "compels us to confront critically the most explosive issue in American civilization: the historical centrality and complicity of law in upholding white supremacy." For those attempting to make sense of the legal and political trends toward ending affirmative action, CRT makes several challenges. First is the importance of keeping race and racism at the centre of the argument. Second is to acknowledge the debate in its historic and social context. Third is the call to pay attention to the real life experiences of African Americans. CRT's usefulness in formulating political and policy strategy remains to be seen, but the utility of some of its principles is demonstrated in two recent works on affirmative action, a study by William Bowen and Derek Bok, and President Clinton's review of federal practices.

In one of the largest studies of African Americans affected by affirmative action, Bowen and Bok (1998) tracked the lives of over 45,000 students admitted to highly selective colleges under racial preferences. Their data underscore the success of affirmative action in creating a generation of African American intellectual, professional, and community leadership. By focusing attention on the experiences of these students and their lives after college, Bok and Bowen help publicize the accomplishments of race-factored admissions policies and reveal us as a nation that has not only rejected, but is actively reversing, its racist past.

President Clinton's 1996 order for a review of the federal government's affirmative action policy also utilized several methods of CRT. By tracing the long history of US racial and gender discrimination, and presenting not only numeric data, but detailed stories of the experiences of random testers documenting widespread racist disparities in hiring practices, the Clinton administration was able to support its "Mend it, don't end it" policy. In this way, the debate was placed in its historical and social context, systemic racist practices were revealed, and valid concerns about fairness and effectiveness could still be addressed (Stephanopoulos and Edley 1995).

What can CRT offer multiculturalism? Both are descendants of that proud forebear, the civil rights movement, and are inspired by centuries of African American resistance. Both must respond to the backlash against affirmative action, even if such efforts, as in the case of I-200, seem in vain. As well as informing the debate on affirmative action, CRT can help articulate and reinvigorate multiculturalism's political roots. A dose of racial realism may be needed to discover a new vision and the will to struggle toward that vision, whether it be the dream of a workforce and classrooms that genuinely reflect our nation's diversity or the hope of a multicultural curriculum so authentic and powerful as to eradicate racism and sexism in our society. The likelihood of this happening may seem as remote a hope as freedom must have seemed for our chained ancestors. Their heroism and ultimate victory lay not in armed revolt or illustrious gestures, but in the cumulative effect of countless small acts of resistance. In the same way, we prevail by the act of resistance itself. For when we begin to question our own assumptions and privileges, to resist stereotyping, classism, and patriarchy, and to critically examine the contextualized, racial meanings of our lives – it is at that point we are triumphant.

Notes

An earlier version of this chapter appeared in *Teachers College Record* 102, 3 (2000): 539-60.

1 State affirmative action hiring programs for Vietnam-era veterans, veterans with disabilities, and disabled persons are exempt from this ban. Collegiate athletic programs are immune. Whether recruiting efforts for minority students would also be prohibited remains unclear.

References

Banks, J.A. 1984. Multicultural education and its critics: Britain and the United States. *New Era* 65: 58-65.

Bell, D. 1980. *Brown* v. *Board of Education* and the interest-convergence dilemma. *Harvard Law Review* 93: 518-33.

–. 1990. After we're gone: Prudent speculations on America in a post-racial epoch. *St. Louis Law Journal* 34: 393, 397-400.

–. 1992. *Faces at the bottom of the well: The permanence of racism.* New York: Basic Books.

Bond, J. 1991. Reconstruction and the southern movement for civil rights – Then and now. *Teachers College Record* 93(2): 221-35.

Bowen, W.G., and D. Bok. 1998. *The shape of the river: Long-term consequences of considering race in college and university admissions.* Princeton, NJ: Princeton University Press.

Brown, W.R. 1992. The convergence of neutrality and choice: The limits of the state's affirmative duty to provide equal educational opportunity. *Tennessee Law Review* 60: 63-133.

Brune, T. 1998. I-200 backers faulted over gifts. *Seattle Times,* 3 July, B1, B2.

Brune, T., and B.A. Serrano. 1998. Signature gatherers, their race becomes issues, Initiative 200 effort. *Seattle Times,* 12 December, A1, A22.

Calmore, J.O. 1995a. Critical race theory, Archie Shepp, and fire music: Securing an authentic intellectual life in a multicultural world. In *Critical race theory: The key writings that formed the movement,* ed. K.W. Crenshaw, N. Gotanda, G. Peller, and K. Thomas, 315-29. New York: New Press.

–. 1995b. Racialized space and the culture of segregation: "Hewing a stone of hope from a mountain of despair." *University of Pennsylvania Law Review* 143: 1233-73.

Crenshaw, K.W. 1988. Race, reform, and retrenchment: Transformation and legitimation in antidiscrimination law. *Harvard Law Review* 101: 1331-87.

–. 1995. Mapping the margins: Intersectionality, identity politics, and violence against women of color. In *Critical race theory: The key writings that formed the movement,* ed. K.W. Crenshaw, N. Gotanda, G. Peller, and K. Thomas, 357-83. New York: New Press.

Delgado, R. 1989. Storytelling for oppositionists and others: A plea for narrative. *Michigan Law Review* 87: 2411-41.

–, ed. 1995. *Critical race theory: The cutting edge.* Philadelphia: Temple University Press.

Egan, T. 1997. Blacks recruited by "rights" drive to end preferences. *New York Times,* December 17, A12.

Feinberg, W. 1997. Affirmative action and beyond: A case for a backward-looking gender- and race-based policy. *Teachers College Record* 97(3): 362-81.

Foster, H. 1997. I-200 nets signatures – and a controversy. *Seattle Post-Intelligencer,* 31 December, A1, A4.

Gay, G. 1983. Multiethnic education: Historical developments and future prospects. *Phi Delta Kappan* 64: 560-63.

Harris, C.I. 1993. Whiteness as property. *Harvard Law Review* 106: 1707-91.

Holmes, S. 1998. Victorious preference foes look for new battlefields. *New York Times,* 10 November, A23.

Initiative process compromised again. 1997. *Seattle Times,* 17 December, A16.

King, M. 1997. Debate over affirmative action moves to this state. *Seattle Times,* 13 November. http://www.seattletimes.com.

Ladson-Billings, G. 1994. *The dreamkeepers: Successful teachers of African American children.* San Francisco: Jossey-Bass.

Ladson-Billings, G., and W.F. Tate. 1995. Toward a critical race theory of education. *Teachers College Record* 97: 47-68.

Lawrence, C.R., M.J. Matsuda, R. Delgado, and K.W. Crenshaw. 1993. *Words that wound: Critical race theory, assaultive speech, and the First Amendment.* Boulder, CO: Westview Press.

Litowitz, D.E. 1997. Some critical thoughts on critical race theory. *Notre Dame Law Review* 72(2): 503-29.

No. I-200 Campaign. Because it's bad for business. 1998. Advertisement. *Seattle Times,* 6 September, A22.

Postman, D., and T. Brune. 1998. Across state, thirst is strong for reforming affirmative action. *Seattle Times,* 12 July, A1, A8-9.

Rubin, E.L. 1996. The new legal process, the synthesis of discourse, and the microanalysis of institutions. *Harvard Law Review* 109: 1393-1438.

Serrano, B.A. 1998. Carlson out at KVI over I-200 focus. *Seattle Times,* 4 February, A1, A10.

Sleeter, C.E. 1996. *Multicultural education as social activism.* Albany: State University of New York Press.

Sniderman, M., and E.G. Carmines. 1997. *Reaching beyond race.* Cambridge, MA: Harvard University Press.

Stephanopoulos, G., and C. Edley. 1995. *Review of federal affirmative action programs.* Report to the President. http://ucblibraries.colorado.edu/govpubs.

Taylor, E. 1998. Critical race theory, a primer. *Journal of Blacks in Higher Education* 6: 122-25.

–. 1999. Critical race theory and interest convergence in the desegregation of higher education. In *Race is ... race isn't: Critical race theory and qualitative studies in education*, ed. L. Parker, D. Deyhle, and S. Villenas, 181-204. Boulder, CO: Westview.

Taylor, Q. 1994. *The forging of a black community: Seattle's Central District from 1870 through the civil rights era*. Seattle: University of Washington Press.

Tushnet, M.V. 1996. The "We've done enough" theory of school desegregation. *Howard Law Journal* 39(3): 767-79.

Verhovek, S.H. 1999. Gates, "Spreading the wealth," makes scholarship gift official. *New York Times*, 17 September, A19.

Washington State Commission on African American Affairs. 1995. *Affirmative action: Who's really benefiting? Part II on public higher education*. November. Olympia: Commission on African American Affairs.

Washington State HECB (Higher Education Coordinating Board). 1987. *The Washington State master plan for higher education*. Olympia: HECB.

–. 1996. Briefing paper on affirmative action and diversity. April. Olympia: HECB.

–. 1997. *1997 Statewide progress report on diversity and participation of people of color in higher education*. December. Olympia: HECB.

West, C. 1995. Foreword. In *Critical race theory: The key writings that formed the movement*, ed. K. Crenshaw, N. Gotanda, G. Peller, and K. Thomas, xi-xii. New York: New Press.

Williams, J. 1991. *The alchemy of race and rights: Diary of a law professor*. Cambridge, MA: Harvard University Press.

Wing, A.K. 1996. Critical race feminism and the international human rights of women in Bosnia, Palestine, and South Africa: Issues for LitCrit Theory. *University of Miami Inter American Law Review* 28(2): 337-60.

15
Dialogue across Borders on Employment Equity/ Affirmative Action
Michelle Goldberg

Over the last several decades we have seen great strides toward equity for racial minority groups and women. Recently, however, we have seen a backlash against the diversity policies that have created the space for such progress. This trend is appearing in countries around the world, but will be analyzed here through a specific focus on employment equity (EE) in Canada and affirmative action (AA) policies in the United States.[1] As discussed in the previous two chapters, diversity policy is being dismantled and the gap between racial minorities and Whites is widening. Furthermore, even where these policies are in place, their ineffectiveness is clear. Drawing on evidence from both Canada and the United States, this chapter will examine how this dismantling process operates, and why the existing policies produce limited results. I will use critical discourse analysis to add another level of explanation to conventional theorizations by examining the similar discursive strategies used in both countries to dismantle and disarm EE/AA policies. My goal is to highlight the strong parallels between Canada and the United States in the EE/AA policy arena and explore how we might work together to inform the debate in each country and develop counterdiscourses as forms of resistance and change.

Discourse Framework
Carol Agocs and Edward Taylor both stress in their chapters that the epistemological frame of reference used to approach a problem affects the solution. Therefore, we need to specify clearly the theoretical lens used when conducting our work, so that our values, beliefs, and assumptions are made visible. For, as Taylor writes, "perceptions of truth, fairness, and justice reflect the mindset, status, and experience of the knower" (Chapter 14). We cannot be objective. Our subjectivity sets the foundation for our work and as such must be outlined before we begin, so that we can recognize its influence on us.

Agocs uses various epistemological programs of feminist thought to analyze the effectiveness of employment equity legislation in Canada. While she agrees that there is a benefit to all approaches, and more specifically to using several approaches to answer the same problem (frame shifting), she claims that we must move beyond traditional assumptions and frames of reference to address the power relations, institutional practices, and political forces that affect policy research. The postpositivist feminist approach she endorses addresses these issues. This postmodern approach "challenges conventional assumptions of rationality and truth, pointing to the social construction of knowledge claims within contexts of power relations" (Agocs, Chapter 13).

Taylor's chapter uses the theoretical framework of critical race theory, which, like postmodern feminist approaches, sees knowledge and truth as socially constructed. According to Taylor, the following points outline the basic tenets of CRT:

1 Race and racism must be kept at the centre of the argument.
2 The debate must be situated in its historical and social context.
3 The study must be grounded in the real life experiences (narratives) of people affected by racism.
4 Racism must be seen as a normal fact of everyday life, because White superiority is so ingrained that it is almost invisible.

Policy and its effects must therefore be studied with an understanding of the surrounding historical institutional power relations enacted through racial hierarchies.

This paper follows in a vein similar to the frameworks described by Agocs and Taylor but goes one step further. That is, while I recognize the social construction of knowledge and truth, I also focus on the role of discourse in this process.[2] Consequently, I investigate how power operates through discourse. This framework builds on Foucault's claim that the study of power must be located in discursive activity, for "relations of power cannot themselves be established, consolidated nor implemented without the production, accumulation, circulation and functioning of a discourse" (1980, 93). I also draw on Foucault's constitutive view of discourses as "practices that systematically form the objects of which they speak ... Discourses are not about objects; they do not identify objects, they constitute them and in the practice of doing so they conceal their own invention" (1974, 49). As a result, I view reality as socially constructed through discourse; that is, reality is discursively constructed. Finally, this framework also draws on Foucault's performative function of discourse. Discourse is action – it is something we both say and do – and thus produces knowledge or what counts as "truth": "Language does not report on the world but is itself performative of action in that world" (Austin quoted in Hughes 1990, 117). As such, the discursive strategies used in debating EE/AA policies actually dismantle and make them ineffective in achieving equality for racial minority groups and women.

Basically, I see discourse operating as a technology. This notion is similar to Foucault's concept of strategy, in that discourse "is the totality of means put into operation to implement power effectively or to maintain it" (1982, 225). Discourse is the series of rules that enable and constrain material relations of power. As the rules develop, they have the tendency to privilege some people and disadvantage others. Discourse organizes knowledge, produces truth, and accomplishes social relations by structuring thoughts and behaviours. Because this discursive process is largely unconscious, it makes invisible the exercise of power. That is why it is so crucial that we study the operation of discourse: discourse is everywhere, it operates in everyday social interactions, and its operation is taken for granted.

But first a word of caution: language on its own is not the cause of inequities. "Language has little power when it is separated from powerful institutions and people. The power of language comes from what it is used to do: the discursive practices in which it is sited" (Corson 1998, 114). Thus, while I do believe in the power of discourse to structure reality, we cannot overvalue the linguistic and representational powers of language in isolation from material arrangements of power. Power is not a function of the text alone. We cannot attribute power to the internal properties and structure of language, because the power in language links to, and stems from, external, material and tactical forms of power. According to Hook (2001, 530), "Power in no uncertain terms cannot be fixed or apprehended in the meanings and significations of texts, but must be grasped and traced through the analysis of tactical and material relations of force." Thus, while racism and discrimination are the cause of inequalities, they operate through the wider discourses that surround us.

The benefit of this discursive framework is that it allows us to recognize discourses for what they are and what they do. More specifically, we can further examine how power operates through discourse in the social construction of material relations. In this way, we see reality as discursively constructed. We also, however, need to recognize discourse as socially constructed. It is important to recognize the dialectical relationship between reality and discourse. If discourse is socially constructed, in that individuals create it, then individuals can also change it. Social actors can, and do, create conditions that allow for the construction and circulation of counterdiscourses as strategies of resistance that work for, rather than against, groups that have not been well-served by dominant discourses (Ryan 1999). We therefore need to analyze discourse to reveal how racism and discrimination operate, and to develop counterdiscourses. This analysis will further illustrate how policy making is inherently political; we cannot ignore power relations operating in the process.

Discourse operates at two levels: the societal and individual. Societal level discourses are similar to the historical and social context of racism in critical race theory. Discourses operating at the individual level are congruent with CRT's focus on narrative. Thus, analyzing discourse is a way of getting at the context and individual personal life experiences that are so critical to understanding a problem. I examine the three major discursive themes that emerge in the media, government press releases, and policy documents as a proxy for societal discourses and link them to individual discourses.

Discursive Strategies That Undermine EE/AA Policies

Symbolic Discourse

In both Canada and the United States, symbolic or decorative discourse is used in EE/AA policies and in empty exercises of review and improvement. In the United States, for example, "the contractor will not discriminate ... and the contractor will take affirmative action" (Equal Employment Opportunity 1965). In Canada, the Employment Equity Act (1995) states that its purpose "is to achieve equality in the workplace" (s. 2). This discourse is effectively empty, because it is so vague that it cannot be enforced. Furthermore, the Employment Equity Act does not require the employer to comply if it would cause "undue hardship." Much of the discussion in both policy documents focuses on the maintaining of records and the completing of compliance reports instead of on what equity means. The Canadian legislation does not have any sanctions for failure to comply with employment equity, only for failure to produce an employment equity plan or report. Both the act and the US regulation say that in such cases action can be referred to another agency (e.g., the Canadian Human Rights Commission or US civil rights legislation). In Canada, however, the Human Rights Commission is ineffective in these cases: an organization can be charged only for an *intent* to discriminate; the charge cannot be based on the outcome that occurred. Furthermore, there are inadequate resources for enforcement of these policies in both countries, which creates a sense of illegitimacy and, more concretely, a backlog of cases.

Another reason the discourse is considered symbolic is that there is no consistency across different diversity policies or across different provinces or states. For example, Canada has a federal Employment Equity Act, but only one province has complementary legislation. A further contradictory message was given in 1995 when the large, diverse province of Ontario replaced its provincial Employment Equity Act with a voluntary Equal Opportunity Plan (discussed below).

Symbolic discourse also occurs in empty legislative review processes. As seen in Agocs' chapter, a lengthy review of the 1995 Employment Equity Act included eleven meetings and testimonies from stakeholders, unions, employers, and expert witnesses. A report with twenty-nine recommendations resulted, but "none of [the recommendations] involved substantial amendments to the Employment Equity Act" (Agocs, Chapter 13). The recommendations mainly suggested further research or fine-tuning. This analysis also lends support to other research conducted on commissions of inquiry (see, for example, Ashforth 1990).

A Discourse of Neoliberalism

A second discursive strategy used to dismantle employment equity and affirmative action policies in Canada and the United States is the reliance upon a neoliberal ideology. This neoliberal discourse claims to be fair and colour-blind as it endorses equal opportunity and meritocracy as the foundation of equity policies. For example, in Ontario the government labels its Equal Opportunity Plan "a merit-based, inclusive and voluntary approach to fairness in the workplace" (Government of Ontario 1995b). Unpacking this discursive umbrella we see three things occurring. First, this neoliberal discourse endorses equal opportunity. This discourse argues for equal treatment instead of equal outcomes, failing to recognize that we can treat people differently in order to treat them fairly. As the premier of Ontario stated: "I want to build an Ontario in which people are judged by their qualifications ... That calls for equality of opportunity – not the legislated equality of outcome" (Government of Ontario 1995c). Employment equity is thus labelled unfair, because instead of treating all people the same, some people are given special treatment. As Ontario citizenship minister Marilyn Mushinski said, "Women, aboriginals, and minorities shouldn't get special treatment when applying for a job" (in Wallace 1995).

Related closely to this theme of equal opportunity is one of meritocracy. As is seen in the government discourse above, the claim is made that people should be hired based on their merit, not because they belong to a designated group. This discourse devalues minority groups by assuming that they are hired based on their membership in a designated group, not based on their qualifications, while the best person for the job is overlooked, that is, the person with "merit." Minority groups and women are thus socially constructed as persons with deficiencies in skills, education, and work experience – as individuals without merit. This discourse is reinforced in the media: "Police forces and fire departments, when faced with the NDP [New Democratic Party] quota law, were forced to lower testing and physical fitness standards to fill employment equity quotas" (Buckorough 1996).

This notion of merit also stems from neoliberalism's individualistic model of social justice. This model fails to recognize that certain rules can have systematic effects on groups and individuals by virtue of their membership in those groups. Neoliberal discourse claims merit criteria are neutral and fair, but critical discourse analysis shows that they are defined by power. We need to critically examine what is defined as merit and whose interests are served by how it is defined.

The two themes above lead to a third outcome, as this discourse of equal opportunity and meritocracy sets the stage for backlash and a complementary discourse of reverse discrimination to emerge. An us/them dichotomy is created that fosters competition between groups. This notion works in combination with a zero-sum mentality that suggests "there is a finite number of opportunities for 'others'" so that the advancement of one group must be to the detriment of another (Bacchi 1996, 24). Groups are thus encouraged to take up positions against one another. Critics are also able to argue that in EE/AA the "rights of the few are affirmed over those of the many" (Ruiz 1984, 13). Backlash and reverse discrimination are seen when White men are portrayed as victims of equity policies, since they are allegedly passed over for jobs that employers must give to unqualified women and members of minority groups.

In sum, we see how a neoliberal ideological discourse of equal opportunity and meritocracy helps to dismantle EE/AA policies and make them ineffective. This discourse claims equal treatment instead of equal outcomes. In so doing, minorities and women are socially constructed as unqualified, for if everyone is treated equally, and minorities do not achieve labour market equality, they must not possess equal skills. This discourse blames the victim. When groups are labelled as different and inferior, it becomes difficult to argue that they should have equal employment outcomes. Under this discursive regime, equity policies are easily dismantled, because regulation is labelled unnecessary and intrusive. Only policies that "encourage" designated groups to apply for jobs, or that remove "obviously discriminatory" policies, are considered acceptable. These soft reforms appear legitimate, and strong measures are rendered illegitimate and inequitable. Corrective measures of hiring from a designated group are thus thwarted, and injustices remain.

Economic Rationalism/Competitive Marketplace Discourse

Tied closely to the neoliberal justice discourse is the discourse of economic rationalism. One of its key features is the use of gender- and race-neutral language in the argument for employment equity and affirmative action policies. Instead of focusing on equity for women and minorities, a discourse on the economic advantage of equitable workforces or "diversity is good for business" is used. For instance, we see claims such as "utilizing the talents of all Ontarians in our workforce is not only fair and equitable, but it also makes good economic sense" (Government of Ontario 1992). An influential report by the Conference Board of Canada (1999) makes the business case for hiring from diverse groups by appealing to an organization's need to compete in the global marketplace and in the increasing ethnocultural diversity of Canadian markets. The Ontario government drew on this discourse as it promoted its Equal Opportunity Plan: "Employers know that maximizing the skills, talents and creativity of a diverse workforce is key to competitive success. Encouraging equal opportunity is one way of gaining and maintaining that competitive edge" (Government of Ontario 1995a).

Ontario employers bought into this discourse. For example, a study of Ontario employers (Goldberg and Corson 2001) found extensive use of the generic managing-diversity-for-economic-advantage discourse. Ontario employers claimed they valued diversity in order to meet local customer service needs, reach global markets, and do international business. They also claimed its value for competitive advantage, competitive hiring, good public relations, and good employee relations. One employer suggested that "leveraging diversity" is a better term than "valuing diversity" because it states more strongly that diversity should be tied to business objectives and used for competitive advantage: "It's not just a nice thing to do" (in Goldberg and Corson 2001, 49).

In the United States, organization gurus also promote the generic "managing/valuing/leveraging diversity" discourse. This discourse expands the definition of diversity beyond gender, race, or physical and intellectual abilities to include diversity in opinions, social customs, and other variations in lives and lifestyles (Gandz 2001). Expanding the definition of diversity in this way actually advances White privilege by including White men under the diversity umbrella. The gap between racial minorities and Whites then continues to widen as resources are redirected back to the dominant group. Moreover, organizations are rewarded for having a workforce of diverse opinions and learning styles, even though it is still made up of White men.

At first I also bought into this discourse, as it seemed like a good way to convince people of the practicality, if not the justice, of equity policies. However, further analysis reveals it to be an inadequate strategy. As Taylor (Chapter 14) claims, "Colour-blindness allows us to ignore the racial construction of Whiteness and reinforces its privileged and oppressive position." Using a discourse of economic rationalism fosters market relationships, competition between groups, and assimilation. Economic rationalism projects a respect for bland sameness instead of respect for the actual diversity the world contains (Corson 2001). Under this economic regime, people matter only for their economic value, and only minority groups with large populations or with strong purchasing power will be accommodated (such as Asian or European language groups).

Furthermore, this discourse creates a marketplace mentality "where the quality of something is decided according to the price it can fetch, rather than according to any intrinsic and real qualities it might have" (Corson 2001, 25). The returns from equitable workforces, however, are difficult to measure, and we see the struggle to "make the business case" and tie objectives to the "bottom line." It also becomes difficult for nonprofit organizations or organizations whose customers are not the average public to buy into this discourse. As Goldberg and Corson (2001) found, as the customer became more ambiguous, organizations became more ambiguous on the benefits of employing minority group members. These organizations felt the benefits appeared in unique or isolated cases only.

This business discourse places the benefits to big business above the rights of the individual: "Many skilled people are underemployed and Ontario *workplaces* lose the contribution these individuals can make" (Government of Ontario 1995b, emphasis added). In addition, the Ontario government claims that it wants to ensure that *Ontario* fully benefits from the skills of immigrants and a diverse workforce. Benefits to society, such as the contribution of taxes by working individuals and increased consumer spending, outweigh the equity benefits to the individuals themselves.

By overtly disallowing any reference to race, this seemingly neutral language also promotes an agenda where race becomes invisible. In Ontario, when the provincial government repealed its Employment Equity Act, it also forced companies to destroy all the data they had collected on the makeup of their organizations and their target populations (self-identification data and employee census data). The lack of this kind of data makes it impossible for minorities to have evidence of racism or "name their reality" (Taylor, Chapter 14).

On the whole, we can see how a generic, race- and gender-neutral economic discourse helps to render EE/AA policies ineffective. First, this discourse helps keep minority groups from achieving equality, for they are no longer the only ones covered under equity policies. Expanding the definition of diversity to include the dominant group allows privileged positions to be maintained. Second, the economic discourse fosters competition between groups and assimilation by forcing individuals to fit a predetermined norm based on a supposedly neutral marketplace. In addition, the benefits of equity policies are difficult to measure, making them easy targets for dismantling. Third, this generic discourse works to render race and gender invisible, making it difficult to find evidence for racism and discrimination. The lack of evidence for racism and the benefits of equity policies also helps render the policies ineffective.

Conclusion

Similar discursive strategies are being used to dismantle and make ineffective EE/AA policies in Canada and the United States. First, symbolic or empty discourses create a watered-down, ineffective policy that lacks resources and sanctions for noncompliance. Second, a neoliberal ideological discourse of meritocracy that promotes equal opportunity, instead of equal outcomes, is used to dismantle diversity policies by opening up space for a discourse of reverse discrimination. This discourse also constructs racial minorities as inferior, further limiting the results equity policies can achieve. Third, a colour-blind economic discourse that appeals to the business-case argument for such policies also works to limit their effectiveness. Recognizing that these discourses are operating in both countries highlights the need to work together as we struggle for change. If we follow this discursive framework and recognize that discourse is socially constructed, we can make change. We can subvert predominant discourses by developing counterdiscourses as forms of resistance and action.

Through this analysis I attempt to provide additional insights into how discourse can constrain policies. We, as researchers, need to think about how discourse creates and constrains public policy and to raise our level of awareness about the influence of discourse in the power equation. To do so we need to make students, teachers, activists, and policy developers aware of the connection between language and power and to enable them to deconstruct discourse, so that they are able to see how language can turn individuals into subjects; that is, individuals who are "divided inside [themselves] or divided from others" (Foucault 1982, 209). Critical language awareness highlights the "constructedness of language and facilitates the process of 'unpacking,' 'unmaking,' 'unpicking,' or 'de-constructing' a text" (Janks 1991, 192). The overall purpose of critical language awareness is to enable the reader/hearer to evaluate a text in order to see whose interests it serves. Thus, we can be taught to contest the language practices "which maintain and reproduce patterns of domination and subordination in society" (Janks and Ivanic 1992, 1). According to Fairclough (1993), such awareness is a prerequisite for democratic citizenship and an urgent priority for language education.

Notes

1 Despite the differences between these policies and their contexts, the goals of employment equity and affirmative action are essentially the same. Therefore I believe there is much to be learned by comparing these diversity policies in the two countries.

2 Specifically, my framework draws mostly from French poststructuralist Michel Foucault, British critical language theorist Norman Fairclough, and French anthropologist Pierre Bourdieu.

References

Ashforth, A. 1990. Reckoning schemes of legitimation: On commissions of inquiry as power/knowledge forms. *Journal of Historical Sociology* 3(1): 1-22.

Bacchi, C.L. 1996. *The politics of affirmative action: "Women," equality, and category politics.* London: Sage Publications.

Buckorough, M. 1996. Letter to the editor. *Niagara Falls Review*, 31 July, A6.

Conference Board of Canada. 1999. *Diversity: An imperative for business success.* http://www.conferenceboard.ca/documents_summary.asp.

Corson, D. 1998. *Changing education for diversity.* Buckingham, UK: Open University Press.

–. 2001. *Language diversity and education.* Mahwah, NJ: Lawrence Erlbaum.

Equal Employment Opportunity. 1965. Executive order 11246, 24 September. Available at US Department of Labor, Employment Standards Administration, Office of Federal Contract Compliance Programs, http://www.dol.gov/esa/regs/statutes/ofccp/eo11246.htm.

Fairclough, N. 1993. Critical discourse analysis and the marketization of public discourse: The universities. *Discourse and Society* 4(2): 133-68.

Foucault, M. 1974. *Archeology of knowledge.* London: Tavistock.

–. 1980. *Power/knowledge: Selected interviews and other writings, 1971-1977.* New York: Pantheon.

–. 1982. The subject and power. In *Beyond structuralism and hermeneutics,* ed. H. Dreyfus and P. Rabinow, 208-26. Sussex, UK: Harvester Press.

Gandz, J. 2001. A business case for diversity. Available at Government of Ontario, *Paths to equal opportunity* website, http://www.equalopportunity.on.ca/eng_g/documents/BusCase.html.

Goldberg, M., and D. Corson. 2001. *Valuing linguistic diversity as a resource.* Toronto: New Approaches to Life Long Learning, Ontario Institute for Studies in Education.

Government of Ontario. 1992. Citizenship Minister Ziemba responds to Stephen Lewis report. Media release. 10 December.

–. 1995a. Bill to repeal job quotas passed by legislature. Media release. December.

–. 1995b. Government provides framework for Equal Opportunity Plan in Ontario. Media release. December.

–. 1995c. Mike Harris and equal opportunity. Media release. 9 June.

Hook, D. 2001. Discourse, knowledge, materiality, history: Foucault and discourse analysis. *Theory and Psychology* 11(4): 521-47.

Hughes, J. 1990. *The philosophy of social research.* London: Longman.

Janks, H. 1991. A critical approach to the teaching of language. *Educational Review* 43(2): 191-99.

Janks, H., and R. Ivanic. 1992. CLA and emancipatory discourse. In *Critical language awareness,* ed. N. Fairclough, 305-31. London: Longman.

Ruiz, R. 1984. Orientations in language planning. *NABE Journal* 8(2): 15-34.

Ryan, J. 1999. *Race and ethnicity in multi-ethnic schools: A critical case study.* Clevedon, UK: Multilingual Matters.

Wallace, J. 1995. Tories to scrap job equity law. *Toronto Star,* 12 October, A5.

Part 6:
Extending the Dialogue

16
Institutional Racism in Education Policy and Practice: A View from England
David Gillborn

The term *multiculturalism* tends to be used somewhat differently in the British literature than in North America. In particular, multiculturalism has often been defined negatively in contrast to a more radical critique offered by theorists and activists under the heading of "antiracism." Such critiques portray multiculturalism as a liberal facade that deflects deeper criticism by attending to superficial matters of "celebrating diversity" and making limited token (often patronizing) curricular changes. Similar criticisms have been made in Canada and are, of course, increasingly prominent in the US literature too, where the notion of critical multiculturalism, and in particular the adoption of critical race theory, has much in common with antiracist theory elsewhere (see Carrim and Soudien 1999; Dei 1996, 1998; Figueroa 1999; Gillborn 2000; Goldberg 1994; Ladson-Billings 1998; May 1999; Nieto 1999; Troyna 1993).

Until recently, antiracism inhabited a role outside the political mainstream in Britain. Its proponents included prominent politicians in local authorities, educators, and community movements, but national policy makers fought shy of the term, which was popularly equated with extreme radicalism (see Gillborn 1995; Sivanandan 1990).[1] This changed in 1999 with the report of a public inquiry proposing that the key institutions of British society in general, and the police in particular, were guilty of institutional racism. In education, one of the most high-profile official responses was to promote compulsory citizenship education for all eleven-to-sixteen-year-olds in state schools in England.[2] This is frequently presented as a bold step to address race equity in education. In this chapter I examine this development as a means of exploring the more general situation of multicultural policies in a racist education system. In particular, I take the recent deployment of citizenship education as a critical case in the issues at the heart of this volume, that is, the symbolic and substantive worth of contemporary multicultural and diversity policies. I conclude that far from promoting antiracism, in England citizenship education operates as a form of placebo: an activity that appears to address the issues (racism and race inequity) but, in reality, manifestly fails to tackle the real problem. Indeed, recent developments suggest that even this analysis may be too optimistic: citizenship education is increasingly implicated in a series of policy developments that threaten to worsen an already dire situation.

Stephen Lawrence: Institutional Racism and Public Policy

As he waited for a bus at 10:30 p.m. on 22 April 1993, Stephen Lawrence, an eighteen-year-old Black college student, was brutally stabbed to death.[3] His killers, a group of White youths, have never been brought to justice. Stephen was by no means the first young Black person to be murdered on British streets because of his race. After years of campaigning by Stephen's parents, Doreen and Neville Lawrence, however, a public inquiry was established into the circumstances surrounding the murder and the police's failure to prosecute. On its publication in February 1999, the Stephen Lawrence Inquiry report (Macpherson 1999) sent shock waves through Britain with its meticulous account of the bungled police investigation and its conclusion that "racism, institutional or otherwise, is not the prerogative of the Police Service. It is clear that other agencies including for example those dealing with housing and education also suffer from the disease" (33).

One of the most significant aspects of the report concerned its attempt to move beyond the superficial and extreme notion of racism that had previously characterized policy debate (in education and beyond). Pre-Lawrence public authorities and commentators tended to work with a view of racism as encompassing only the more obvious and deliberate forms of race hatred, as if "racism is restricted to a few 'rotten apples' in a basket that is basically sound" (Rizvi 1993, 7, after Henriques 1984, 62). Remarkably, for a report that stemmed from a racist murder (surely the most crude and vicious form of racism), the Stephen Lawrence Inquiry insisted on a broad reworking of the term *institutional racism* to explicitly include unintended and thoughtless acts that have the *effect* of discriminating (regardless of their intent). The report defined institutional racism as the "collective failure of an organisation to provide an appropriate and professional service to people because of their colour, culture, or ethnic origin. It can be seen or detected in processes, attitudes and behaviour which amount to discrimination through unwitting prejudice, ignorance, thoughtlessness and racist stereotyping which disadvantage minority ethnic people. It persists because of the failure of the organisation openly and adequately to recognise and address its existence and causes by policy, example and leadership" (Macpherson 1999, 28).

Needless to say, this definition has been subject to endless scrutiny and debate. It is by no means a simple paraphrasing of previous approaches and it is not without its problems. Nevertheless, one thing this perspective shares with longer-established definitions is its fundamental challenge to liberal complacency about the realities of contemporary racial politics and inequities. As Stokely Carmichael and Charles V. Hamilton observed in 1967, institutional racism "is less overt, far more subtle, less identifiable in terms of *specific* individuals committing the acts. But it is no less destructive of human life. [It] originates in the operation of established and respected forces in the society, and thus receives far less public condemnation" (original emphasis, reprinted in Cashmore and Jennings 2001, 112).

Speaking in Parliament on the day of publication, Prime Minister Tony Blair hailed the Lawrence Inquiry as a turning point in British political life: "The publication of today's report on the killing of Stephen Lawrence is a very important moment in the life of our country. It is a moment to reflect, to learn and to change. It will certainly lead to new laws but, more than that, it must lead to new attitudes, to a new era in race relations, and to a new more tolerant and more inclusive Britain" (UK *Parl. Deb.*, Commons, 326:380). Similarly, Jack Straw, then home secretary (with responsibility for policing, public order, immigration, etc.), stated: "I want this report to serve as a watershed in our attitudes to racism. I want it to act as a catalyst for permanent and irrevocable change, not just across our public services but across the whole of our society. The report does not place a responsibility on someone else; it places a responsibility on each of us. We must make racial equality a reality" (UK *Parl. Deb.*, Commons, 326:393).

These statements were repeated across the popular media where, for a brief but notable period, the question of institutional racism headed the news and current affairs agenda. Significantly, the Education Department[4] lost no time in issuing a press briefing on its response to the Lawrence Inquiry. On the same day the inquiry report was published, the department announced that it would be "carefully considering" the report, but was already confident enough to trumpet its major response, citizenship education:

Education and Employment Secretary David Blunkett today reaffirmed the Government's commitment to equality of opportunity in the wake of the publication of the Stephen Lawrence Inquiry Report. Mr Blunkett said the Department for Education and Employment would be carefully considering the Inquiry Report's recommendations. Mr Blunkett said: "The tragedy of Stephen Lawrence's death shows how much more needs to be done to promote social justice in our communities. This is about how we treat each other and, importantly, how we learn to respect ourselves and one another as citizens. That learning comes from within the home, at school and the wider community. That is why we are promoting the teaching of citizenship at school, to help children learn how to grow up in a society that cares and to have real equality of opportunity for all." (UK DfEE 1999)

The Education Department's response is vitally important because its discursive construction achieves a remarkable double act. Initially, the department presents itself as accepting the Lawrence Inquiry's analysis and sharing in its aims. Hence, its first sentence *"reaffirms"* a "commitment to equality of opportunity in the wake of the publication." And yet the detail of the announcement refuses the most central part of the report's analysis, namely, the concern with institutional racism as a characteristic of policy and practice that resides in the system itself. Rather, the department assumes a minimalist and crude definition of the problem, in terms of individual race hatred: "This is about how we treat each other and, importantly, how we learn to respect ourselves and one another as citizens." The institutional dimension is thus erased. The slogan of "equality of opportunity" is repeated in a vague fashion that appears to confirm a meaningful commitment but actually carries no weight at all (not unlike the situation in Canada highlighted by Goldberg in Chapter 15). In this way, "equality of opportunity" serves as what Barry Troyna called a condensation symbol: "Condensation symbols have a specific political purpose: to create symbolic stereotypes and metaphors which reassure supporters that their interests have been taken into account. But these symbols have a contradictory meaning so that the proposed solutions to perceived problems might also be contradictory, or ambiguously related to the way in which proponents and supporters initially viewed the issue" (1993, 36, after Edelman 1964).

The ritualistic citation of "equality of opportunity" acts as a marker that seems to accept the Lawrence Inquiry while simultaneously offering nothing concrete in response. The only clear commitment is a restatement of the government's already existing work on citizenship education. This position became clearly established as the government firmed up its response to the Lawrence Inquiry over the following weeks. In a debate dedicated to the inquiry report, for example, the home secretary stated: "The inquiry also made recommendations on education. My right hon. Friend the Secretary of State for Education and Employment is taking a number of steps aimed at promoting cultural diversity and preventing racism in our schools. Citizenship education, which will foster an understanding of cultural diversity in Britain, has a prominent place in the revised national curriculum" (UK *Parl. Deb.*, Commons, 327:767).

This statement is important because it indicates how quickly citizenship education came to be invested with the official role of leading the education system's response to the charge of institutional racism.[5] In the following sections I consider the background to this move and identify its inherent problems. First, however, it may be useful to briefly examine some of the evidence of institutional racism in the English educational system: this will provide a context for the critique by outlining the scope and depth of the inequities that currently shape young people's experience of education.

Education and Institutional Racism in England: "Standards" for Some
If we take the Stephen Lawrence Inquiry report's definition of institutional racism as a starting point, there is compelling evidence that the English education system has a case to answer. The first element concerns "the collective failure of an organisation to provide an appropriate and professional service to people because of their colour, culture, or ethnic origin."

For the last twenty or thirty years, the debates around "race" and education in England have been dominated by a concern with the relatively lower attainments of some minority ethnic groups. These inequities have been documented by numerous pieces of research and are widely accepted. The latest data show that Black/African Caribbean students and their peers of Bangladeshi and Pakistani origin continue to fare less well in terms of educational certification at the end of compulsory schooling – a pattern that holds regardless of social class background (Gillborn and Mirza 2000). In 2002, for example, 52 percent of White sixteen-year-olds attained five or more higher grade passes in the General Certificate of Secondary Education examinations that mark the end of compulsory schooling in England.[6] The same was true for 41 percent of Bangladeshi young people, 40 percent of Pakistanis, and 36 percent of Black students (see Table 16.1).

The statistics in Table 16.1 are drawn from a nationally representative sample of young people, with a new cohort contacted roughly every two years. This project, the Youth Cohort Study (YCS), is funded by central government and provides the best available guide to the changing attainments of different ethnic groups during a period of educational reform unprecedented in peacetime Britain. The Education Reform Act (1988) heralded the beginning of a series of major reforms of state education that started under the Conservative administrations of Margaret Thatcher and have continued under successive governments, including the "New" Labour administrations headed by Tony Blair. These reforms have included the creation of a statutory National Curriculum, the erosion of power from the local state, the establishment of a punitive regime of school inspections (run by the Office for Standards in Education, or Ofsted), and the enforcement of statutory testing across all state schools for children at the ages of seven, eleven, fourteen, and sixteen. The latter have been used as the basis for annually published "school performance tables" that list every school in the country according to crude measures of pupils' performance with no indication of background factors such as social class disadvantage.

The YCS, like all social science research, is far from perfect. Although the samples are relatively large (30,000 in 2002) and nationally representative, the findings must be treated with some caution because several factors reduce the size of many subsamples. For example, less than 60 percent of young people sampled in 2002 actually responded (UK DfES 2003, Table 1). In addition, subsamples are greatly reduced in number to match overall population

Table 16.1

Ethnic origin and GCSE attainment:
Percentage gaining five higher grade GCSEs and percentage point difference with White group

	1989		1991		1992		1994		1996		1998		2000		2002	
	%	gap	%	gap	%	gap	%	gap	%	gap	%	gap	%	gap	%	gap
White	30		35		37		43		45		47		50		52	
Black	18	-12	19	-16	23	-14	21	-22	23	-22	29	-18	39	-11	36	-16
Indian	n/a		n/a		38	+1	45	+2	48	+3	54	+7	60	+10	60	+8
Pakistani	n/a		n/a		26	-11	24	-19	23	-22	29	-18	29	-21	40	-12
Bangladeshi	n/a		n/a		14	-23	20	-23	25	-20	33	-14	29	-21	41	-11

Source: Adapted from UKDfES 2003, table A.

sizes, where around 10 percent of the overall population is estimated to have community backgrounds outside Britain (Runnymede Trust 2000, 372). In view of these limitations, therefore, the YCS is best seen as indicating broad trends of significance.

Despite the limitations of the YCS, the data in Table 16.1 are particularly striking in several ways. First, they show the impact of the relentless drive by politicians to measure standards according to a single crude measure, in this case the proportion of sixteen-year-olds attaining five or more high grade (A+ to C) passes. The overall rate mirrors the data for White students in the table: this has risen from 30 percent in 1989 to 52 percent in 2002. The reforms noted above, and especially the publication of so-called school league tables based on this same benchmark figure, means that secondary schools have prioritized it above all else – what Deborah Youdell and I have called the "A-to-C economy" (Gillborn and Youdell 2000). To some extent this emphasis has affected all the main ethnic groups for whom data are gathered officially: students in each group are now significantly more likely to attain the benchmark figure than they were when data were first gathered in 1990.

But not all groups have improved equally. Only one ethnic group, White students, has actually shown an improvement in every year of the YCS. Indian students, whose overall attainment now outstrips that of their White peers, showed no change in the most recent data. More worryingly, each of the other main groups sampled (Pakistani, Bangladeshi, and Black students) have experienced relative declines in their attainment at some point: most recently Black students between 2000 and 2002.

The data also show that, despite periodic fluctuations, the scale of inequity in attainment remains significant.[7] Although Bangladeshi students' attain-ment is closer to that of their White counterparts than it was in 1992 (when separate values were first calculated for South Asian groups), they remain significantly behind overall. Pakistani students (who are 12 percentage points behind White students) are actually further adrift than they were a decade ago. Black students, for whom data stretch back to 1989, experienced a con-siderable increase in the inequity of attainment during the 1990s. Although the current situation is an improvement, it is striking that their percentage point difference from White students is worse now than when the education reforms were first introduced in the late 1980s.

Black-White inequities do not encompass only attainment at the end of compulsory education. Indeed, a disproportionately large number of Black students are permanently excluded (expelled) from full-time schooling before they have a chance to enter examinations. Whenever statistics on school exclusion have been broken down by ethnicity in England, Black students have always been disproportionately overrepresented in the figures. The national rate of overrepresentation varies between two and four times the rate experienced by White students (Gillborn 1995; Osler 1997); in some local areas the difference is as high as thirteen times the White rate (Thornton 1999). For many of these young people exclusion represents the end of their full-time education in mainstream settings, as they find themselves in specialist "units" or left to survive on a few hours of "home tuition" each week. Not surprisingly, permanent exclusion is strongly associated with unemployment and contact with the criminal justice system in adult life (UK Audit Commission 1996).

The historical (and in some cases growing) inequities of attainment experienced by some minority ethnic groups, plus the continued overrepresentation of Black youth among the ranks of the permanently excluded, offer compelling evidence that the English education system is institutionally racist in terms of its failure to provide "an appropriate and professional service." There is also disturbing evidence in relation to a further part of the Lawrence Inquiry's definition: "attitudes and behaviour which amount to discrimination through unwitting prejudice, ignorance, thoughtlessness and racist stereotyping."

Detailed school-based qualitative research conducted since the mid-1980s is highly relevant to this question (see, for example, Bhatti 1999; Connolly 1998; Gillborn 1990; Gillborn and Youdell 2000; Mac an Ghaill 1988; Mirza 1992; Nehaul 1996; Sewell 1997; Troyna and Hatcher 1992; Wright 1986, 1992; Youdell 2003). These studies suggest that many White teachers hold systematically lower expectations of Black and other minority ethnic students and often respond more quickly and more harshly to perceived signs of unruly behaviour or inappropriate attitudes. These processes are given institutional force through the use of selective pupil grouping (through tracking, streaming, setting, and the like) that have been found consistently to place disproportionate numbers of Black students in the lowest-ranked teaching groups (Hallam 2002; Hallam and Toutounji 1996; Oakes 1990; Sukhnandan and Lee 1998). Such approaches have become increasingly common as schools try to deliver on the government's requirement for ever higher standards, and the effects are predictably destructive (Ball 2003; Hallam 2002).

Education has been one of the most prominent policy fields in British politics since the wide-ranging legislation in 1988 began a period of unrelenting calls for schools to improve standards. The standards mantra has been repeated by all major political parties and, as discussed above, is usually interpreted in relation to the proportion of young people attaining five or more higher (A* to C) grade General Certificate of Secondary Education (GCSE) passes at age sixteen. The drive to improve standards has been enforced through numerous measures, few more powerful than the annual publication of the school performance tables that list the results of every school in the country. These are frequently rearranged by the news media to list schools in the form of national and local league tables, as if reporting the latest sports standings. In these cases the calculations are almost always based on a simple percentage of students attaining five or more higher grade passes: the distribution of those passes among students of different ethnic groups, genders, and class backgrounds is not calculated. The imperative to raise standards in this crude form has increased the use of internal selection between different teaching groups. Black students find themselves disproportionately placed in the lowest groups, facing a restricted curriculum and lower teacher expectations. The opportunity for the racist structuring of opportunities exists whenever the system offers teachers the possibility of separating students into selective groups in this way.

Indeed, the GCSE examination itself (in which success is so crucial) offers a further level of selection. The GCSE was introduced in the late 1980s as a unified examination that would be open to all students. However, most GCSE examinations have since adopted a system of tiered examination papers, whereby students are entered for different question papers within the same subject specialization. Teachers decide which examination a student will take, and this decision is important because each tier only offers a limited number of grades (see Figure 16.1).

Figure 16.1

Tiering in GCSE examinations

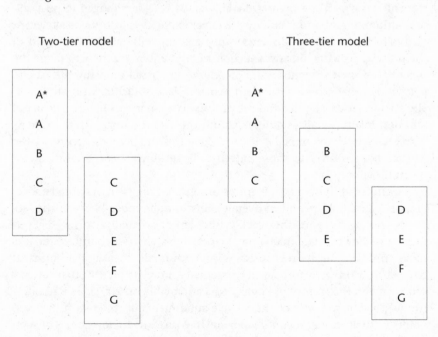

Two-tier model   Three-tier model

The most common system is the two-tier model. Here, students in the higher tier can achieve grades A to D. If they perform below the level of a grade D, then rather than be awarded a grade between E and G (the remaining "pass" grades) in most subjects they will effectively fall through the tier floor and be awarded a U (ungraded) result.[8] Students entered in the Foundation (lower) tier cannot exceed a grade C regardless of how well they perform. In mathematics, a subject with a long history of selection, the examination is structured by a three-tier model. In this case the best grade available to the Foundation tier is a grade D – while grade C is the usual minimum required for study at an advanced level or entry to professional training.

Decisions on tiering systematically disadvantage Black students: in comparison with their White peers, Black young people are less likely to be placed in the higher tiers and more likely to be entered at Foundation level (Gillborn and Youdell 2000, 102-32). In the two London schools I studied with Deborah Youdell, 66 percent of Black students were entered at Foundation level in mathematics.[9] Consequently, *before they had even answered a question,* it had been determined that two-thirds of Black children would effectively fail their math exams.

Tiering and the related differential selection of students by ethnic origin provide a clear example of how multiple factors can come together to deny educational opportunity. It is difficult to think of a clearer example of institutional racism than an examination, disproportionately taken by Black students, in which the highest possible grade is widely judged to be a failure. Although race and ethnicity are never explicitly positioned as relevant factors in the dominant discourse, they are implicitly at the very heart of the process. Selective practices such as tiering require teachers to judge the potential of their students: these judgments are based on assumptions and perceptions that work to the detriment of Black students, who are generally seen as lacking ability and presenting disciplinary problems. The act of selection institutionalizes differences in expectation by presenting students with markedly different pedagogical experiences and denying access to basic educational resources to those judged to be lacking. This is a clear case of institutional racism.

The effects of these multiple forms of selection are clear. As noted above, despite a sustained period of overall gains in attainment between the late 1980s and the present, the Black-White gap has actually worsened. Even more revealing are data that show the growing scale of inequity as students move through education. The obsession with crude, measurable standards has led to a drive to formally test students more frequently than at any other time in the history of English education (Wiliam 2001). As a result, it is now possible to compare the relative attainments of students at different points in their formal schooling. Figure 16.2 presents the outcomes of such monitoring in a large metropolitan area of England. The illustration shows the attainment of Black and White students in relation to the overall average for all students in the area as a whole (that is, the Local Education Authority, or LEA).[10] The data show that Black students attained 20 percentage points *above* the local average when tested at age five. Their relative attainments plummet with age, however, such that their sixteen-year-old counterparts attained 21 percentage points *below* the local average.

Figure 16.2

Performance relative to local average, by age and ethnicity

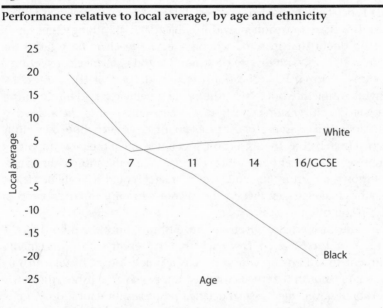

Source: Adapted from Gillborn and Mizra 2000, figure 5.

To summarize, the Stephen Lawrence Inquiry report's proposition that institutional racism is a characteristic of the English educational system is strongly supported by the evidence. As I have noted, Black students consistently finish compulsory schooling with lesser qualifications than their White counterparts. This "Black-white gap" (Drew and Gray 1991) has widened since the late 1980s, when the official drive to improve standards was at its height. Qualitative research suggests that this gap results from internal practices of selection and separation, whereby teachers increasingly place Black students in lower-ranked teaching groups where they experience inferior curricula and may even be denied the formal possibility of the highest examination grades. These processes are reflected in the growing inequity of attainment between Black children and their White counterparts as they move through schooling between age five and age sixteen. In the face of such evidence, only a thorough and unreservedly antiracist response by the education system would appear to adequately meet the requirements of the Lawrence Inquiry. Unfortunately, the government's commitment to extending citizenship education as its principal response in the education system does not meet this need.

Citizenship Education and Institutional Racism

Citizenship education has traditionally offered curricular space for the discussion of social and moral issues, especially those seen as either too general or too controversial for treatment within subject specializations (Osler 1999). There is no doubt that in some schools – where teachers have taken the opportunity to work with diverse communities and challenge conventional assumptions – citizenship education *can* provide part of the context for meaningful antiracist work.[11] Nevertheless, as a vehicle for addressing institutional racism, citizenship education is at best only part of the answer: at worst, it can leave key aspects of the problem intact, or even more powerfully entrenched than before. In this section, I set out some of the most important problems with the current promotion of citizenship education as an answer to institutional racism in England. The mismatch could scarcely be clearer between the challenge identified by the Lawrence Inquiry and the poverty of citizenship education as a response.

Despite the prominence given to citizenship education following the publication of the Stephen Lawrence Inquiry report, the government's commitment to citizenship education has a much longer history. In July 1997, the same month that the Lawrence Inquiry was established, the newly elected Labour government issued detailed proposals for education. Among these plans was an advisory group "to discuss citizenship and the teaching of democracy in our schools" (UK DfEE 1997, 63). Interestingly, race equity was absent from this discussion of citizenship, which stressed the need to bind young people into a sense of their duties and responsibilities: "Schools can help to ensure that young people feel that they have a stake in our society and the community in which they live by teaching them the nature of democracy and the duties, responsibilities and rights of citizens. This forms part of schools' wider provision for personal and social education, which helps more broadly to give pupils a strong sense of personal responsibility and of their duties towards others" (63).

The focus here, as with character education in the United States and Canada (Chapter 1), is not on challenging inequity and empowering students but on "personal responsibility" and "duties towards others." In fact, neither placing citizenship on the curriculum nor emphasizing stability and control were new ideas: both were established long before Blair's "New" Labour Party was elected to power in 1997. Previous Conservative administrations had long since adopted citizenship, especially the notion of "active citizenship" (see

Kirton and Brighouse 2001), which, as Carol Vincent (2000, 7) has noted, "meant an emphasis on citizens' duties towards their communities, particularly where the prevention of crime was concerned." Similarly, in 1990, an inquiry into citizenship recommended that the subject be taught to all school children (UK Speaker's Commission 1990).

The Conservatives' attempt to define a specific role for citizenship education dates back more than a decade, when it was defined as one of five so-called cross-curricular themes (UK NCC 1990a). These themes were aspects of education that were identified as being of great importance but had effectively fallen between the cracks of the statutory National Curriculum imposed in 1988 on all state-maintained schools in England and Wales. The separate subject specializations (now established in law) did not see the themes as intrinsically "their" business, and so action was taken to establish the themes across the entire span of the curriculum.[12] The specific guidance for citizenship education (UK NCC 1990b) included a component entitled "A Pluralist Society," which many educators saw as the perfect opportunity to develop multicultural or antiracist initiatives (Taylor 1992, 2-3). However, this was a weak and marginal place to concentrate such efforts. By 1992 only one in four schools claimed even to have a written policy on the subject, compared with three-quarters of schools that could boast a policy on information technology (Whitty, Aggleton, and Rowe 1992, 2). Furthermore, the curriculum guidance itself embodied a predictably narrow and uncritical reading of society, where justice and fair play were assumed to be the norm and racial prejudice and discrimination were presented as aberrations born of tensions around perceived difference. Racism, as a persistent and systematic feature of society, was notably absent (see, for example, Gillborn 1995, 135-6). These same criticisms can be made of the latest developments, which, predictably, echo Labour's initial thrust toward control and participation within the strict limits laid down by "socially acceptable behaviour" and "the development of active citizenship" (UK DfEE 1998, 1).

The Labour government's Advisory Group on the Teaching of Citizenship and Democracy was established in November 1997 under the chairmanship of Professor Bernard Crick, a long-time advocate of political education and political literacy in schools. The advisory group reported in 1998 (UK QCA 1998), before the publication of the Stephen Lawrence Inquiry report. The Crick Report, as it became known, was immediately criticized by those who hoped citizenship education would be a vehicle for antiracist change.

First, racism was conspicuously absent from the report. As Audrey Osler has argued powerfully, although ethnicity and diversity are raised, they "are not addressed in relation to inequality or differences in power ... Race and racism, either institutional or interpersonal, receive no mention" (Osler 2000, 8). Second, the report itself adopts a perspective on minority ethnic communities that is at best patronizing and at worst racist. It treats minorities as if they were a homogeneous mass and speaks of "the homelands of *our* minority communities" (UK QCA 1998, 18, quoted in Osler 2000, 7, emphasis added) as if such groups are somehow a possession, assumed to look outside the UK for their true home. By default, such groups are clearly not the anticipated audience for the report. The report manifestly fails to appreciate the complex nature of contemporary cultural identities (there is no room here for hybridity or contestation; see, for example, Appiah 1999; Leonardo 2002; Osler 2000) or that around half of Britain's minority ethnic population were born in the UK (UK Office for National Statistics 1996, 12).

Worse still, the Crick Report stated that minorities "must learn and respect the laws, codes and conventions as much as the majority" (UK QCA 1998, 17-18, quoted in Osler 2000, 7). This astonishing statement seems to presume that minority communities are somehow outside current conventions in a way that is not true for White people. Indeed, as Osler argues, it could be interpreted as supposing that minority ethnic groups represent a greater threat to law and social stability – a well-established stereotype.[13] Undoubtedly, the statement exemplifies the tendency of citizenship education to become a vehicle for moralistic preaching that emphasizes conformity and control.

From September 2002, building largely on the recommendations of the Crick Report, citizenship education became a compulsory part of the curriculum for eleven-to-sixteen-year-olds in state-maintained schools in England. Schools have considerable scope to add their own ideas and directions; they can also decide to cover a bare minimum. As in the past, communities, activists, and academics have attempted to produce useful tools and additions (see, for example, Citizenship Foundation and Me Too 2002). For the most part, however, the antiracist potential of citizenship education remains unrealized. A recent publication aimed specifically at helping teachers deliver the new curriculum, for example, contains no index references to "race," "racism," nor even the more limited notions of "discrimination" and "prejudice" (Arthur and Wright 2001).

Early in 2003, as part of its response to the Lawrence Inquiry, the Qualifications and Curriculum Authority[14] established a website meant to promote multicultural and antiracist work across the curriculum. Branded "political correctness gone mad" in one national daily newspaper (Political correctness 2003, 15), the site brings together examples of "good practice" that are meant to "provide effective learning opportunities for pupils to value diversity and challenge racism" (UK QCA 2003a). The aims are laudable but, as in the past, the focus is almost exclusively on addressing relations between students (leaving teachers out of the equation), and the treatment of racism lacks a wider critical understanding.

For example, at its launch the citizenship strand contained at least one example activity for each of the four official "key stages" (age-related phases of the curriculum) between five and sixteen. There was no activity on racism, but the site did include an activity (aimed at students aged twelve to thirteen) entitled "racial discrimination." In this model lesson, students are "asked to brainstorm the term 'racial discrimination'" and then given a series of incidents to consider, including the following: "A white boy starts a fight with a smaller Asian boy. Afterwards he speaks of his opponent as 'one of them' ... In a geography lesson pupils are learning about unemployment. A girl says 'Unemployment keeps going up because immigrants took all the best jobs.'" Subsequently the students are asked to decide which of the following labels "best described the event":

· racist and serious
· serious but not racist
· racist but not too serious
· probably not racist (but need to ask more questions to be sure).

The students' responses are used to generate a discussion about "types of racial discrimination," its effects, and students' "responsibility to speak out against injustice" (UK QCA 2003b).

Much could be said about this model lesson but, for the purposes of this chapter, the key issue is how this treatment fails to engage with one of the central concerns of the Stephen Lawrence Inquiry report. I have already noted at some length how the report placed institutional racism at centre stage. Part of this involved recommending a simple and clear definition of a racist incident, a definition that is now officially accepted by the government and enshrined in law: "A racist incident is any incident which is perceived to be racist by the victim or any other person" (UK Home Office 2000).

This definition cuts through the mire of intentions and focuses unequivocal attention on the perceptions of those involved in an incident. It encapsulates the antiracist analysis of the Lawrence report and attempts to shift the balance of evidence in all relevant cases. It represents a fundamental challenge to White liberal assumptions that racism can somehow be quantified or identified in any purportedly objective sense. And yet the QCA's exemplar activity seems to take for granted that racial discrimination *can* be identified through the application of a reasoned and rational set of criteria that will arise through structured debate. In microcosm, and despite its best intentions, the model lesson stands as a further example of how the English education system in general, and citizenship education in particular, have fundamentally failed to address the real challenge laid out in the Lawrence report.

Despite the efforts of campaigners and advocates, therefore, in practice citizenship education in England has not seriously addressed institutional racism. Historically, citizenship education has been used as a force for stability and control. Where issues of racism and inequity are discussed at all, the context typically reduces racism to issues of personal prejudice and adopts a moralizing tone that seeks to ensure compliance and passivity where resistance and protest must be held within the bounds of supposedly accepted democratic principles, most obviously formal parliamentary elections. The current focus on citizenship has been paraded by the Labour government as a cornerstone of how the education system is responding to the Stephen Lawrence Inquiry report, and yet the impetus for the reforms, and indeed much of their eventual detail, was already shaped before the inquiry was even concluded. Although some scope remains for meaningful antiracist work, overall the citizenship reforms are piecemeal and wholly inadequate as a response to institutional racism. In some respects, the reforms themselves embody precisely the form of thinking that is part of the problem.

Policy and Practice: Struggle and Assimilationism

Marcus Wood (2000, 1-6) begins his study of the Western visual representation of slavery by considering the case of Thomas Clarkson's abolition map. Produced in 1808, this document was an attempt to chart all the important people and events involved in bringing about abolition. As Wood states, the map "summed up in cartographic fantasy ... abolition as a series of tributary streams and rivers, each with the name of a supposed abolitionist attached. The waterways unite to form two mighty rivers in England and America, and these in turn unite when they flow into the open sea, presumably the sea of emancipation and spiritual renewal" (1, 4). Incredibly, not a single slave is mentioned in the map.

Clarkson's map is an object lesson in the reimagining of history to present a unified tale of the triumph of White civilizing values over the forces of repression. The erasure of Black people as an active and ultimately irresistible force for change is both obscene and significant. In a similar fashion, policy makers tend to present education policy as evolving over time, sometimes with dramatic changes in focus, but always with the best of intentions for all "consumers" (regardless of age, class, and ethnicity). In this view, the role of resistance and protest is lost in the effort to present policy as a rational procession of changes, each building on its predecessors in a linear and evolutionary fashion. In fact, the history of race and educational reform in England is marked by bloodshed and destruction. Much as in the United States (see Chapter 2), meaningful advances in race equity are typically preceded by public uprisings (usually labelled riots by a media keen to present minority communities as hotbeds of criminality and alienation), by deaths (at the hands of police or other White racist groups and individuals), or, at the very least, by concerted public protest by minority communities. This pattern is repeating itself in contemporary education policy in England: "The unrelenting struggle of the Lawrences has put institutional racism back on the agenda ... they changed the whole discourse on race relations and made the government and the media and the people of this country acknowledge that there is a deep, ingrained, systemic racism in the institutions and structures of this society" (Sivanandan 2000, 7).

The impact upon English popular culture of the Stephen Lawrence Inquiry is difficult to describe: in some respects it stands as the nearest thing yet in England to the kinds of shock waves experienced in the United States over the Rodney King affair. The inquiry offered a fundamental challenge to White liberal complacency about the essentially sound and just nature of race relations in the country; it propelled race and White racism to the top of the popular news agenda; and it had repercussions throughout the justice system. In the field of education, however, the Lawrence report stands as an opportunity for change that is rapidly slipping away.

As I have shown in this chapter, the report's accusation of institutional racism in education stands up to scrutiny through both quantitative and qualitative analyses of contemporary schooling. The inequities of attainment between Black and White students are not only persisting but growing, year by year and from one generation of students to another. The Education Department consistently presents citizenship education as one of its leading initiatives in this area. Citizenship education in England, however, has historically been limited to a focus on students (leaving school structures and teachers' perspectives largely untouched) and a vision of society based on liberal universalistic principles that require all students to be aware of their particular duties and responsibilities. In this way, citizenship education can be seen as a policy placebo: "a substance or procedure which a patient accepts as a medicine or therapy but which actually has no specific therapeutic activity for his [sic] condition or is prescribed in the belief that it has no such activity ... an epithet given to any medicine adapted more to please than benefit the patient," according to the *Oxford English Dictionary* online.

In relation to institutional racism in the education system, citizenship education is currently being deployed as a fake treatment, meant to placate concern, but making no actual attempt to address the central problem. Institutional racism has been diagnosed, not least by Black communities (who have protested at their children's mistreatment for decades) and by the Lawrence Inquiry, and citizenship education is the sugar pill meant to demonstrate the seriousness of a system that continues systematically to exclude and fail Black children. In the current political context, however, the concern with citizenship education may even prove to be a malign factor, part of a wider refusal to combat racism that threatens ultimately to worsen the situation.

The events of 11 September 2001 triggered a dramatic increase in anti-Islamic feeling in the West, especially in North America and Britain (Taylor and Singh 2001). Even before these events, however, Britain witnessed an increasingly vociferous discourse attacking multiculturalism in general (and the Stephen Lawrence Inquiry in particular). This was given impetus by a series of disturbances involving conflict between police and South Asian young people in Oldham, Burnley, and Bradford (towns and cities in the north of England) in the summer of 2001.[15] It was widely acknowledged at the time that each of the English disturbances had been sparked by the activities of White supremacist groups, namely the British National Party and the National Front. However, history suggests that blame has a strange way of shifting sides when race is involved. In the late 1950s, for example, White mobs caused widespread damage and launched physical attacks on migrant communities in Nottingham and London. Although these (and later) disturbances were clearly started by Whites, they formed a backdrop to immigration controls and wider policy moves that shifted the blame onto the minority communities (Ramdin 1987).

Similarly, the protests in 2001 prompted David Blunkett (by this time promoted from the Education Department to home secretary) to argue that minority communities must do more to foster a "sense of belonging" (Blunkett 2001). He subsequently introduced a policy of "Integration with Diversity" that included proposals to discourage marriage outside the "settled community" (in other words, marriage that involves bringing a spouse to the UK from a person's country of origin), to speed up deportation, and to test the English-language skills of new immigrants (UK Home Office 2002). These developments have an unmistakably assimilationist character (see, for example, J.A. Banks 1994; Mullard 1982; Tomlinson 1977). In education they have been matched by a renewed focus on English-language teaching and an attack on so-called monocultural schools, which seem predominantly to be those with a disproportionate number of minority ethnic, rather than a majority of White, students (see Cantle 2001). These dimensions have become particularly heated in the context of an increasingly rabid discourse that constructs asylum seekers as criminals or parasites determined to take advantage of state benefits.

The tone of the debate was further inflamed when the home secretary voiced his fears that "asylum seekers are swamping some British schools" (BBC News 2003). The popular press took this claim to new heights when they covered the 2003 report by the official schools inspectorate for England. Although the chief inspector was quoted as saying that only around 3 percent of schools in England have more than one in ten asylum-seeker pupils, this detail was lost amid the incendiary headlines: "OFFICIAL: asylum rush causes crisis for schools – BRITISH kids are suffering as schools struggle to cope with a flood of asylum seekers' children, an official report warned yesterday" (Official 2003, 14-15) and "'Threat' of asylum pupils – The huge influx of asylum seeker children is threatening the education of tens of thousands of pupils, a report warned yesterday" (Threat of asylum 2003, 18-19).

Such headlines are indicative of an increasingly vitriolic attack on minority communities in general, and asylum seekers in particular. Assimilationist sentiments among policy makers, such as Blunkett's statements about South Asian communities[16] and asylum seekers, have done nothing to reduce tensions: indeed, there is evidence that things are getting worse. When mainstream politicians use "common sense" and a rejection of "political correctness" as an excuse for thinly veiled attacks on minority communities, the number of race hate crimes rises and neo-Nazi groups gain electoral muscle. In 2001, for example, London's Metropolitan Police confirmed that racist attacks increase when asylum and race are made political footballs: "The most serious trend we have seen is a rise in reports of [racist] incidents when the issue of asylum and refugees is brought into the public domain by reputable politicians making inflammatory statements" (a "Scotland Yard source" quoted in Ahmed and Bright 2001, 2). Since the uprisings of 2001 the far-right British National Party has experienced unparalleled electoral success in northern English towns, including becoming the second-largest party on Burnley council in May 2003 (Brunsdon 2003).

In this context, the government's response to the Lawrence Inquiry is exposed as largely cosmetic. The current emphasis on citizenship education is especially weak. The central educational reforms (all proclaimed as part of "the standards agenda") pursue policies that are known to have a markedly negative effect on certain minoritized groups, especially Black students. For example, the Labour government continues to encourage school specialization, promote even more "setting by ability," and extend the use of published school performance tables. There is the possibility of citizenship education drawing on past successes elsewhere to open up new and controversial areas of debate and, within a critical whole-school approach, advance antiracist developments. In Britain, however, the dominant tradition has been for citizenship education to reinforce the status quo by binding students to a superficial and sanitized version of pluralism that is long on duties and responsibilities, but short on popular struggles against race inequity. The Stephen Lawrence Inquiry laid down a fundamental challenge to the institutional racism that characterizes the English educational system; unfortunately, policy makers' readiness to invoke citizenship education as a remedy indicates just how little has been learned so far. In contradiction of the government's apparently positive response to the Lawrence report, the ensuing years have seen a failure to address the institutionalized nature of educational race inequity while, at the same time, the engines of educational injustice (in the use of setting, selection, tiering, etc.) have been further strengthened.

Conclusion

The chapters in this volume illustrate the range, variety and complexity of the issues that face educators who want to work toward greater race equity in education. Despite the sometimes markedly different specificities of region and context, there are clearly many commonalities. Policy borrowing has reached a global scale, and education systems in North America and Europe increasingly pursue policies that share a reliance on crude measures of standards and a top-down approach to public schooling. These policies threaten the fabric of education for working-class and minoritized students. To date the academy has been slow to produce responses that are both theoretically informed and relevant to the struggles facing diverse communities. It is to be hoped that the critiques outlined in this chapter, and in the rest of this collection, can add to a growing project of critical scholarship with a truly international perspective and a local applicability.

Notes

In part this chapter arises from the conference "Ethnic Diversity and Citizenship Education in Multicultural Nation-States' (Bellagio, Italy, June 2002), chaired by James A. Banks and sponsored by the Center for Multicultural Education, University of Washington. The conference was supported by grants from the Rockefeller Foundation, New York, and the Spencer Foundation, Chicago. I am grateful to all the conference participants for so generously sharing their experiences, knowledge, and concerns. This particular treatment of the issues was produced in response to an invitation to contribute to the conference "Dialogue on Multicultural and Diversity Policies in Canada and the United States: Symbol or Substance?" at the University at Buffalo, Baldy Center for Law and Social Policy (May 2003). I am especially grateful to Lauri Johnson and Reva Joshee for inviting me to contribute and for their insightful comments on an earlier version. This chapter has also benefited from the input of numerous colleagues and friends. In particular, the following commented in detail on earlier drafts: Stephen Ball, Gregg Beratan, Dorn Gillborn, Jan McKenley, Audrey Osler, Claudine Rausch, Nicola Rollock, Kalwant Sidhu, Sally Tomlinson, and Deborah Youdell. Any remaining problems and inaccuracies are, of course, solely my responsibility.

1 For a consideration of differing national traditions of antiracism, see Bonnett 2000.
2 A limited form of devolution within the United Kingdom means that although a single British Parliament resides in Westminster, certain powers (including those to determine the curriculum) are now held separately in England, Wales, Scotland, and Northern Ireland. In this chapter I focus specifically on the situation in England.
3 In common with current conventions in the United Kingdom, I use the word *Black* as a collective term for people who self-identify as of Black Caribbean, Black African, and other "Black" ethnic origins, including "Black British." Although flawed in numerous respects, this usage does at least correspond to the term used most frequently by the people so labelled (see Mason 2000).
4 The government department responsible for education has been subject to several reorganizations in recent years. For the sake of clarity I adopt the term *Education Department* for that arm of government most recently known as the Department for Education and Employment (DfEE) and the Department for Education and Skills (DfES).
5 The education service is also subject to the Race Relations (Amendment) Act 2000, which arose as a result of the Lawrence Inquiry and placed a duty on all public authorities (including schools and universities) to proactively pursue race equality. The system was largely unprepared for the consequences of the act, despite having two years to prepare for its implementation (Rooney 2002). In addition, there is no reliable indication that the act has so far had any tangible effect on most schools. Despite the formal scope of the act, therefore, citizenship education was clearly the preferred and most public response of the education system itself.
6 The General Certificate of Secondary Education is the most common examination at the

end of compulsory schooling in England. The highest pass grades (A*, A, B, and C) are often required for entry into higher education, training, and the professions. Attaining these grades in at least five separate subjects has become the benchmark for academic success at this age (see Gillborn and Youdell 2000).

7   The notion of underachievement is often associated with differences in attainment between minority ethnic groups and the larger White population (e.g., Swann 1985). However, this concept has increasingly come to be corrupted in policy discourse so that "underachievement" is seen as a problem residing in particular populations rather than the system itself. For this reason I prefer an alternative formulation such as "inequity of attainment" (see Gillborn and Mirza 2000).

8   In examinations in English and science a small "safety net" has been created to provide a grade E for those who narrowly miss a grade D.

9   The equivalent figure for White students was 48 percent.

10   I draw on locally based data here because no national data are available for the entire span of age groups from five to sixteen years. For the sake of simplicity the figure presents the relative attainments of White and Black students only, removing the other main minority ethnic groups in the area. A fuller version of the data is available in Gillborn and Mirza 2000.

11   Such approaches are likely to be limited unless other aspects of the school (across all of its pastoral and academic functions) are also subject to antiracist developments (see, for example, Dadzie 2000).

12   The five themes were defined as economic and industrial understanding; careers, education and guidance; health education; citizenship; and environmental education (UK NCC 1990a).

13   See Gillborn 2001 for a discussion of such fears in relation to the development of UK education policy since the Second World War.

14   The QCA, successor to NCC, is an official body with a statutory duty to monitor and promote the formal curriculum.

15   Scotland also witnessed an increase in racist attacks (and public demonstrations), especially against asylum seekers.

16   In 2002 David Blunkett, then Britain's home secretary, introduced a White Paper on immigration and citizenship called "Secure Borders, Save Haven." The document linked the issue of terrorism threats with worries about preserving a traditional notion of British citizenship. In so doing, Blunkett singled out the South Asian community as one that used its tradition of arranged marriage to bring in young women and men from the subcontinent. He depicted British citizens of South Asian origin as people who could easily be "duped" into marriage with individuals who "may have paid someone to go through a marriage ceremony with them or used an organized crime group, a corrupt solicitor or immigration advisor to arrange a bogus marriage for them" (Blunkett cited in Kapur 2002).

References

Ahmed, K., and M. Bright. 2001. Labour failing to meet pledges on race. *Observer* (London), 22 April, 1-2.

Appiah, L. 1999. Multicultural citizenship. *Multicultural Teaching* 18(1): 20-23.

Arthur, J., and D. Wright. 2001. *Teaching citizenship in the secondary school.* London: David Fulton.

Ball, S.J. 2003. *The more things change ... Educational research, social class and "interlocking" inequalities.* Centenary lectures series. London: Institute of Education, University of London.

Banks, J.A. 1994. *Multiethnic education: Theory and practice.* 3rd ed. Boston: Allyn and Bacon.

BBC News Online. 2003. Blunkett revels in straight talking image. January 23. http://news.bbc.co.uk.

Bhatti, G. 1999. *Asian children at home and at school.* London: Routledge.

Blunkett, D. 2001. Interview. *Independent on Sunday* (London), 9 December, 4.

Bonnett, A. 2000. *Anti-racism.* London: Routledge.

Brunsdon, J. 2003. Burnley takes stock of BNP vote. *BBC News Online,* May 3. http://news.bbc.co.uk.

Cantle, T. 2001. *Community cohesion: A report of the independent review team.* London: Home Office.

Carmichael, S., and C.V. Hamilton. 1967. *Black power: The politics of liberation in America.* London: Penguin.

Carrim, N., and C. Soudien. 1999. Critical antiracism in South Africa. In *Critical multiculturalism: Rethinking multiculturalist and antiracist education,* ed. S. May, 153-71. London: Falmer.

Cashmore, E., and J. Jennings, eds. 2001. *Racism: Essential readings.* London: Sage.

Citizenship Foundation and Me Too. 2002. *Education for citizenship, diversity and race equality: A practical guide.* London: Citizenship Foundation and Me Too.

Connolly, P. 1998. *Racism, gender identities and young children: Social relations in a multi-ethnic, inner-city primary school.* London: Routledge.

Dadzie, S. 2000. *Toolkit for tackling racism in school.* Stoke-on-Trent, UK: Trentham.

Dei, G.J.S. 1996. *Anti-racism education: Theory and practice.* Halifax: Fernwood Publishing.

–. 1998. The denial of difference: Reframing anti-racist praxis. *Race, Ethnicity, and Education* 2(1): 17-37.

Drew, D., and J. Gray. 1991. The black-white gap in examination results: A statistical critique of a decade's research. *New Community* 17(2): 159-72.

Edelman, M. 1964. *The symbolic uses of politics.* Chicago: University of Illinois Press.

Figueroa, P. 1999. Multiculturalism and anti-racism in a new ERA: A critical review. *Race, Ethnicity, and Education* 2(2): 281-301.

Gillborn, D. 1990. *"Race," ethnicity, and education: Teaching and learning in multi-ethnic schools.* London: Unwin Hyman.

–. 1995. *Racism and antiracism in real schools: Theory, policy, practice.* Buckingham, UK: Open University Press.

–. 2000. Anti-racism: From policy to praxis. In *Routledge international companion to education,* ed. B. Moon, S. Brown, and M. Ben-Peretz, 476-88. London: Routledge.

–. 2001. Racism, policy and the (mis)education of Black children. In *Educating our Black children: New directions and radical approaches,* ed. R. Majors, 13-27. London: Routledge-Falmer.

Gillborn, D., and H.S. Mirza. 2000. *Educational inequality: Mapping race, class and gender: A synthesis of research evidence.* Report no. HMI 232. London: Office for Standards in Education. http://www.ofsted.gov.uk.

Gillborn, D., and D. Youdell. 2000. *Rationing education: Policy, practice, reform and equity.* Buckingham, UK: Open University Press.

Goldberg, D.T., ed. 1994. *Multiculturalism: A critical reader.* Oxford: Blackwell.

Hallam, S. 2002. *Ability grouping in schools.* Perspectives on Education Policy no. 13. London: Institute of Education, University of London.

Hallam, S., and I. Toutounji. 1996. *What do we know about the grouping of pupils by ability? A research review.* London: Institute of Education, University of London.

Henriques, J. 1984. Social psychology and the politics of racism. In *Changing the subject: Psychology, social regulation, and subjectivity,* ed. J. Henriques, W. Holloway, C. Urwin, C. Venn, and V. Walkerdine, 11-25. London: Methuen.

Kapur, R. 2002. Monsoon in a teacup. *Legal Affairs* http://www.legalaffairs.org/issues/September-October-2002.

Kirton, A., and H. Brighouse. 2001. Compulsory citizenship education in England: Problems and prospects. *Delta* 53(1-2): 61-78.

Ladson-Billings, G. 1998. Just what is critical race theory and what's it doing in a *nice* field like education? *International Journal of Qualitative Studies in Education* 11(1): 7-24.

Leonardo, Z. 2002. The souls of white folk: Critical pedagogy, whiteness studies, and globalization discourse. *Race, Ethnicity, and Education* 5(1): 29-50.

Mac an Ghaill, M. 1988. *Young, gifted and Black: Student-teacher relations in the schooling of Black youth.* Milton Keynes, UK: Open University Press.

Macpherson, W. 1999. *The Stephen Lawrence inquiry.* CM 4262-I. London: Stationery Office.

Mason, D. 2000. *Race and ethnicity in modern Britain*. Oxford: Oxford University Press.

May, S. 1999. Critical multiculturalism and cultural difference: Avoiding essentialism. In *Critical multiculturalism: Rethinking multiculturalist and antiracist education*, ed. S. May, 11-41. London: Falmer.

Mirza, H.S. 1992. *Young, female and Black*. London: Routledge.

Mullard, C. 1982. Multiracial education in Britain: From assimilation to cultural pluralism. In *Race, migration and schooling*, ed. J. Tierney, 120-33. London: Holt, Rinehart and Winston.

Nehaul, K. 1996. *The schooling of children of Caribbean heritage*. Stoke-on-Trent, UK: Trentham.

Nieto, S. 1999. Critical multicultural education and students' perspectives. In *Critical multiculturalism: Rethinking multiculturalist and antiracist education*, ed. S. May, 191-215. London: Falmer.

Oakes, J. 1990. *Multiplying inequalities: The effects of race, social class, and tracking on opportunities to learn mathematics and science*. Santa Monica, CA: Rand Corporation.

Official: Asylum rush causes crisis for schools. 2003. *Sun* (London). 6 February, 14-15.

Osler, A. 1997. *Exclusion from school and racial equality*. London: Commission for Racial Equality.

–. 1999. Citizenship, democracy and political literacy. *Multicultural Teaching* 18(1): 12-15, 29.

–. 2000. *Citizenship and democracy in schools: Diversity, identity, equality*. Stoke-on-Trent, UK: Trentham.

Political correctness gone mad. 2003. *Daily Mail* (London). 27 February, 15.

Ramdin, R. 1987. *The making of the Black working class in Britain*. Aldershot, UK: Wildwood House.

Rizvi, F. 1993. Critical introduction. In *Racism and education: Research perspectives*, ed. B. Troyna, 1-17. Buckingham, UK: Open University Press.

Rooney, B. 2002. Ready for a racial policy? *Times Educational Supplement*, May 31. http://www.tes.co.uk.

Runnymede Trust. 2000. *The future of multi-ethnic Britain: Report of the commission on the future of multi-ethnic Britain established by the Runnymede Trust*. London: Profile Books.

Sewell, T. 1997. *Black masculinities and schooling: How Black boys survive modern schooling*. Stoke-on-Trent, UK: Trentham.

Sivanandan, A. 1990. *Communities of resistance: Writings on Black struggles for socialism*. London: Verso.

–. 2000. Reclaiming the struggle – one year on. *Multicultural Teaching* 18(2): 6-8, 20.

Sukhnandan, L., and B. Lee. 1998. *Streaming, setting, and grouping by ability*. Slough, UK: National Foundation for Educational Research.

Swann, L. 1985. *Education for all: Final report of the Committee of Inquiry into the education of children from ethnic minority groups*. Command 9453. London: HMSO.

Taylor, K., and S. Singh. 2001. Hatred born out of tragedy. *Searchlight*, October, 4-5.

Taylor, M.J. 1992. *Multicultural antiracist education after ERA: Concerns, constraints, and challenges*. Slough, UK: National Foundation for Educational Research.

Threat of asylum pupils. 2003. *Daily Mail* (London). 6 February, 18-19.

Thornton, K. 1999. Exclusion still highest in minority groups. *Times Educational Supplement*, 9 July, 2.

Tomlinson, S. 1977. Race and education in Britain 1960-77: An overview of the literature. *Sage Race Relations Abstracts* 2(4): 3-33.

Troyna, B. 1993. *Racism and education: Research perspectives*. Buckingham, UK: Open University Press.

Troyna, B., and R. Hatcher. 1992. *Racism in children's lives: A study of mainly white primary schools*. London: Routledge.

UK. 1999. *Parliamentary Debates*, Commons, 6th series, vol. 326-7.

UK. Audit Commission. 1996. *Misspent youth: Young people and crime*. London: Audit Commission.

UK. DfEE (Department for Education and Employment). 1997. *Excellence in Schools*. CM 3681. London: DfEE.

–. 1998. *New report points the way to citizenship education for all pupils*. Press notice 1998/0433. 22 September.

–. 1999. Ethnic minority pupils must have the opportunity to fulfill their potential – Blunkett. Press release 90/99. 24 February.

UK. DfES (Department for Education and Skills). 2003. *Youth cohort study: The activities and experiences of 16-year-olds: England and Wales*. SFR 04/2003. London: DfES.

UK. Home Office. 2000. *Code of practice on reporting and recording racist incidents in response to recommendation 15 of the Stephen Lawrence Inquiry Report*. London: Home Office.

–. 2002. *Secure borders, safe haven: Integration with diversity in modern Britain*. CM 5387. London: Home Office.

UK. NCC (National Curriculum Council). 1990a. *Curriculum guidance 3: The whole curriculum*. York: NCC.

–. 1990b. *Curriculum guidance 8: Education for citizenship*. York: NCC.

UK. Office for National Statistics. 1996. *Social focus on ethnic minorities*. London: Office for National Statistics.

UK. QCA (Qualifications and Curriculum Authority). 1998. *Education for citizenship and the teaching of democracy in schools*. QCA/98/155. London: QCA.

–. 2003a. *Respect for all: PSHE and citizenship KS1-4*. http://qca.org.uk/1590.html.

–. 2003b. *Respect for all in PSHE and citizenship: Racial discrimination (KS 3)*. http://qca.org.uk/1590_2362.html.

UK. Speaker's Commission on Citizenship. 1990. *Encouraging citizenship*. London: Speaker's Commission on Citizenship.

Vincent, C. 2000. *Including parents? Education, citizenship and parental agency*. Buckingham, UK: Open University Press.

Whitty, G., P. Aggleton, and G. Rowe. 1992. *Cross curricular work in secondary schools: Summary of results of a survey carried out in 1992: Report to participating schools*. London: Institute of Education, University of London.

Wiliam, D. 2001. What is wrong with our educational assessment and what can be done about it? *Education Review* 15(1): 57-62.

Wood, M. 2000. *Blind memory: Visual representations of slavery in England and America 1780-1865*. Manchester, UK: Manchester University Press.

Wright, C. 1986. School processes – an ethnographic study. In *Education for some: The educational and vocational experiences of 15-18 year old members of minority ethnic groups*, ed. J. Eggleston, D. Dunn, and M. Anjali, 127-79. Stoke-on-Trent, UK: Trentham.

–. 1992. *Race relations in the primary school*. London: David Fulton.

Youdell, D. 2003. Identity traps or how Black students fail: The interactions between biographical, sub-cultural, and learner identities. *British Journal of Sociology of Education* 24(1): 3-20.

17
Multicultural Policies and Practices in North America: A Dialogue with the View from England
Catherine Cornbleth, Rinaldo Walcott,
Carlos J. Ovando, and Terezia Zoric

Editors' note: David Gillborn's insights about diversity policy in England extend our policy dialogue beyond North America to a third national context and help us to reconsider issues surrounding diversity policies within our two countries. In this dialogue chapter, four educators with different views on multicultural education policy respond to issues raised by Gillborn. Catherine Cornbleth, an influential scholar from the United States, who has studied multicultural education curriculum and policy making, uses her extensive understanding of the field to highlight the uses and need for policy. Rinaldo Walcott, a noted scholar in Canada, approaches the issue of policy from a cultural studies perspective and explores issues of identity. Carlos Ovando, a distinguished scholar from the United States, draws on his work with teacher educators to raise questions about how to proceed from critique to constructive practice. Terezia Zoric, an activist educator known across Canada for her groundbreaking work in the development and implementation of diversity education policies, draws on her experiences in the Toronto schools to address the question of moving from rhetoric to policy activism. These four responses raise new issues and underscore the need for continued conversation and work on multicultural education policy in both Canada and the United States.

Catherine Cornbleth
David Gillborn has provided us with a compelling case – of opportunity lost, of symbolic reform, of bureaucracies doing what bureaucracies do, that is, muting or mediating external demands in order to maintain the status quo in the interests of those who benefit from it. I am reminded of Jules Henry, a US anthropologist, who in his 1963 book *Culture against Man* (I assume that he meant women too) argued well that schooling serves to transmit the dominant culture (euphemized as mainstream) and that social studies, including history and citizenship education, teach students to be "stupid" by both overwhelming them with supposedly factual information and discouraging questioning. "It

couldn't be otherwise," Henry observed, "if the culture, the dominant culture that is, is to survive" (287-88).

And here we are, trying to undermine or subvert at least parts of that dominant culture. Clearly, that's not easy to do. It's not easy to undermine institutional or structural racism given the very strong individualistic bias that masks it in the United States and in England. The reduction of institutional or structural racism to individual prejudice is the simplest example here.

The focus of my own research in this area is on curriculum practice: what we teach, how we go about it, and who benefits from it. I have been studying what shapes that practice with respect to the political policy-making processes, as well as the policies regarding more multicultural or inclusive history and social studies education. In our book *The Great Speckled Bird: Multicultural Politics and Educational Policymaking* (Cornbleth and Waugh 1999), Dexter Waugh and I examine the multicultural politics and the history of social studies curriculum policy making in New York and California. Gillborn's comments about citizenship education in England sound painfully familiar. As he notes: "Schools have considerable scope to add their own ideas and directions; they can also decide to cover a bare minimum. As in the past, communities, activists, and academics have attempted to produce useful tools and additions ... For the most part, however, the antiracist potential of citizenship education remains unrealized." The same can be said for New York, California, and probably at least a few places in between.

Let me briefly suggest two possible grounds for hope and for hard work. First, teachers who *are* incorporating antiracist practices should be identified, supported, and their stories shared with other teachers. Waugh and I found in both New York and California teachers whose classroom curriculum practices went beyond their state's multicultural policies and their textbook's pages. I think we can start with the good things that are happening and see what we can do to make them more common. A second possibility is to maintain the pressure and to refuse to be silenced so that minimalist responses or symbolic policies and practices are unable to hold or to appease. This requires patience, persistence, and organization, attributes not usually associated with academics. As Gillborn notes: "Meaningful advances in race equity are typically preceded by public uprisings (usually labelled riots by a media keen to present minority communities as hotbeds of criminality and alienation), by deaths (at the hands of police or other White racist groups and individuals), or, at the very least, by concerted public protest by minority communities. This pattern is repeating itself in contemporary education policy in England."

I'm not advocating violence, but concerted public protest in a range of forums does appeal. What can be learned from how the Stephen Lawrence Inquiry and report came to be and how it came to say what it did? It seems to me, from my location in Buffalo, that even a public conversation about institutional or structural racism is something. When is the last time that you encountered that kind of conversation in print or verbally outside the university? How might the spirit of the Lawrence Inquiry be kept alive and translated into curriculum practice, if not education policy?

In Chapter 2, Lauri Johnson discusses how local multicultural policies in the United States have been largely reactive and crisis-oriented, resulting from the advocacy of a particular board member or grassroots activists. This observation seems to point to some similarity with the Stephen Lawrence case in England worth further examination and action.

Finally, some comments on symbolic policy. Symbolic policies vary in their potential and largely unintended utility. Some symbolic policies *are* empty. They are perhaps decorative but otherwise intended only to give the appearance of doing something worthwhile. Other policies *become* symbolic because, whether by accident or on purpose, they are not implemented widely or at all. They do, however, provide space, language, leverage, and legitimation for those who care to use them and have the resources to do so. It's here that both research and programmatic efforts might focus their subversive energies.

Rinaldo Walcott

My comments are framed within the context of the official nation-state policy of multiculturalism in Canada, that is, the policy that was enacted in 1971 and then made an act in 1988. My comments must be understood within that context because of the ways in which I want to address the question of citizenship and the making of the nation.

I was pleased to see that David Gillborn framed his paper through the racist murder of Stephen Lawrence, because I think that the murder sets up a useful paradigm for thinking about how discourses of multiculturalism and antiracism work at the level of nation-state rhetoric and governmental procedures. I would argue, along with others, that Canadian multicultural policy is a policy that attempts to imagine how those who are not of British ancestry or Québécois are part of the nation. Without such a policy, all those who are not anglophone or Québécois are seen as outsiders. The preamble of the Canadian Multiculturalism Act (1988) restates that Canada is a bilingual nation and leaves anglophone Canadians and Québécois outside the category of the ethnic. They are seen as the "real" Canadians; all others have to be imagined as a part of the nation. So, for example, to imagine me as a Canadian, legislation is needed. This Canadian narrative of two founding peoples discounts a long history of Black belonging to the nation.

Multiculturalism in that sense is about managing diversity and managing multiple cultures. When we think about multiculturalism we should separate the discourse, rhetoric, and practice of managing diversity from the everyday lived realities of multiple cultures in particular spaces encountering each other and negotiating how to live on some kind of civil terms.

For me, multiculturalism is about the crisis of the multicultural moment for modern nation-states. The murders of Reena Virk[1] and Stephen Lawrence are symptoms of a deep crisis of belonging within particular national landscapes. Their bodies become representative of something that has to be rooted out of the nation, because it represents an aberration. The nation imagines itself as White, so how can Stephen Lawrence exist, being Black and British? The nation imagines itself as White, so how can Reena Virk exist, being South Asian and Canadian? In part, we must change the popular imagination regarding who belongs to the nation. This lies beyond ideology but this is also quite phenotypically coded. It's no accident that it's usually coloured bodies who die in these skirmishes.

What is really at stake are questions of race, questions of nation, and questions of citizenship. Heritage discourse in the multiculturalism policy Act is important because it leads you somewhere else. It leads you outside the nation, back to Greece or Barbados, no matter how many generations removed you are.

Borrowing from Stuart Hall (2000), I don't think that multiculturalism is a term that we can throw out. It now exists in our popular consciousness and, as Hall says, we have to struggle to reclaim it. One of the places where we can struggle over this new multicultural logic is the realm of popular culture. In North America and globally we live to the soundtrack of African American music. Popular culture contains some possibilities for opening up a new kind of multiculturalism – a multiculturalism about the everyday intimacies of life. It seems to me that the important conceptual shift is to think about the ways of living intimately with multiple cultures in the urban context: how to talk about that and how to translate that into social policy and political action.

Carlos J. Ovando

Carlos Fuentes (1988), the Mexican novelist and author of *The Old Gringo*, among other books, has said that the biggest challenge facing humanity is dealing with the other. We see ourselves through the mirror of others and how they reflect who we are. When I read David Gillborn's chapter I was frustrated, challenged, and angry, because there is so little optimism. There is strong critique, with which I agree, but the course of action to address or remedy the situation seems to be absent. I say this with the utmost respect to him as a scholar, because it's easy for any of us to critique, but it's not that easy to offer solutions. I've been looking at education for many years. The situation in England parallels that in the United States so much: the marginalization of students, the tracking, and the widening achievement gap. I'm rereading things that I read in graduate school. The schools can serve as the engine either to mobilize society or to perpetuate inequities.

I would like to toss a set of questions back at David: Why does it take violence or a death to produce or stimulate change? Examples of this are the

Rodney King case[2] in the United States and the Stephen Lawrence Inquiry in England. Why do policies reflect the lack of political will on the part of policy makers? David, you're very eloquent with your critique. Is your voice being heard among your colleagues who are determining policy in the British system? How can we create dialogue so that we're not just talking to the converted but other people are listening to us?

When I look at multicultural education in the United States, "to know, to care, and to act" is the mantra of the field. Citizenship education is accepted by many people as a vehicle of that reform. If I were a teacher in England today implementing this curriculum, what would I say to you? How would I respond to those allegations that citizenship education is a placebo, that it's the problem? Many teachers have been told this is what they are supposed to do, and they do it because they think it is the right thing to do.

I am struggling with where we go from here. I disagree with very little in the paper, but what I don't see here is a path whereby things are going to change either in the United States or England. I'd like us to continue the conversation.

Terezia Zoric

I want to discuss the issues David Gillborn's paper raises from the perspective of a front-line equity worker. I define myself as a bureaucratic activist, someone who tries to implement diversity policies in the schools. I worked as a high school teacher for six years, mainly in inner city schools, but the systemic problems associated with teaching students who were not getting the resources they deserve were making it impossible for me to do my job. Because I've always been interested in some kind of institutional reform, I eventually became a coordinator of equity in my school board in Toronto.

Toronto schools are the most multilingual and multicultural in the world. About half of our students, and there are 300,000 in the Toronto District School Board, are a racial minority within Canada. About 53 percent of our students have English as their first language, but 41 percent of our students are born outside of Canada. Our students speak over eighty different languages at home. We get eight thousand newcomers from more than 170 countries every year. Twelve percent of our secondary students have been in Canada for three years or less. Half of our students are female. One in three lives in poverty. One in ten is gay, lesbian, bisexual, or transgender. One in ten has an identified physical, psychological, or learning disability. The Toronto schools thus include a very diverse and global population.

With this diversity has come some exceptionally strong community activist groups who have seen education as a vehicle for social progress. Activist antiracist organizations have existed for more than twenty-five years. We have trustees who were members of national human rights commissions and have been elected to the school board on antiracist and antisexist platforms. There has been a very activist community presence and a long history of antiracist and equity work. Six years ago I was able to work to develop an extensive equity policy inclusive of race, religion, gender, class, sexual orientation, and ability with the input of thirty-five activist community groups such as Anti-Racist Multicultural Educators, the Chinese Canadian National Council, the Labour Council, Parents of Black Children, antihomophobia groups, special education advocacy groups, public education advocacy groups, and Justice for Children and Youth. The list goes on and on – the who's who of activism was involved. When it came time to pressure the school board to adopt an inclusive and extensive equity policy, we presented more than eight hundred oral and written deputations to the board. There were two years of constant conversation in the community about the extent to which race ought or ought not to be the central focus of these policies, whether we were going to support antihomophobia work like all other kinds of work, and so on.

In the end we achieved dramatic and ambitious language (see, for example, Toronto District School Board 2005). The Toronto District School Board acknowledges institutional racism, sexism, homophobia, and able-ism. It recognizes that what exists in society exists in the schools, and that the schools are responsible for creating it and addressing it. We have the policy; the challenge is implementation in the face of the current neoliberal assault.

Neoliberalism in Canada, as in the United States and the United Kingdom, has led to high-stakes testing, zero tolerance for violence, and increasing failure rates for marginalized students. We thought that the equity policy would be an important tool for those who were trying to resist neoliberal practices. We knew from the start we were working against the odds. Six equity workers had $300,000 to implement the equity policy in six hundred schools in one year. That is a budget of one dollar per student. We knew at the end of a five-year process there would be no more money available and there would be tremendous cuts to the Toronto District School Board. We hoped we could reculture the school board in those five years. We thought that it was important to train the principals, vice principals, and superintendents, and to produce policy documents in order to gain a foothold in the school system.

Why did we bother? We thought it was possible to create a momentum working with those people who were already "on side," to give them powerful tools that they could use. Our equity policy allowed me to disseminate materials into schools on antihomophobia education, books that had been banned in other provinces. We could remove hate materials because they were contrary to the policy. We created a cadre of defenders of equity who could justify their activities based on the policy. We were able to produce minimal literacy about equity that is still present in the system today. Those school principals who had never talked about equity before began to understand the difference between treating everyone the same and treating people according to their needs in order to achieve similar outcomes. The equity policy became a lens through which other policies were viewed and changed.

In summary, I believe that you can be symbolic and substantive at the same time. Policies may contain inspiring language, but the real challenge is to move beyond the words. In Toronto we attempted to do this through strategic political and bureaucratic action. From my experience, the key is not so much the high quality of the policies you produce, as the leverage of the policies when they hit the ground.

Notes

1 In 1997 Reena Virk, a fourteen-year-old South Asian girl described by the media as someone who "didn't fit in," was beaten and drowned by a group of teenagers (six girls and one boy) in Victoria, British Columbia.

2 The 1991 police beating of Rodney King, an African American man stopped for a traffic violation in Los Angeles, was captured on videotape and broadcast to the world. When the police officers involved in the incident were found not guilty in 1992, the verdict became the catalyst for several days of violence in South Central Los Angeles that resulted in fifty-three deaths, 10,000 arrests, and $1 billion in damages.

References

Cornbleth, C., and D. Waugh. 1999. *The great speckled bird: Multicultural politics and education policymaking*. New York: St. Martin's Press.

Fuentes, C. 1988. *Myself with others*. New York: Farrar, Strauss Giroux.

Hall, S. 2000. The multicultural question. In *Un/Settled multiculturalisms: Diasporas, entanglements, transruptions*, ed. B. Hesse, 209-41. London: Zed Books.

Henry, J. 1963. *Culture against man*. New York: Random House.

Toronto District School Board. 2005. *Equity foundation statement and commitments to equity policy implementation*. http://www.tdsb.on.ca.

Contributors

Carol Agocs is a professor emerita in the Department of Political Science at the University of Western Ontario. Her research examines employment equity, gender and racial discrimination in employment, and workplace change.

Adrienne S. Chan is an adjunct professor at the University of British Columbia and a faculty member in the School of Social Work and Human Services at the University College of the Fraser Valley. Her research interests include the relationships between policy and practice, change, and institutional culture – with an emphasis on race, gender, class, diversity, social inclusion, and social justice.

Catherine Cornbleth is a professor in the Department of Learning and Instruction at the University at Buffalo. Her teaching and research interests include curriculum studies (politics, policies, and practices), social studies and history education, and social identities (individual, group, and national). She has also published extensively on multicultural policy implementation and climates of constraint/restraint on teaching.

Tracey M. Derwing is the co-director of the Prairie Centre of Excellence in Immigration and Integration and a professor in the Department of Educational Psychology at the University of Alberta. Her principal research interests are second language acquisition and native speaker-non-native speaker intelligibility, as well as citizenship education for adult immigrants and refugee issues.

David Gillborn is a professor in the sociology of education and chair of the Department of Educational Foundations and Policy Studies at the Institute of Education, University of London. He is best known for his work on inequality in working-class, multiethnic schools and the racialized consequences of educational reform.

Michelle Goldberg is a recent graduate of the PhD program in the Department of Theory and Policy Studies, Ontario Institute for Studies in Education, University of Toronto. Previously she worked for the Ontario government for ten years researching equity issues affecting immigrants and their ability to access professions in Ontario.

Karen M. Gourd is a visiting professor of education at Waseda University in Tokyo, Japan. Her teaching and research interests focus on the preparation of critical multicultural educators, with particular interest in the use of forum theatre in education, diverse cultural perspectives on the philosophy of education, and language instruction and policy issues.

Jan Hare is an Anishinaabe and member of the M'Chigeeng First Nation, located on Manitoulin Island in northern Ontario. A former primary school teacher, she is currently an assistant professor with the Department of Language and Literacy Education at the University of British Columbia. Her research is concerned with Aboriginal responses to various points of contact between Aboriginal peoples and Europeans, with a particular focus on families and literacy.

Lauri Johnson is an associate professor in the Department of Educational Leadership and Policy at the University at Buffalo. A former administrator with the New York City public schools, her research examines educators' conceptualizations of race, community activism in urban school reform, the development and implementation of diversity policies, and successful urban school leadership.

Reva Joshee is co-director of the Centre for Leadership and Diversity and an associate professor in the Department of Theory and Policy Studies of the Ontario Institute for Studies in Education, University of Toronto. She has worked with the Canadian government as a community development officer in the area of multiculturalism. Her research examines issues of diversity and policy in India, Canada, and the United States.

Augustine McCaffery is a senior administrator who works with academic program review in the School of Graduate Studies at the University of Washington, where she is also responsible for the recruitment of American Indian and Alaskan Native students. As a doctoral student in educational leadership and policy studies at the university, her research focuses on issues of equity and retention for American Indian and Alaskan Native students in graduate school.

Murray J. Munro, a professor of linguistics at Simon Fraser University, has a long-standing interest and involvement in citizenship education for adult immigrants. His chief area of research is phonetic learning by speakers of English as a second language. This work has led him to study the linguistic aspects of foreign accents, how people respond to second language speech, and the problem of discrimination against people with non-native patterns of speaking.

Carlos J. Ovando is a professor of curriculum and instruction and former associate dean of teacher education in the College of Education at Arizona State University. He has written extensively on culture, language, and curriculum-related issues pertaining to language minority student populations.

Yoon K. Pak is an associate professor in educational policy studies and a core faculty member of the Asian American Studies Program at the University of Illinois at Urbana-Champaign. She teaches on the history of American education from a multicultural perspective and on issues and developments in Asian American education. Her research interests include the history of intercultural education and democratic citizenship education between the world wars.

Rashid V. Robinson is a doctoral student in educational policy studies at the University of Illinois at Urbana-Champaign. His research interests include the history of American higher education and representations of higher education in popular culture.

Sabrina Redwing Saunders is a PhD candidate at the Ontario Institute for Studies in Education at the University of Toronto. As a Haudenosaunee woman, mother, and educator, she self-identifies as a stakeholder in Native school improvement and challenges all readers to take up the struggle for first-class Native education.

Christopher M. Span is an assistant professor at the University of Illinois at Urbana-Champaign. A historian of education in the Department of Educational Policy Studies, his research interests pertain to the educational history of nineteenth- and twentieth-century African Americans.

Edward Taylor is vice provost at the University of Washington, an associate professor in educational leadership and policy studies, and a faculty associate of the Center for Multicultural Education, University of Washington. His areas of teaching and research are related to the sociocultural foundations of education, multicultural education, policy issues, and leadership and organizational change.

John W. Tippeconnic III is a professor of education and the director of the American Indian Leadership Program at Pennsylvania State University. He began his educational career as a middle school teacher in New Mexico and Arizona, and served as vice president of the Navajo Community College (now Diné College). Dr. Tippeconnic was also the director of the Office of Indian Education Programs for the Bureau of Indian Affairs, and of the Office of Indian Education (OIE) in the US Department of Education.

Charles Ungerleider is director of research and knowledge mobilization for the Canadian Council on Learning while on leave from his position as professor of the sociology of education in the Department of Educational Studies at the University of British Columbia. Formerly deputy minister of education for the province of British Columbia, he has published widely on educational governance, student assessment, race relations, intergroup relations and multiculturalism, and the impact of media on Canadian society.

Trinidad Molina Villegas is a doctoral student at the University of Illinois at Urbana-Champaign, pursuing a degree in educational policy studies. Her research interests include the educational experiences of immigrant students in the United States, bilingual education, and undocumented immigrant students' access to higher education.

Rinaldo Walcott is an associate professor in the Department of Sociology and Equity Studies, Ontario Institute for Studies in Education, University of Toronto, where he holds the Canada Research Chair in Social Justice and Cultural Studies. His teaching and research has been in the area of cultural studies, queer theory, and postcolonial studies with an emphasis on Black diaspora studies.

Njoki Nathani Wane is an associate professor in the Department of Sociology and Equity Studies, Ontario Institute for Studies in Education, University of Toronto, where she teaches in both the pre-service and graduate programs. Her research interests include gender, colonialism and development, Black feminism, African immigrant women in Canada, and antiracism education.

Terrence G. Wiley is professor and director of the Division of Educational Leadership and Policy Studies, and co-director of the Language Policy Research Unit of the Educational Policy Studies Laboratory, at Arizona State University. He is the author of numerous publications on language policy, literacy, biliteracy, and current and historical issues related to language diversity.

Susan Winton is a PhD student at the Ontario Institute for Studies in Education at the University of Toronto. She is an experienced teacher who has taught in Canada, the United States, and Mexico. Her current research focuses on character education in Canada.

Terezia Zoric is a lecturer in the pre-service teacher education program at the Ontario Institute for Studies in Education at the University of Toronto. A former high school teacher, she previously worked for the Toronto District School Board as the district-wide co-coordinator of equity, helping develop and implement a comprehensive equity and human rights policy.

Index

achievement gap. *See* educational attainment.

Acoose, Janice, 56

Act for the Gradual Enfranchisement of Indians (1869) (Canada), 52

Administrative Committee on Intercultural and Interracial Relations (US), 33

Advisory Group on the Teaching of Citizenship and Democracy (UK), 229

affirmative action, 11, 188, 191-92, 195-200, 207-8, 208-9, 209-11

Agocs, Carol, 10

Akwesasne Science and Math Curriculum, 63

Alberta, Canada, 96, 100, 101, 102, 104, 139

Alvarez v. The Board of Trustees of the Lemon Grove School District (US), 153-55

American Civil Liberties Union, 155, 194

American Council on Education, 86

American Jewish Congress, 30-31, 155

American Service Institute of Allegheny County, 35, 38

Americans All, 20, 21

Americans All, Immigrants All (CBS 1938-39), 7, 20, 30, 39n4, 43-46

Ancheta, Angelo, 44

antiracism, 140-42, 217, 242, 245-46

anti-Semitism, 29, 30

asylum seekers (UK), 234-35

Baldy Center for Law and Social Policy, at the University at Buffalo, 8

Bangura, Yusuf, 5

Bilingual Education Act (1968) (US), 120, 123

bilingual education programs, 10, 28, 96, 102, 104, 107-9, 112-17, 121, 123-24, 126. *See also* English as a second language (ESL)

bilingualism, xi, 10, 95-98, 127, 243

Black Learners Association, 140

Black Panther Party, 39n1

Blair, Tony, 219

Blunkett, David, 219, 234, 237n16

boarding schools. *See* residential schools

British Columbia, Canada, 56, 99, 102-3, 132, 134, 135, 139, 142

British National Party, 234, 235

British North America Act (1867) (Canada), 52

Brooklyn, NY, 30-31

Brown, Homer, 34-35, 39

Brown v. Board of Education of Topeka (US), 27, 28, 36, 146

Building One Nation, Indivisible, (Detroit public schools), 33

Bureau for Intercultural Education (US), 30, 33, 34, 37, 43

Bureau of Indian Affairs (US), 70, 77, 78, 109

Bureau of Public Information (Canada), *Canadians All*, 20

Burlingame Treaty (US), 150

Calgary Board of Education, 103

California, US, 123, 126, 152-56

Canada: A Source Book for Orientation, Language and Settlement Workers, 99

Canadian Alliance, 179, 185

Canadian American Studies Association, xvii

Canadian Association for Adult Education, 24

Canadian Broadcasting Corporation, xiv

Canadian Citizenship Council, 19, 21, 23, 24

Canadian Committee on Cultural
Relations, 21
Canadian Human Rights Act (1977), 138,
172
Canadian Human Rights Commission,
172
Canadian Multiculturalism Act (1988),
96, 120, 132, 137-38, 243, 244
Canadian Studies Center, xvii, 8
Canadians All (Bureau of Public
Information, Canada), 7, 20, 46
Canadian/US Conference on
Multicultural Policy, xvii
Cardinal, Harold, 57
Carlson, John, 193, 194, 197
Carmichael, Stokely, 219
Carter, Robert L., 155
Chalfant, Mrs. F.B., 35-36
Chan, Adrienne, 10
Character Counts (US), 24, 25
character education, 24-25, 228
Character Education Partnership (US), 24
Character Matters (US), 24, 25
Charter of Rights and Freedoms (1982)
(Canada), 96, 132, 138
Cherokee language, 109
Chinese Canadian National Council, 246
Chinese Exclusion Act (1923) (Canada),
131
Citizens Plus (Indian Association of
Alberta 1970), 58
Citizenship Act (1947) (Canada), 17, 18,
23
Citizenship Branch (Canada), 19-20, 23
citizenship education, 11, 19-22, 43, 217,
219, 220, 228-32, 233, 235
City-Wide Citizens' Committee on
Harlem (CWCCH), 31-32
Cole Harbour School District High
School, 140-42
Committee on Education, Training and
Research in Race Relations (US), 20
Constitution Act (1982) (Canada), 54
Coordinating Committee for Democratic
Human Relations (US), 33
Cornbleth, Catherine, 11
Cowessess Indian Residential School, 56
Crick, Bernard, 229
Crick Report, 229-30
critical discourse theory, 204-7, 211-12
critical race theory, 11, 188, 189-91, 199,
200-1, 205
Culture against Man (Henry 1963), 241

Davin, Nicholas, 55
Delaney, Martin, 35

demographics, for Canada, xiv, 93-95,
168-69, 174
demographics, for United States, 32,
34-35, 73, 78, 108, 112, 153, 191
Denman, James, 149-50
Department of Indian Affairs (Canada),
60
Derwing, Tracey, 10, 122-23
Detroit Intercultural Code, 33-34
Detroit, Michigan, African-American
population of, 32
Detroit Public Schools, 32-34
Detroit riot, 32
Diné College, 84-85
diversity policies, 11, 18, 28-39, 167-212.
See also multicultural policies
DuBois, Rachel Davis, 30, 35, 43, 44

Economic Opportunity Act (US), 84
education, Aboriginal, in Canada, 9,
51-66, 83-84, 140-42
education, American Indian/Alaska
Native, in the United States, 9, 69-81,
83-88
Education Department (UK), 219, 220
education policy development, 11
Education Reform Act (UK), 221
educational attainment, 51, 57, 61, 71-73,
77-78, 85-88, 192, 221-24, 226-27, 233
educational equity, 6, 115-16, 124-25, 246
Elementary and Secondary Education Act
(US), 84
Employment and Immigration Canada,
99
employment equity, 10-11, 167-68,
207-11
Employment Equity Act (1986/1995)
(Canada), 167-82, 184-86, 207
Employment Equity Review Tribunal
(Canada), 172
England, Robert, 19
English as a second language (ESL), 19,
98-104, 116-17, 126
Executive Order 13096 on American
Indian and Alaska Native Education, 72

Federal Contractors Program (1986)
(Canada), 167, 171
Forbes, Steve, 193
Foucault, Michel, 185, 205, 206
Foulds, Frank, 23
foundational myths, 22-23
Fuentes, Carlos, 244

Gaynor, Florence, 19
General Certificate of Secondary

Education (UK), 224-27, 236-37n6,
Georgia, US, 147
Gillborn, David, 11
Goldberg, Michelle, 11
Gourd, Karen, 10
The Great Speckled Bird: Multicultural Politics and Educational Policymaking (Cornbleth and Waugh 1999), 242
Gus, Ramona, 56

Halligan, Alice, 36
Hamilton, Charles V., 219
Harding, Sandra, 181
Hare, Jan, 9, 17
Harlem, 30
Harlem Committee (New York City Teachers Union), 31, 37
Harlem riot (1943), 30
Hawthorn, H.B., 51
Hawthorn Report, 51-52, 58
Henry, Jules, 241
Hill v. *Camden* (Canada), 134
Human Resources and Development Canada, 179
Humphrey, John, 23

identity, in Canada, xii, xvi, 10, 17-19, 23, 52, 58, 97, 99
identity, in United States, 75-76, 80, 83, 84, 87
immigrants, in Canada, xiv, 46, 93-95, 97-98, 100, 103, 125-26, 168-69, 170
immigrants, in United States, xiv, 34-35, 43-45, 112, 149-50
Immigration Act (1910/1978) (Canada), 94, 137
immigration policies, 4, 10, 44, 93-95, 112, 120, 122, 126, 234-35
Indian Act (1876) (Canada), 52, 57, 58, 60, 131, 161
Indian Control of Indian Education (National Indian Brotherhood 1972), 58, 63
Indian Education: A National Tragedy – A National Challenge (US Senate Subcommittee 1969), 70-71
Indian Education Act (1972/1988) (US), 71
Indian Nations at Risk Task Force (US), 71, 73
Indian School Days (Johnston 1988), 56
Indian Self-Determination and Education Assistance Act (1975) (US), 71
Initiative 200 (US), 188, 193-201
institutional racism, 217, 218-19, 220, 224, 226-32, 241. *See also* racism

intercultural education (US), 7, 8, 20-22, 23, 29-39, 43
International Reading Association, 115, 125
internment of Japanese Americans and Japanese Canadians, 46, 135-36

Jackson, Andrew, 109
Japanese-American Citizens League, 155
Jefferson, Thomas, 109
Jewish Labor Committee (US), 20-21
Johnson, Lauri, 9, 200, 243
Johnston, Basil, 56
Joint Labour Committee to Combat Racial Intolerance (Canada), 21
Joshee, Reva, 9
Justice for Children and Youth (Canada), 246

Kamloops Indian Residential School, 56
Kaplansky, Kalmen, 21
Kennedy Report, 70
Kidd, John, 23
Kidd, Roby, 24
Kirkness, Verna, 62
Klein, Phillip, 35
knowledge: Eurocentric, 79; indigenous, 79

Labour Council (Canada), 246
language education in Canada, 56, 95-104, 120, 121-27. *See also* bilingual education; English as a second language (ESL)
language education in United States, 10, 76, 107-17, 123-27, 120-27. *See also* bilingual education programs; English as a second language
Language Instruction for Newcomers to Canada (LINC), 98-100
language, loss of heritage, xv, 52, 56, 76, 109-10, 112, 121
language, official, in United States, 122-23, 126
languages, official, in Canada, xiv, 10, 64, 95-97, 104, 120-23
Lau v. *Nichols* (US), 103-4, 112, 117, 120, 124
Lawrence Inquiry. *See* Stephen Lawrence Inquiry report
Lawrence, Stephen, 218, 243, 244
Lemon Grove Grammar School, 153
Liberal Party, xiv, 137, 179
liberalism, 188-89, 191, 200. *See also* neoliberalism
Lindlof, Johanna M., 29, 37, 39n3

Longboat, Dianne, 60
Louisiana, US, 147
Lum v. *Rice* (US), 152

Macdonald, John A., 55
Manitoba, Canada, 95, 96, 139
Marshall, Thurgood, 155
Martin, Sr., Paul, 23
McCaffery, Augustine, 9
McCormick, Paul J., 156
McWilliams, Carey, 36
melting pot thesis, xii, xiii, 113
Mendez v. *Westminster School District of Orange County* (US), 153, 155-56
Meriam Report, 70, 72
meritocracy, myth of, 190, 208-9, 210
Miller, Clyde, 36
Minister's National Working Group on Education (Canada), 60, 63, 64
model minority, myth of, 43-47
Montague, Ashley, 20
Morris, Robert, 148
Mujica, M.E., 122, 123
multicultural education, 3-12, 17, 20, 22, 25, 29, 33, 38, 142, 189. *See also* antiracism; intercultural education (US)
multicultural policies, 3-8, 42-43, 121, 139, 140, 142-43, 217, 242-43. *See also* diversity policies
multiculturalism, xi, 17-18, 54, 96, 137-39, 141-43, 161, 188-89, 201, 217, 243-44
Munro, Murray, 10

National Association for Bilingual Education (US), 115
National Association for the Advancement of Colored People (US), 32-33, 155
National Center for Education Statistics (US), 86
National Conference of Christians and Jews (US), 36, 37
National Council of Teachers of English (US), 115-16, 125-26
National Curriculum (UK), 221, 229
National Defense Education Act (1958) (US), 111
National Film Board of Canada, xiv, 20, 21
National Front (UK), 234
National Indian Brotherhood (US), 58
Nationalities Branch (Canada), 19
Native American Languages Preservation Act (1990) (US), 71, 109
Navajo Community College, 84-85

Neighours' Committee of Lemon Grove, 154
neoliberalism, 11, 24, 25, 208-9, 211, 246
New Brunswick, Canada, 96, 132, 133
New York City, 29, 31-32
New York City Board of Education, 29, 31, 37
Nisga'a Treaty, 65
Nixon, Richard, 71
No Child Left Behind Act (US), 72, 74, 76-78
Nova Scotia, Canada, 99, 132, 134, 140

Oakland, California, 110, 116
O'Connor, Julia, 6
Office of the Commissioner of Official Languages (Canada), 95-96
Office for Standards in Education (UK), 221
Official Languages Act (1969) (Canada), 96, 97, 137
Ontario, Canada, 21, 95, 102, 132, 133, 134, 139
Ontario Equal Opportunity Plan, 207, 208
Ontario Ministry of Education Advisory Committee on Race Relations, 140-41
Osler, Audrey, 229-30
Ovando, Carlos, 10, 11

Pak, Yoon, 7, 9
Parents of Black Children (Canada), 246
Park, Robert, 20
Parliamentary Standing Committee on Human Resources Development and the Status of Persons with Disabilities, 168
Pearson, Lester B., 23
Pittsburgh School Board, 34-36
Pittsburgh Urban League, 34, 35
Plessy v. *Ferguson* (US), 148, 149, 156
policy analysis, xvi, 4, 7, 12, 181, 183-86
policy borrowing, 7, 17, 19-22, 24, 25, 236
policy dialogue, 4, 5, 6-8
policy webs, 5-6
The Problem of Indian Administration (Meriam 1928), 70
Promising Practices in Intergroup Education, 33
Proposition 227 (US), 113, 124

Qualifications and Curriculum Authority (UK), 230-31
Quebec Act of 1774, 22
Quebec, Canada, 20, 95, 96-97, 98

Race Relations (Amendment) Act (UK),

236n5
race-based policy in Canada, 10, 132-37,
159-63
race-based policy in United States, 10,
146-57, 159-63
racialization, 10, 44, 131-32, 136, 137,
142, 143, 159, 162
racism, 10, 21, 140-43, 189-90, 195-96,
199-200, 205, 206, 212, 218-19. *See also*
institutional racism; race-based policy
in Canada; race-based policy in United
States
*Report of the Royal Commission on
Aboriginal Peoples* (1996), 59, 63-64
residential schools, 55-57, 70, 83, 84, 109,
161
Reyhner, Jon, 71-72
Rhode Island, US, 148
Roberts v. *City of Boston* (US), 148-49
Robinson, Rashid, 10
Royal Commission on Bilingualism and
Biculturalism, 64, 96, 137, 161
Royal Commission on Equality in
Employment, 167-68
Royal Proclamation of 1763, xii, 22, 53

San Francisco school board, 150
Saskatchewan, Canada, 56, 96, 139
Saunders, Sabrina Redwing, 9
School Act (1849) (Ontario), 133
segregated schools in Canada, 132-36,
160. *See also* residential schools
segregated schools in United States, 32,
36, 146-56, 160. *See also* residential
schools
self-determination, tribal, in United
States, 70-71, 73-76, 80-81
self-governance, Aboriginal, in Canada,
53-66
Separate School Act (1850) (Ontario), 133
Sequoyah, 109
Service Bureau for Intercultural Education
(US). *See* Bureau for Intercultural
Education (US)
Settlement Language Program, 98
Shaw, Lemuel, Chief Justice of the
Massachusetts Supreme Court, 149
Siddle-Walker, Vanessa, 37
Simmons v. *Chatham* (Canada), 134
South Carolina, US, 147
Span, Christopher, 10
Spence, Lucile, 31, 37, 38
Springfield Plan, 21, 36, 38
standards, academic, 72, 77, 110, 115-17,
125, 192, 195, 221, 223, 224-25
Standards for the English Language Arts, 115

Stanton, Elizabeth Cady, 39n1
Statement on Race (UNESCO 1950), 20
Stephen Lawrence Inquiry report, 218,
224, 227, 231, 233
Straw, Jack, 219
Sumner, Charles, 148

Tape v. *Hurley* (US), 150
Taylor, Edward, 11
Teachers of English to Speakers of Other
Languages (TESOL), 116, 125
Tiering (UK), 224-27
Tippeconnic, John, 9
Toronto Civil Liberties Association, 21
Toronto Committee on Intercultural
Education, 21
Toronto School Board, 140, 245, 246
Toronto schools, 245
*Tradition and Education: Towards a Vision
of Our Future* (Assembly of First Nations
1988), 58
tribal colleges and universities (US), 73,
75, 80, 84-85, 86
Ts"kel (graduate program at University of
British Columbia), 65

UN Declaration on Human Rights, 23,
161
UNESCO, Management of Social
Transformations program, 3; *Statement
on Race*, 20
University at Buffalo, 7; Baldy Center for
Law and Social Policy, xvii; Graduate
School of Education, xvii
University of Alberta, 102
University of British Columbia, 7, 65
University of Washington, xvii; 7;
Canadian Studies Center, 8
*The Unjust Society: The Tragedy of Canada's
Indians* (Cardinal 1969), 57-58
US Department of Justice Immigration
and Naturalization Service, 19
US English, 113
US Office of Education, 43

Vancouver, British Columbia, 7, 101, 135,
169
Vancouver School Board, 102, 134, 135,
141-42
Vann, Robert, 35
Victoria School Board, 134
Viegas, Trinidad Molina, 10

Wade, John, 31
Walcott, Rinaldo, 11
Wane, Njoki Nathani, 10

Washington State, 188, 191-93
Washington State Civil Rights Initiative,
  192-93
Washington State Commission on African
  American Affairs, 192
Washington State Higher Education
  Coordinating Board, 192
Waugh, Dexter, 242
Whose Science? Whose Knowledge?
  (Harding 1991), 181
Wiley, Terrence, 10
Winton, Susan, 9
Wirth, Louis, 20
Wood, Marcus, 232
Works Progress Administration, 43

York Region District School Board, 24
Youth Cohort Study, 221-223
You Are an American (American Service
  Institute 1942), 35

Zoric, Terezia, 11, 241